Texting with a Stranger

The True Story of a Celebrity Imposter Romance Scam

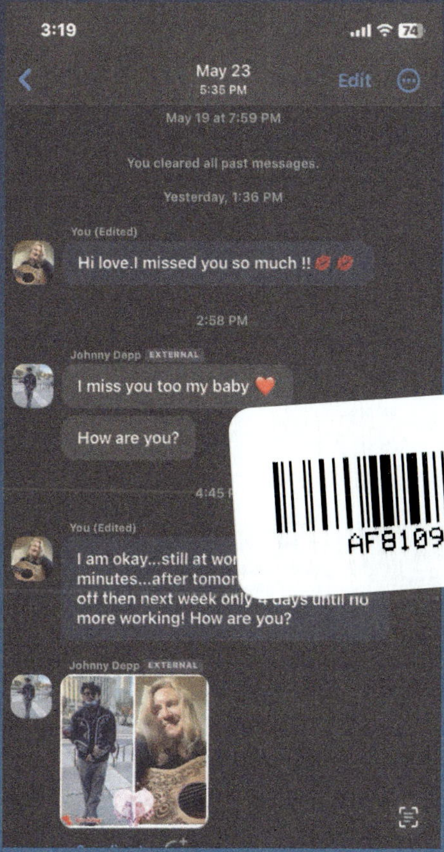

3:19
May 23
5:35 PM
Edit
May 19 at 7:59 PM
You cleared all past messages.
Yesterday, 1:36 PM
You (Edited)
Hi love.I missed you so much !!
2:58 PM
Johnny Depp EXTERNAL
I miss you too my baby
How are you?
You (Edited)
more working! How are you?
Johnny Depp EXTERNAL

ISBN:978-0-9983486-6-7
Library of Congress Reg. No. TX 9-390-327

Manufactured in the United States of America

DISCLAIMER

The text communication included in this book is not between the author and Johnny Depp or anyone known to be affiliated with Mr. Depp. The identity of the imposter(s) is/are unknown. The gender is unknown. The text source whereabouts is unknown. Whether or not all or some of the texts received that are included in this book were sent by a human or were AI generated is unknown. All the images of Johnny Depp used by the imposter(s) as his/her/its profile pictures are assumed to be fairly used but used without the permission of Mr. Depp or his management team.

DISCLOSURE

This publication is a true story about my on-line relationship with someone/something claiming to be Johnny Depp. Although at first I did not believe I was communicating with Johnny Depp, after numerous texts occurring daily, I believed it was possible. That belief brought a flood of emotions. What began as a casual acquaintance quickly morphed into something more. My feelings grew stronger as I navigated the murky waters. The love I felt deepened as we shared interests, experiences, and expectations. I genuinely felt cared for and for the first time in a very long time opened my heart. To this day I still struggle with detachment.

Although screenshots of many texts are included in this book, they are not exhaustive of all those sent and received between me and multiple imposters all claiming to be Johnny Depp over the course of approximately one year. The texts selected for this book were selected to best tell my story in a concise and linear manner.

A 50% portion of any net proceeds realized from the sale of this book will be donated to charities providing mental health services.

DEDICATION

This book is dedicated to anyone who has ever commented on or liked a social media internet page or post. I sincerely hope that individuals reading this book will recognize how our written words can trigger real emotion in others, even one as strong as love. We all have a need to connect. Communicating with someone virtually can fill a temporary void when meeting in person is not plausible; but, beware of the dangers such communication may present before accepting it as a permanent replacement for connecting in the physical world.

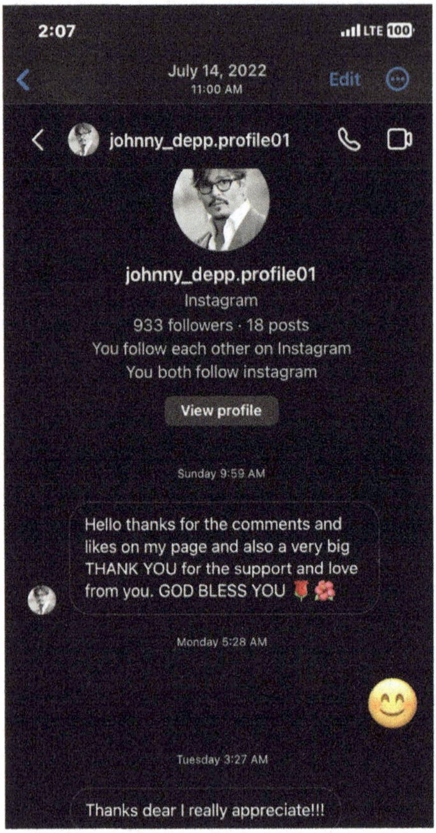
2:07
LTE 100
July 14, 2022
11:00 AM
Edit
johnny_depp.profile01
johnny_depp.profile01
Instagram
933 followers · 18 posts
You follow each other on Instagram
You both follow instagram
View profile
Sunday 9:59 AM
Hello thanks for the comments and likes on my page and also a very big THANK YOU for the support and love from you. GOD BLESS YOU 🌹🌺
Monday 5:28 AM
😊
Tuesday 3:27 AM
Thanks dear I really appreciate!!!

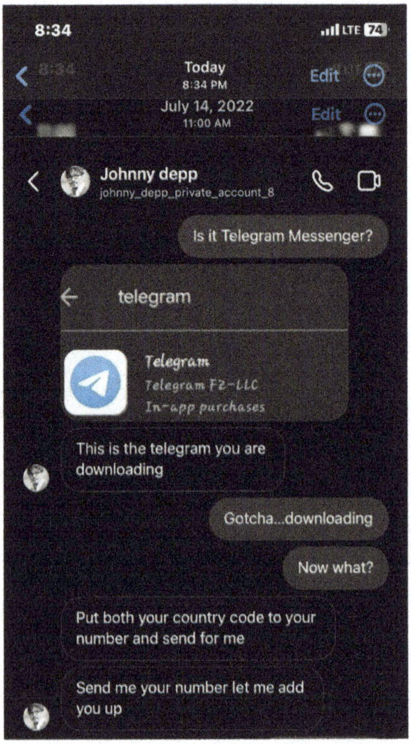
8:34
LTE 74
Today
8:34 PM
Edit
July 14, 2022
11:00 AM
Edit
Johnny depp
johnny_depp_private_account_8
Is it Telegram Messenger?
telegram
Telegram
Telegram FZ-LLC
In-app purchases
This is the telegram you are downloading
Gotcha...downloading
Now what?
Put both your country code to your number and send for me
Send me your number let me add you up

THE BEGINNING, end (twice), and another beginning.

Have you ever liked a social media post or made a comment to one? If your answer is yes, you are subject to internet fraud. What seems like an innocent interaction can quickly turn ugly. I knew this before I ever "liked" any social media post or wrote a comment to one. Why then did I begin to interact on social media sites? The answer is complicated.

I had no real interest in Johnny Depp before the highly publicized 2022 defamation trial. I may have seen him in Hollywood during my years living in California, but I never met him or had a conversation with him. I watched some of the trial footage from an an objective perspective with my interest limited to that of a legal professional. I never commented publicly about the trial; however, I did follow several Depp support web pages.

My first private messaging with a Depp imposter began after I had liked an Instagram post. I received a separate text asking me to communicate on Telegram then received instruction.

The conversation was light and easy, like that one would have if speaking with a new acquaintance. The fact that Depp is famous was not lost on me, but at the same time it had no great effect on me. I had met famous people in the past and was regularly in the company of wealthy individuals, so having a simple text chat with a celebrity was not extraordinary.

It did not occur to me that this could be an imposter. I suppose my naïveté was due partly to my inexperience with social media interaction.

During this initial texting I was on vacation visiting family and attending a wedding. The Telegram texting was just another fun thing to do. I had no expectation of continued communication. I suppose I just figured Depp was bored or that he may genuinely reach out to people who posted kind comments on the web after all the negative publicity he had received.

It may seem incredible that anyone could actually believe texting like this was real. If you consider that anyone living in California for a long time has the opportunity to meet and/or work with celebrities, you may see why texting with one is not a far stretch. I had been fortunate enough to have had on camera experience and was at one time married to the son of a celebrity. I was not nervous or afraid to chat with one.

8:45
8:16
TELEGRAM
Back
Johnny Depp
last seen recently
1:18 PM 10:18 AM
Alright,hope you have had your lunch 10:36 AM
Not yet but had a late breakfast...slept in...a vaca indulgence...almost at our destination so have to go. Have a beautiful day:)
Oh you have something dear 10:40 AM
Eating later is probably not good okay 10:41 AM
You can have snacks and coffee 10:42 AM
Murals are everywhere!
10:48 AM
Yeah 10:49 AM
Where are you now 10:49 AM
Hello friend 2:51 PM
Hello 2:52 PM
Message

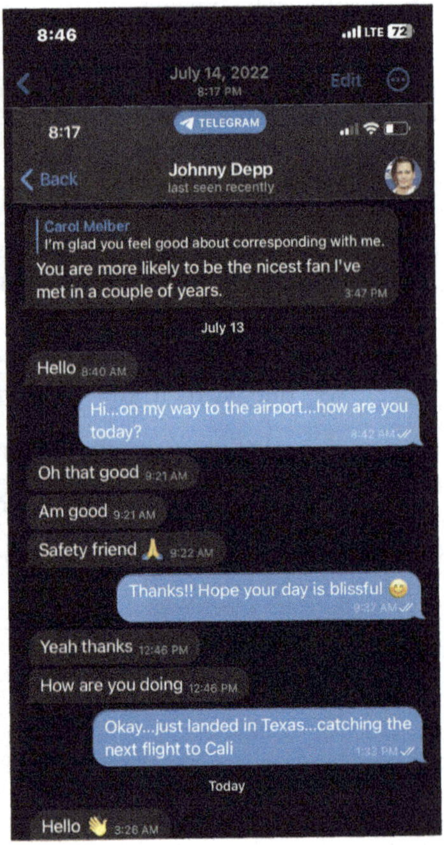
8:46
July 14, 2022
8:17 PM
Edit
8:17
TELEGRAM
Back
Johnny Depp
last seen recently
Carol Melber
I'm glad you feel good about corresponding with me.
You are more likely to be the nicest fan I've met in a couple of years. 3:47 PM
July 13
Hello 8:40 AM
Hi...on my way to the airport...how are you today?
Oh that good 9:21 AM
Am good 9:21 AM
Safety friend 🙏 9:22 AM
Thanks!! Hope your day is blissful 😊
Yeah thanks 12:46 PM
How are you doing 12:46 PM
Okay...just landed in Texas...catching the next flight to Cali
Today
Hello 👋 3:26 AM

This chat was fun and I wanted to continue it as long as I was comfortable. The conversation continued after I returned to California; but, when I saw the post (below right) I realized how unlikely it was that I was communicating with Johnny Depp and so called the imposter out on it. After I ended the chat the imposter came back with a "hello" wave, as if at an attempt to start over, but I deleted it without any response. That brought about the first end.

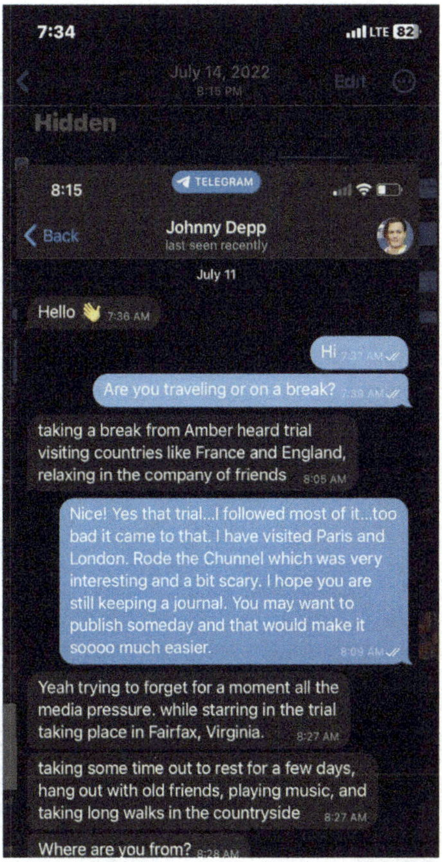
7:34
July 14, 2022
8:15 PM
Edit
Hidden
8:15
TELEGRAM
Back
Johnny Depp
last seen recently
July 11
Hello 👋 7:36 AM
Hi
Are you traveling or on a break?
taking a break from Amber heard trial visiting countries like France and England, relaxing in the company of friends 8:05 AM
Nice! Yes that trial...I followed most of it...too bad it came to that. I have visited Paris and London. Rode the Chunnel which was very interesting and a bit scary. I hope you are still keeping a journal. You may want to publish someday and that would make it soooo much easier. 8:09 AM
Yeah trying to forget for a moment all the media pressure. while starring in the trial taking place in Fairfax, Virginia. 8:27 AM
taking some time out to rest for a few days, hang out with old friends, playing music, and taking long walks in the countryside 8:27 AM
Where are you from?

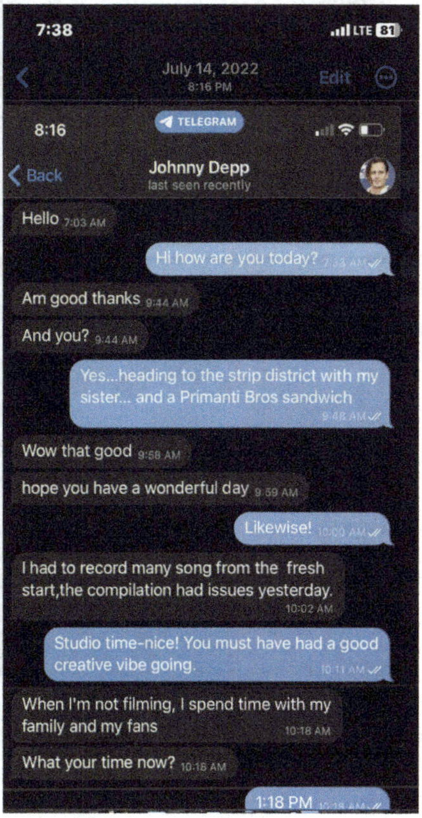
7:38
July 14, 2022
8:16 PM
Edit
8:16
TELEGRAM
Back
Johnny Depp
last seen recently
Hello 7:03 AM
Hi how are you today?
Am good thanks 9:44 AM
And you? 9:44 AM
Yes...heading to the strip district with my sister... and a Primanti Bros sandwich
Wow that good 9:58 AM
hope you have a wonderful day 9:59 AM
Likewise!
I had to record many song from the fresh start,the compilation had issues yesterday. 10:02 AM
Studio time-nice! You must have had a good creative vibe going.
When I'm not filming, I spend time with my family and my fans 10:18 AM
What your time now? 10:18 AM
1:18 PM

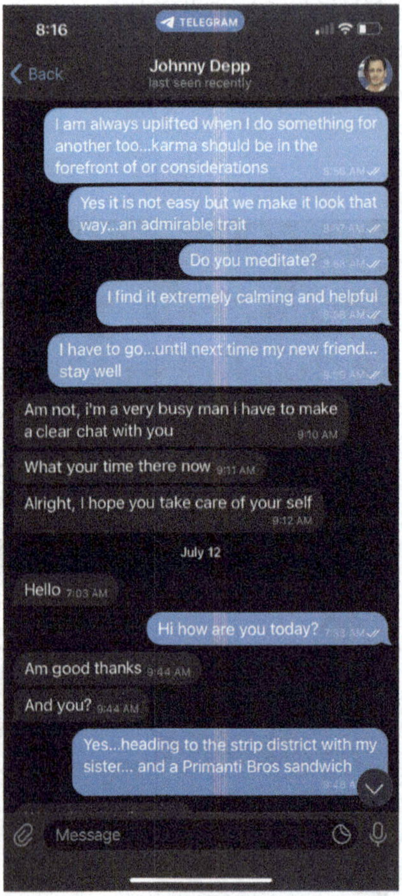
8:16
TELEGRAM
Back
Johnny Depp
last seen recently
I am always uplifted when I do something for another too...karma should be in the forefront of or considerations
Yes it is not easy but we make it look that way...an admirable trait
Do you meditate?
I find it extremely calming and helpful
I have to go...until next time my new friend... stay well
Am not, i'm a very busy man i have to make a clear chat with you 9:10 AM
What your time there now 9:11 AM
Alright, I hope you take care of your self 9:12 AM
July 12
Hello 7:03 AM
Hi how are you today?
Am good thanks 9:44 AM
And you? 9:44 AM
Yes...heading to the strip district with my sister... and a Primanti Bros sandwich
Message

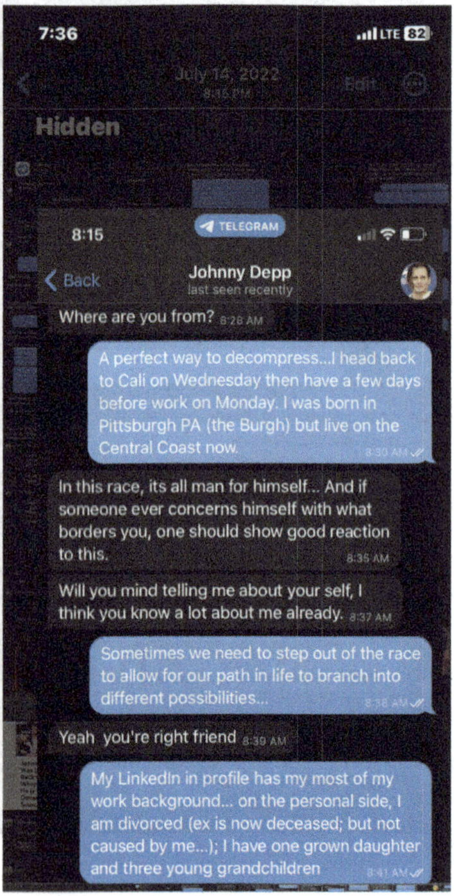
7:36
LTE 82
Hidden
8:15
TELEGRAM
Back
Johnny Depp
last seen recently
Where are you from? 8:28 AM
A perfect way to decompress...I head back to Cali on Wednesday then have a few days before work on Monday. I was born in Pittsburgh PA (the Burgh) but live on the Central Coast now. 8:30 AM
In this race, its all man for himself... And if someone ever concerns himself with what borders you, one should show good reaction to this. 8:35 AM
Will you mind telling me about your self, I think you know a lot about me already. 8:37 AM
Sometimes we need to step out of the race to allow for our path in life to branch into different possibilities... 8:38 AM
Yeah you're right friend 8:39 AM
My LinkedIn profile has my most of my work background... on the personal side, I am divorced (ex is now deceased; but not caused by me...); I have one grown daughter and three young grandchildren 8:41 AM

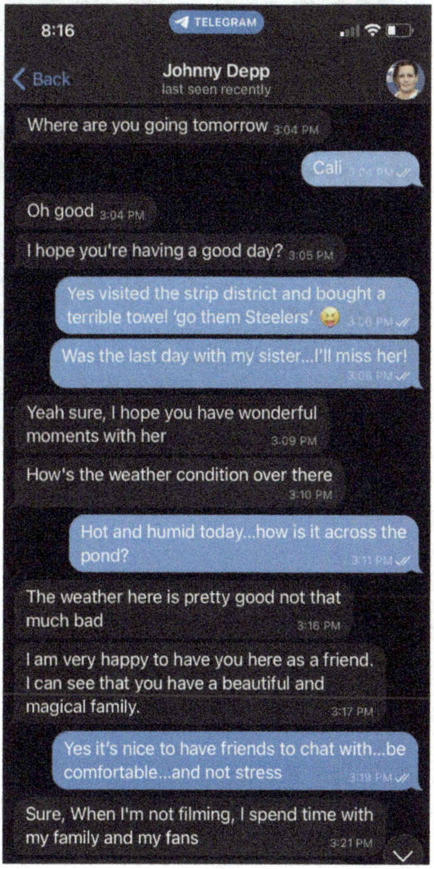
8:16
TELEGRAM
Back
Johnny Depp
last seen recently
Where are you going tomorrow 3:04 PM
Cali
Oh good 3:04 PM
I hope you're having a good day? 3:05 PM
Yes visited the strip district and bought a terrible towel 'go them Steelers' 😜
Was the last day with my sister...I'll miss her!
Yeah sure, I hope you have wonderful moments with her 3:09 PM
How's the weather condition over there 3:10 PM
Hot and humid today...how is it across the pond? 3:11 PM
The weather here is pretty good not that much bad 3:16 PM
I am very happy to have you here as a friend. I can see that you have a beautiful and magical family. 3:17 PM
Yes it's nice to have friends to chat with...be comfortable...and not stress 3:19 PM
Sure, When I'm not filming, I spend time with my family and my fans 3:21 PM

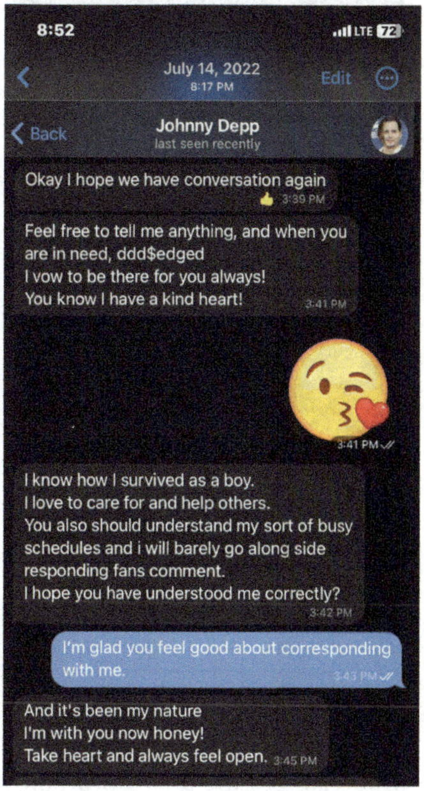
8:52
LTE 72
July 14, 2022
8:17 PM
Edit
Back
Johnny Depp
last seen recently
Okay I hope we have conversation again 👍 3:39 PM
Feel free to tell me anything, and when you are in need, ddd$edged
I vow to be there for you always!
You know I have a kind heart! 3:41 PM
3:41 PM
I know how I survived as a boy.
I love to care for and help others.
You also should understand my sort of busy schedules and i will barely go along side responding fans comment.
I hope you have understood me correctly? 3:42 PM
I'm glad you feel good about corresponding with me. 3:43 PM
And it's been my nature
I'm with you now honey!
Take heart and always feel open. 3:45 PM

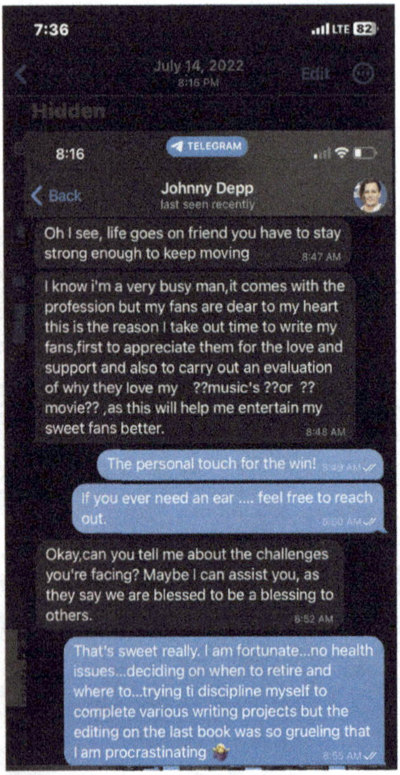
7:36
July 14, 2022
8:16 PM
Edit
8:16
TELEGRAM
Back
Johnny Depp
last seen recently
Oh I see, life goes on friend you have to stay strong enough to keep moving 8:47 AM
I know i'm a very busy man,it comes with the profession but my fans are dear to my heart this is the reason I take out time to write my fans,first to appreciate them for the love and support and also to carry out an evaluation of why they love my ??music's ??or ?? movie?? ,as this will help me entertain my sweet fans better. 8:48 AM
The personal touch for the win!
If you ever need an ear .... feel free to reach out.
Okay,can you tell me about the challenges you're facing? Maybe I can assist you, as they say we are blessed to be a blessing to others. 8:52 AM
That's sweet really. I am fortunate...no health issues...deciding on when to retire and where to...trying ti discipline myself to complete various writing projects but the editing on the last book was so grueling that I am procrastinating 8:55 AM

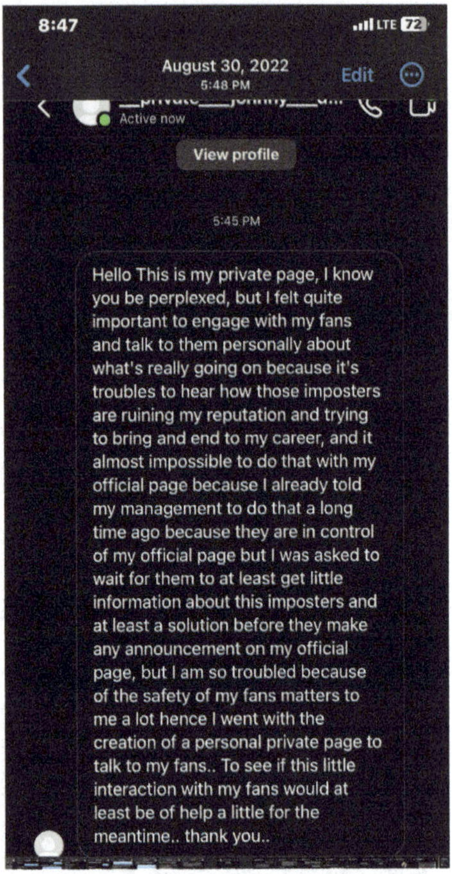
8:47
August 30, 2022
5:48 PM
Edit
Active now
View profile
5:45 PM
Hello This is my private page, I know you be perplexed, but I felt quite important to engage with my fans and talk to them personally about what's really going on because it's troubles to hear how those imposters are ruining my reputation and trying to bring and end to my career, and it almost impossible to do that with my official page because I already told my management to do that a long time ago because they are in control of my official page but I was asked to wait for them to at least get little information about this imposters and at least a solution before they make any announcement on my official page, but I am so troubled because of the safety of my fans matters to me a lot hence I went with the creation of a personal private page to talk to my fans.. To see if this little interaction with my fans would at least be of help a little for the meantime.. thank you..

Interestingly, the post I saw (above right) may not have been official because the profile picture was removed. Still, I heeded the warning.

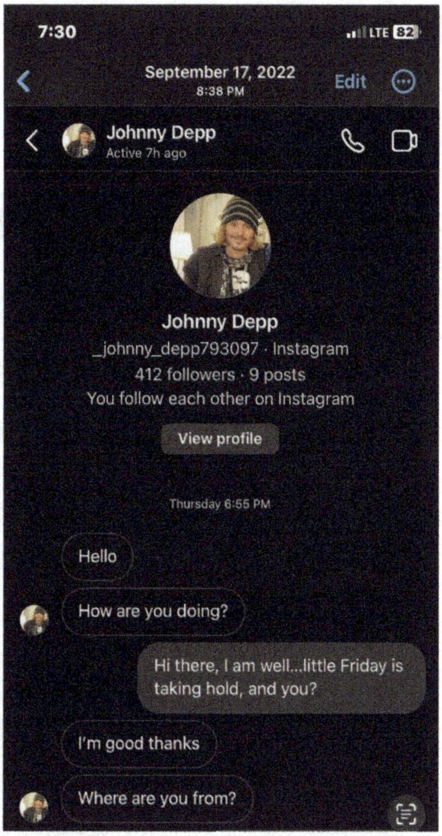
7:30
LTE 82
September 17, 2022
8:38 PM
Edit
Johnny Depp
Active 7h ago
Johnny Depp
_johnny_depp793097 · Instagram
412 followers · 9 posts
You follow each other on Instagram
View profile
Thursday 6:55 PM
Hello
How are you doing?
Hi there, I am well...little Friday is taking hold, and you?
I'm good thanks
Where are you from?

In September I received a message on Instagram and just like that, I was texting with another Johnny Depp imposter.

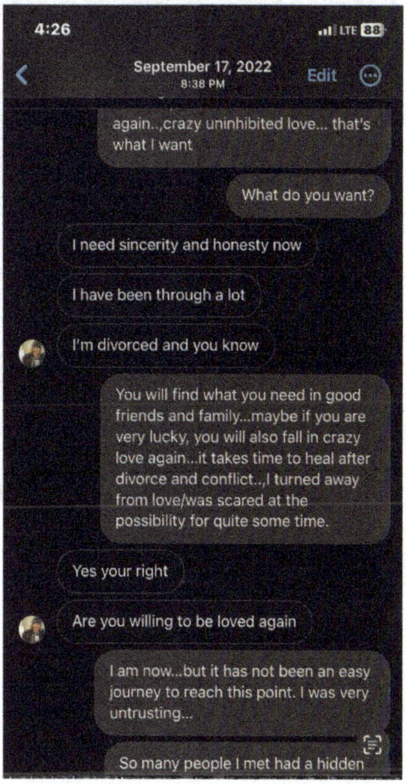
4:26
LTE 88
September 17, 2022
8:38 PM
Edit
again..,crazy uninhibited love... that's what I want
What do you want?
I need sincerity and honesty now
I have been through a lot
I'm divorced and you know
You will find what you need in good friends and family...maybe if you are very lucky, you will also fall in crazy love again...it takes time to heal after divorce and conflict..,I turned away from love/was scared at the possibility for quite some time.
Yes your right
Are you willing to be loved again
I am now...but it has not been an easy journey to reach this point. I was very untrusting...
So many people I met had a hidden

We did not chat for a long time because I received another request message to chat that was similar to the first one while the texting was happening which was a 'red flag'. I decided to 'cut through the chase' and just asked what the end game was. The response was something like, "Well, you already know."

Tip: Imposters will use a celebrity photo found on the internet as their profile picture. Web search the user name and picture to find their true identity.

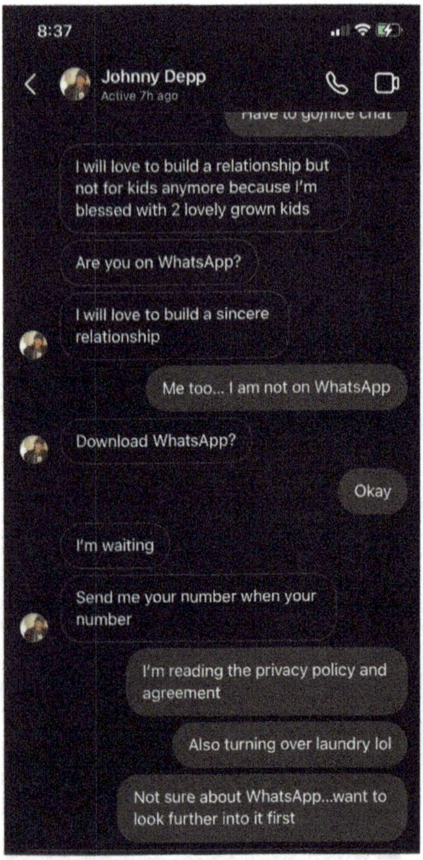
8:37
Johnny Depp
Active 7h ago
I will love to build a relationship but not for kids anymore because I'm blessed with 2 lovely grown kids
Are you on WhatsApp?
I will love to build a sincere relationship
Me too... I am not on WhatsApp
Download WhatsApp?
Okay
I'm waiting
Send me your number when your number
I'm reading the privacy policy and agreement
Also turning over laundry lol
Not sure about WhatsApp...want to look further into it first

4:26
LTE 88
September 17, 2022
8:38 PM
Edit
Where are you?
Hello I'm here
Happy Saturday:)
Good tho
Thanks
How's your day going?
I just had a very relaxing pedicure... do you like them?
Okay
What do you do for a living?
I work for Superior Court
Do you like pedicures?
Men should get them-they are wonderful

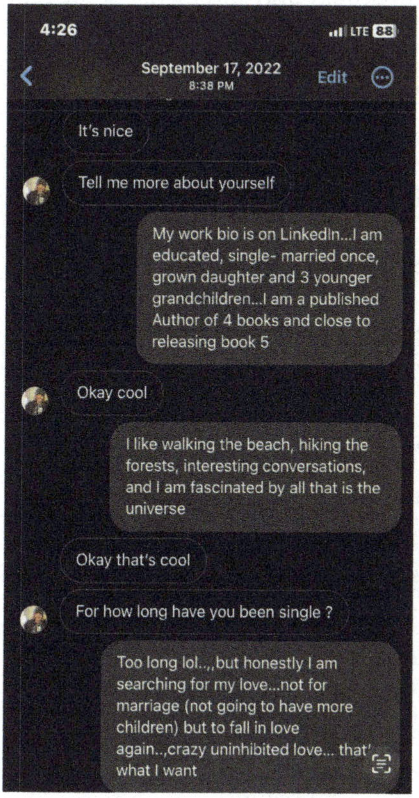
4:26
LTE 88
September 17, 2022
8:38 PM
Edit
It's nice
Tell me more about yourself
My work bio is on LinkedIn...I am educated, single- married once, grown daughter and 3 younger grandchildren...I am a published Author of 4 books and close to releasing book 5
Okay cool
I like walking the beach, hiking the forests, interesting conversations, and I am fascinated by all that is the universe
Okay that's cool
For how long have you been single ?
Too long lol..,,but honestly I am searching for my love...not for marriage (not going to have more children) but to fall in love again..,crazy uninhibited love... that' what I want

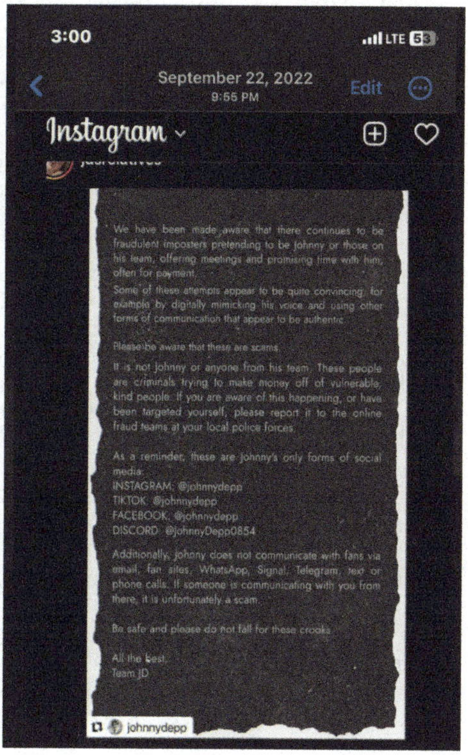
3:00
LTE 53
September 22, 2022
9:55 PM
Edit
Instagram
We have been made aware that there continues to be fraudulent imposters pretending to be Johnny or those on his team, offering meetings and promising time with him, often for payment.
Some of these attempts appear to be quite convincing, for example by digitally mimicking his voice and using other forms of communication that appear to be authentic.
Please be aware that these are scams.
It is not Johnny or anyone from his team. These people are criminals trying to make money off of vulnerable, kind people. If you are aware of this happening, or have been targeted yourself, please report it to the online fraud teams at your local police forces.
As a reminder, these are Johnny's only forms of social media:
INSTAGRAM: @johnnydepp
TIKTOK: @johnnydepp
FACEBOOK: @johnnydepp
DISCORD: @JohnnyDepp0854
Additionally, Johnny does not communicate with fans via email, fan sites, WhatsApp, Signal, Telegram, text or phone calls. If someone is communicating with you from there, it is unfortunately a scam.
Be safe and please do not fall for these crooks.
All the best,
Team JD
johnnydepp

So, after downloading and chatting on WhatsApp I saw the above post on a Depp site warning about imposters, so I removed my contact information and off-loaded WhatsApp. I did not save that conversation. This was the second end to my communication with a Depp imposter.

Was I still following Depp on social media? Yes. I did follow the Fall 2022 Jeff Beck tour and I continued to comment on the social media posts which I found entertaining. I had a busy and somewhat stressful work schedule so welcomed the distraction. I was aware that the tour included a concert in San Jose in late November, just before the Thanksgiving holiday. If I had an escort I would have considered going. Ironically, during the time period between the end of November and into December I experienced a few encounters that contributed to my mounting curiosity about Johnny Depp. These few incidents also made the possibility that I could have been in communication with Johnny Depp seem credible.

In the early morning of November 28th I saw Jeff Beck (or his doppelgänger) at a crosswalk near the marina in Monterey. I recall that exact date because early that morning I was taking my car to a nearby shop for repair and I happened to be in the first car stopped at the light where I watched the man as he crossed the street. On another occasion (not sure of the exact date) while on my way to work I spied someone who looked remarkably like Depp driving in the car behind me. What caught my eye were the rings on the hands gripping the steering wheel. Whoever it was wore glasses and a hat. My vantage did not include a view of any identifying tattoos so I can not be certain who it was.

After a tennis game one evening I saw who looked like one of the Hollywood Vampires group (Alice Cooper) peering from the window of a large black SUV while it passed by the Monterey Tennis Center. A tennis friend and I were chatting on the sidewalk when the vehicle passed by directly in front of where we stood. Was Alice in Monterey California in late 2022? I do not know.

Another unexpected thing took place on New Years Eve 2022. After a storm knocked out power to a portion of the peninsula that included my residence, I decided to eat out and see a movie in town. While I sat at a window in a candle lit restaurant I saw Depp's sister Kristie walking fast past the restaurant. Why did I think it was Kristie? Because Kristie (or someone posing as her) had sent several requests to follow my Instagram account prior to that and I recognized her from her profile picture. At the time I reasoned that her requests stemmed from me making favorable comments to various media posts about her brother. I did not know who she was at first so removed her. When I received another request stating that she was Kristie Depp I accepted. The profile picture of whoever it was bore a striking resemblance to Kristie Dembrowski. Seeing that woman on New Years Eve strengthened my belief in the possibility that I could have been communicating with Johnny Depp.

Here's what happened on January 8, 2023:

2:34
LTE 57
January 8
5:07 PM
Edit
5:07
Cheryl spellins
Active 23m ago
Johnny depp said I shall collect your contact details
Tuesday 3:28 AM
??
Wednesday 8:09 PM
Contact details?
Wednesday 9:59 PM
Do you use zoom apk
Thursday 6:43 PM
Here is an email writes2create@gmail.com
Friday 12:40 PM
Johnny said he try to contact you but he didn't go through

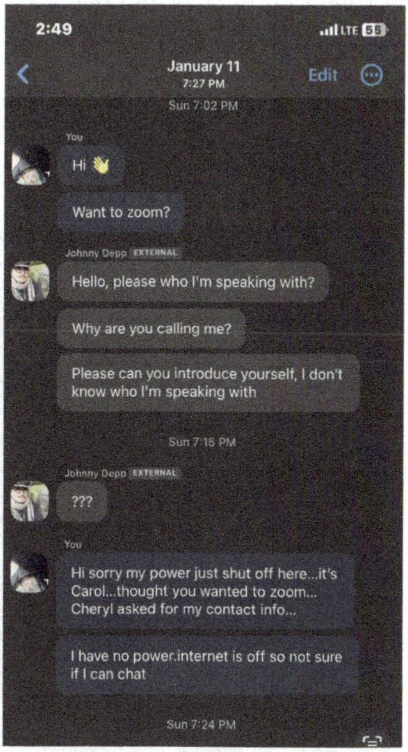
2:49
LTE 56
January 11
7:27 PM
Edit
Sun 7:02 PM
You
Hi 👋
Want to zoom?
Johnny Depp EXTERNAL
Hello, please who I'm speaking with?
Why are you calling me?
Please can you introduce yourself, I don't know who I'm speaking with
Sun 7:15 PM
Johnny Depp EXTERNAL
???
You
Hi sorry my power just shut off here...it's Carol...thought you wanted to zoom... Cheryl asked for my contact info...
I have no power.internet is off so not sure if I can chat
Sun 7:24 PM

For the third time I was communicating with someone/something claiming to be Johnny Depp. One may ask why was I so naive to believe someone like Johnny Depp would ask to communicate with me? I asked myself that same question many times. Aside from the previous disclosures, during the 21 years I lived in California my path crossed A-listers on numerous occasions so I thought perhaps I had possibly met Depp before and he recognized me, but I never confirmed this. I lived in Florida on and off from late 1975 through most of 1989 but I have no direct recollection of ever meeting him there.

Getting back to the texting, this time the mode of communication was Zoom. At the beginning the conversation was simple, polite, and continuous. I soon found my world infused with thoughts of Depp throughout the day and night. Admittedly, this was a welcomed change from my busy but lonely life.

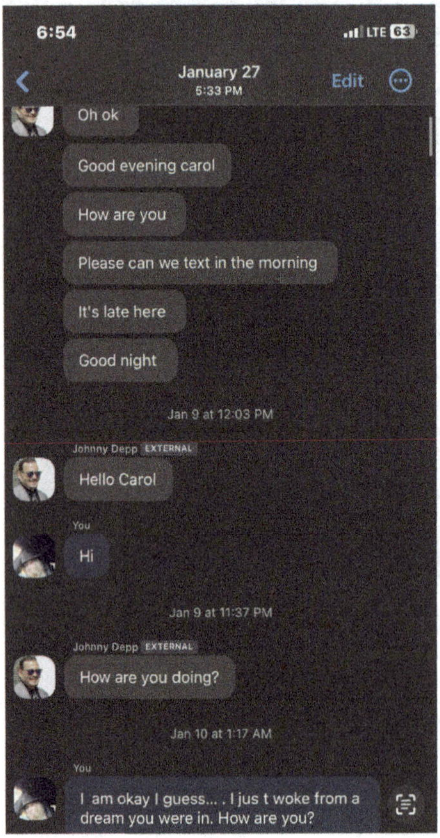
6:54
LTE 63
January 27
5:33 PM
Edit
Oh ok
Good evening carol
How are you
Please can we text in the morning
It's late here
Good night
Jan 9 at 12:03 PM
Johnny Depp EXTERNAL
Hello Carol
You
Hi
Jan 9 at 11:37 PM
Johnny Depp EXTERNAL
How are you doing?
Jan 10 at 1:17 AM
You
I am okay I guess... . I jus t woke from a dream you were in. How are you?

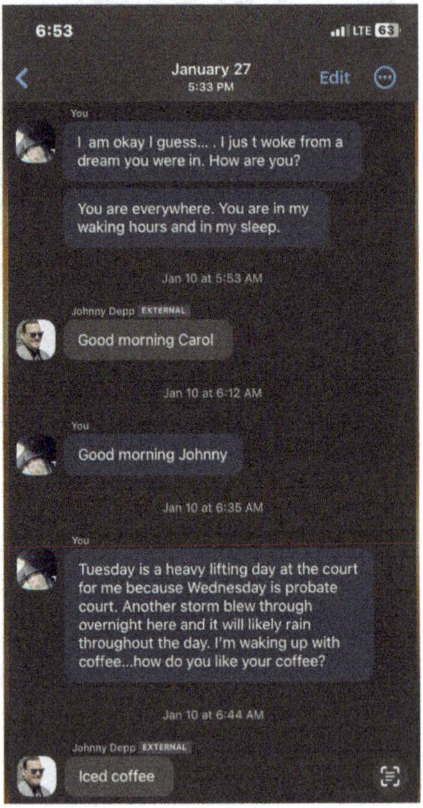
6:53
LTE 63
January 27
5:33 PM
Edit
You
I am okay I guess... . I jus t woke from a dream you were in. How are you?
You are everywhere. You are in my waking hours and in my sleep.
Jan 10 at 5:53 AM
Johnny Depp EXTERNAL
Good morning Carol
Jan 10 at 6:12 AM
You
Good morning Johnny
Jan 10 at 6:35 AM
You
Tuesday is a heavy lifting day at the court for me because Wednesday is probate court. Another storm blew through overnight here and it will likely rain throughout the day. I'm waking up with coffee...how do you like your coffee?
Jan 10 at 6:44 AM
Johnny Depp EXTERNAL
Iced coffee

The first hint I had that this connection was not on the level was when Jeff Beck died. News was not wide-spread on the day he died-January 10, 2023, so when I received multiple texts from the imposter(s) throughout the day and night I didn't really think about it. I learned of the sad news on January 11th. Then I learned that Beck's good friend Johnny Depp was by his side in England when he died. So, while I am receiving the texts throughout the day on January 10th the only thing that seems to interrupt the communication is a visit from Depp's daughter that was used as an excuse to temporarily end the conversation.

I allowed myself to justify this huge red flag with thinking that it was possible Depp could not share information with me; but, while thinking about the situation later I became more and more suspicious.

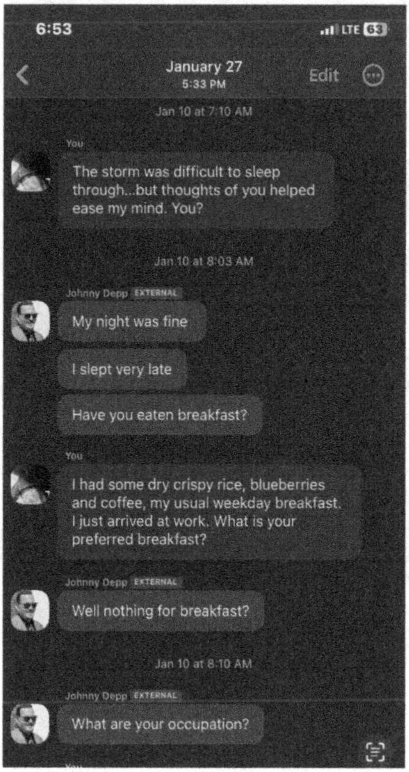
6:53
LTE 63
January 27
5:33 PM
Edit
Jan 10 at 7:10 AM
You
The storm was difficult to sleep through...but thoughts of you helped ease my mind. You?
Jan 10 at 8:03 AM
Johnny Depp EXTERNAL
My night was fine
I slept very late
Have you eaten breakfast?
You
I had some dry crispy rice, blueberries and coffee, my usual weekday breakfast. I just arrived at work. What is your preferred breakfast?
Johnny Depp EXTERNAL
Well nothing for breakfast?
Jan 10 at 8:10 AM
Johnny Depp EXTERNAL
What are your occupation?

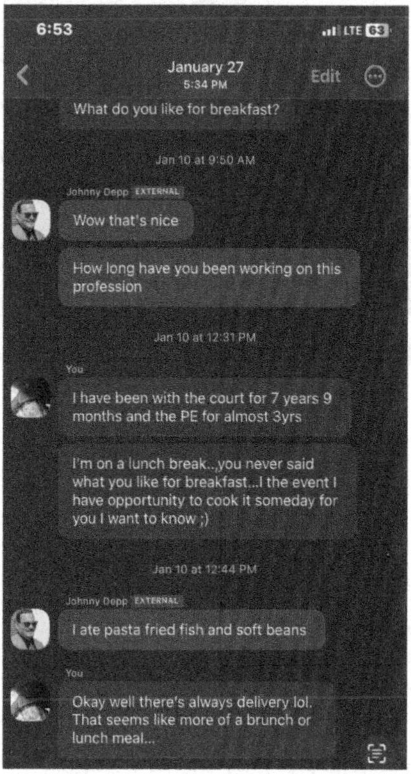
6:53
LTE 63
January 27
5:34 PM
Edit
What do you like for breakfast?
Jan 10 at 9:50 AM
Johnny Depp EXTERNAL
Wow that's nice
How long have you been working on this profession
Jan 10 at 12:31 PM
You
I have been with the court for 7 years 9 months and the PE for almost 3yrs
I'm on a lunch break..,you never said what you like for breakfast...I the event I have opportunity to cook it someday for you I want to know ;)
Jan 10 at 12:44 PM
Johnny Depp EXTERNAL
I ate pasta fried fish and soft beans
You
Okay well there's always delivery lol. That seems like more of a brunch or lunch meal...

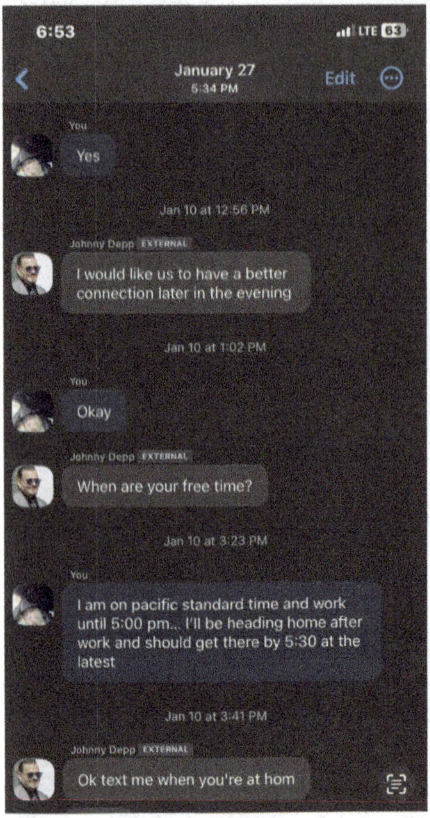
6:53
LTE 63
January 27
5:34 PM
Edit
You
Yes
Jan 10 at 12:56 PM
Johnny Depp EXTERNAL
I would like us to have a better connection later in the evening
Jan 10 at 1:02 PM
You
Okay
Johnny Depp EXTERNAL
When are your free time?
Jan 10 at 3:23 PM
You
I am on pacific standard time and work until 5:00 pm... I'll be heading home after work and should get there by 5:30 at the latest
Jan 10 at 3:41 PM
Johnny Depp EXTERNAL
Ok text me when you're at hom

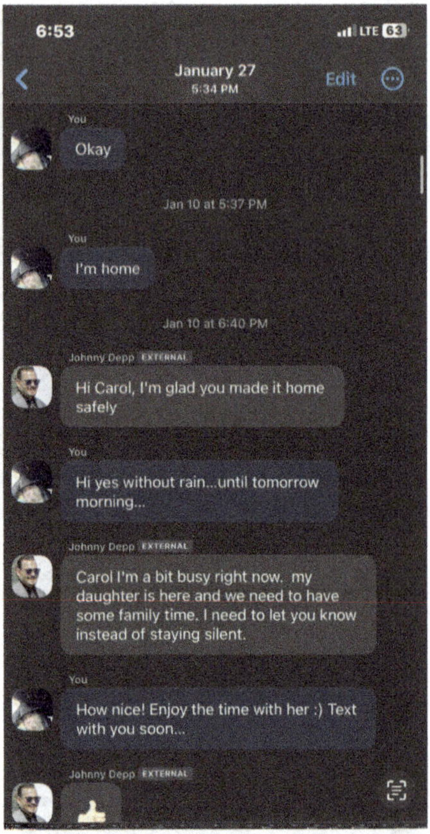
6:53
LTE 63
January 27
5:34 PM
Edit
You
Okay
Jan 10 at 5:37 PM
You
I'm home
Jan 10 at 6:40 PM
Johnny Depp EXTERNAL
Hi Carol, I'm glad you made it home safely
You
Hi yes without rain...until tomorrow morning...
Johnny Depp EXTERNAL
Carol I'm a bit busy right now. my daughter is here and we need to have some family time. I need to let you know instead of staying silent.
You
How nice! Enjoy the time with her :) Text with you soon...
Johnny Depp EXTERNAL

Whatever the truth, I chose to turn a blind eye to my doubts. I actually enjoyed the communication. Whoever this was, he/she/it made me feel cared for and as long as it was just texting I did not find any reason to stop.

After Jeff Beck's death I especially wanted to be supportive, caring and present for who I thought could have been Johnny. I saw our new connection as serendipitous and found more purpose in communicating. I knew the stages of grief, having lost several family members. I genuinely felt I could be of help to someone for whom I was starting to have other feelings. At this point, the nurturing woman in me came to surface and I allowed her to take over.

The conversations we had were pretty ordinary, liken to those of any couple sharing moments of their day. While sharing these moments I began to share my related experiences and desires about those moments. I am uncertain I would have necessarily done this in the early stage of the relationship had we been dating in the physical world. Texting removes the distractions that can occur in the physical presence of attraction. It allows you to feel safer and somewhat removed from the dangers of emotional attachment while exposing your vulnerabilities.

The text words began to include hints that a deeper friendship was brewing and I became more and more accustomed to the connection. I was also beginning to get a little frustrated and more suspicious when the text threads showed that I was sharing more information than I was receiving.

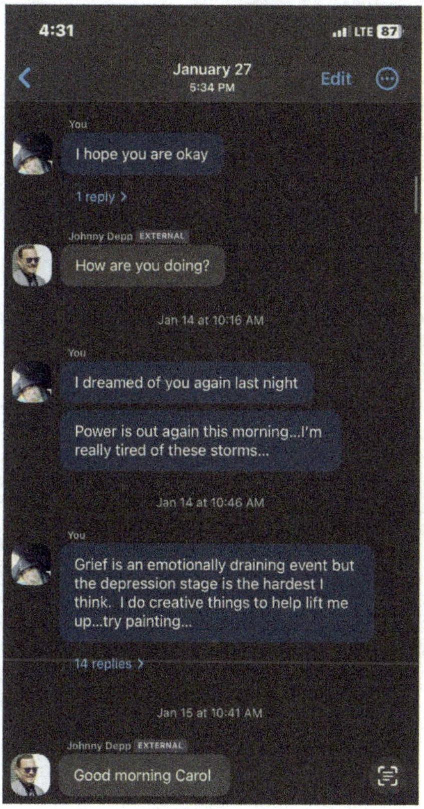
4:31
LTE 87
January 27
5:34 PM
Edit
You
I hope you are okay
1 reply >
Johnny Depp EXTERNAL
How are you doing?
Jan 14 at 10:16 AM
You
I dreamed of you again last night
Power is out again this morning...I'm really tired of these storms...
Jan 14 at 10:46 AM
You
Grief is an emotionally draining event but the depression stage is the hardest I think. I do creative things to help lift me up...try painting...
14 replies >
Jan 15 at 10:41 AM
Johnny Depp EXTERNAL
Good morning Carol

SHARING INFORMATION and GETTING CLOSER

We shared our likes and dislikes about food though there was some misunderstanding in our communication as seen in the texts below about pizza toppings. When I read the response I wondered if English was their first language.

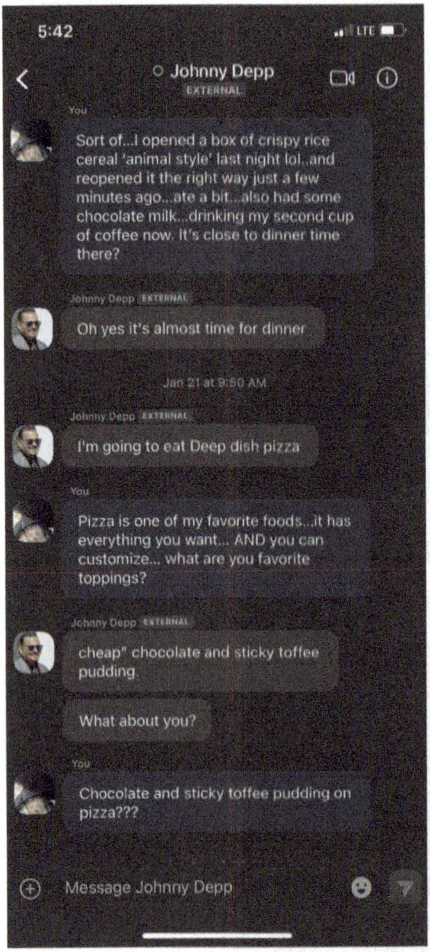
5:42
Johnny Depp
EXTERNAL
You
Sort of...I opened a box of crispy rice cereal 'animal style' last night lol..and reopened it the right way just a few minutes ago...ate a bit...also had some chocolate milk...drinking my second cup of coffee now. It's close to dinner time there?
Johnny Depp EXTERNAL
Oh yes it's almost time for dinner
Jan 21 at 9:50 AM
Johnny Depp EXTERNAL
I'm going to eat Deep dish pizza
You
Pizza is one of my favorite foods...it has everything you want... AND you can customize... what are you favorite toppings?
Johnny Depp EXTERNAL
cheap" chocolate and sticky toffee pudding
What about you?
You
Chocolate and sticky toffee pudding on pizza???
Message Johnny Depp

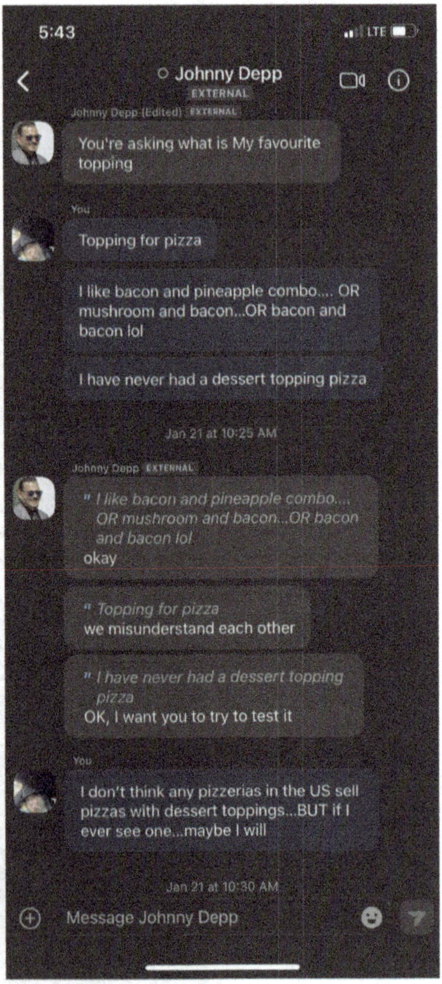
5:43
Johnny Depp
EXTERNAL
Johnny Depp (Edited) EXTERNAL
You're asking what is My favourite topping
You
Topping for pizza
I like bacon and pineapple combo.... OR mushroom and bacon...OR bacon and bacon lol
I have never had a dessert topping pizza
Jan 21 at 10:25 AM
Johnny Depp EXTERNAL
" I like bacon and pineapple combo.... OR mushroom and bacon...OR bacon and bacon lol
okay
" Topping for pizza
we misunderstand each other
" I have never had a dessert topping pizza
OK, I want you to try to test it
You
I don't think any pizzerias in the US sell pizzas with dessert toppings...BUT if I ever see one...maybe I will
Jan 21 at 10:30 AM
Message Johnny Depp

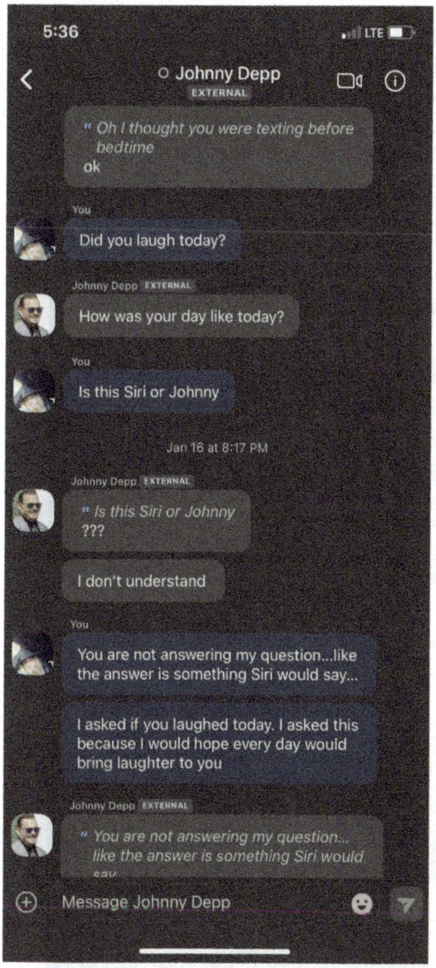
5:36
LTE
Johnny Depp
EXTERNAL
" Oh I thought you were texting before bedtime
ok
You
Did you laugh today?
Johnny Depp EXTERNAL
How was your day like today?
You
Is this Siri or Johnny
Jan 16 at 8:17 PM
Johnny Depp EXTERNAL
" Is this Siri or Johnny
???
I don't understand
You
You are not answering my question...like the answer is something Siri would say...
I asked if you laughed today. I asked this because I would hope every day would bring laughter to you
Johnny Depp EXTERNAL
" You are not answering my question... like the answer is something Siri would
Message Johnny Depp

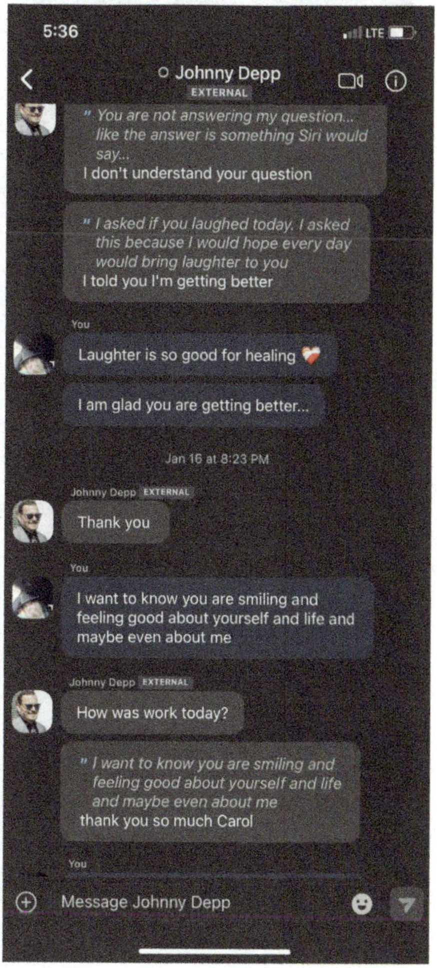
5:36
LTE
Johnny Depp
EXTERNAL
" You are not answering my question... like the answer is something Siri would say...
I don't understand your question
" I asked if you laughed today. I asked this because I would hope every day would bring laughter to you
I told you I'm getting better
You
Laughter is so good for healing
I am glad you are getting better...
Jan 16 at 8:23 PM
Johnny Depp EXTERNAL
Thank you
You
I want to know you are smiling and feeling good about yourself and life and maybe even about me
Johnny Depp EXTERNAL
How was work today?
" I want to know you are smiling and feeling good about yourself and life and maybe even about me
thank you so much Carol
You
Message Johnny Depp

Sometimes the communication was unclear like in the above text where my question was not answered. This could have been because my text was not read or it could have been that I was no communicating with a native English speaker.

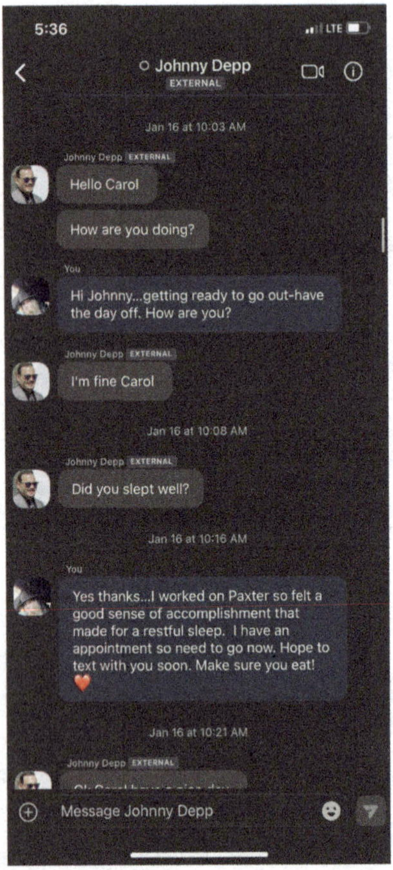
5:36
LTE
Johnny Depp
EXTERNAL
Jan 16 at 10:03 AM
Johnny Depp EXTERNAL
Hello Carol
How are you doing?
You
Hi Johnny...getting ready to go out-have the day off. How are you?
Johnny Depp EXTERNAL
I'm fine Carol
Jan 16 at 10:08 AM
Johnny Depp EXTERNAL
Did you slept well?
Jan 16 at 10:16 AM
You
Yes thanks...I worked on Paxter so felt a good sense of accomplishment that made for a restful sleep. I have an appointment so need to go now. Hope to text with you soon. Make sure you eat!
Jan 16 at 10:21 AM
Johnny Depp EXTERNAL
Message Johnny Depp

Regardless, I was getting used to the daily texts and I started to look forward to them.

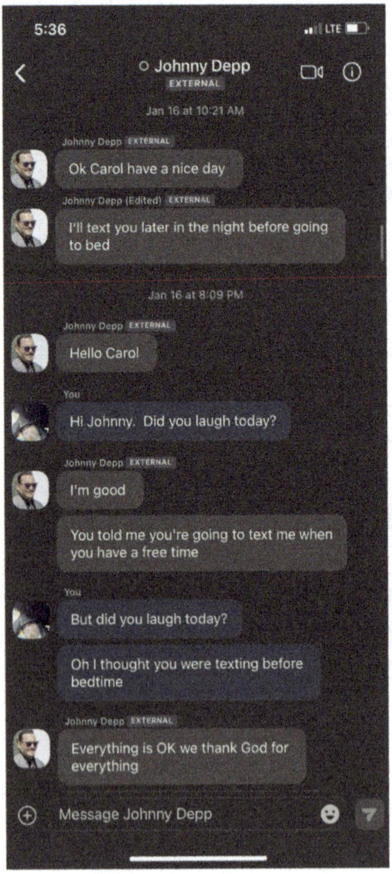
5:36
LTE
Johnny Depp
EXTERNAL
Jan 16 at 10:21 AM
Johnny Depp EXTERNAL
Ok Carol have a nice day
Johnny Depp (Edited) EXTERNAL
I'll text you later in the night before going to bed
Jan 16 at 8:09 PM
Johnny Depp EXTERNAL
Hello Carol
You
Hi Johnny. Did you laugh today?
Johnny Depp EXTERNAL
I'm good
You told me you're going to text me when you have a free time
You
But did you laugh today?
Oh I thought you were texting before bedtime
Johnny Depp EXTERNAL
Everything is OK we thank God for everything
Message Johnny Depp

Although little red flags telling me that the relationship was a sham appeared regularly, I chose to ignore them because I was beginning to have real feelings for the person I wanted to believe was texting me. Waking up to a text, receiving one during working hours, and one before I went to sleep made me feel special and cared for. I did not want it to end.

The chats we had made me feel like there was a real person who was genuinely interested in me and what was going on

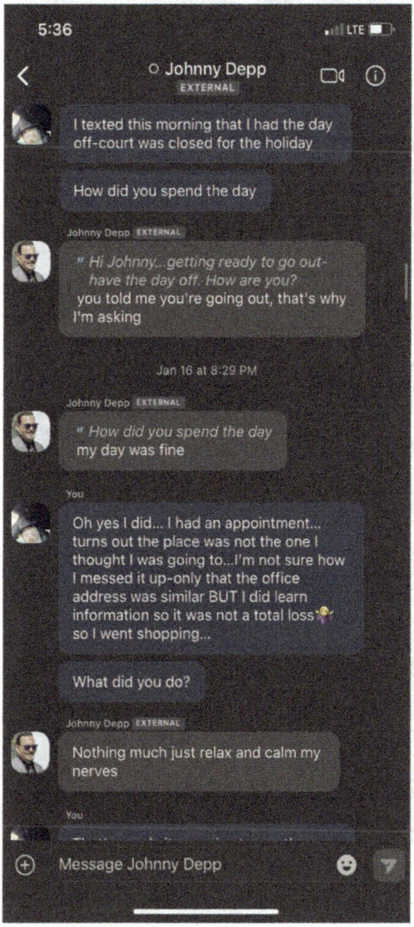

5:36
LTE
Johnny Depp
EXTERNAL
I texted this morning that I had the day off-court was closed for the holiday
How did you spend the day
Johnny Depp EXTERNAL
" Hi Johnny...getting ready to go out- have the day off. How are you?
you told me you're going out, that's why I'm asking
Jan 16 at 8:29 PM
Johnny Depp EXTERNAL
" How did you spend the day
my day was fine
You
Oh yes I did... I had an appointment... turns out the place was not the one I thought I was going to...I'm not sure how I messed it up-only that the office address was similar BUT I did learn information so it was not a total loss
so I went shopping...
What did you do?
Johnny Depp EXTERNAL
Nothing much just relax and calm my nerves
You
Message Johnny Depp

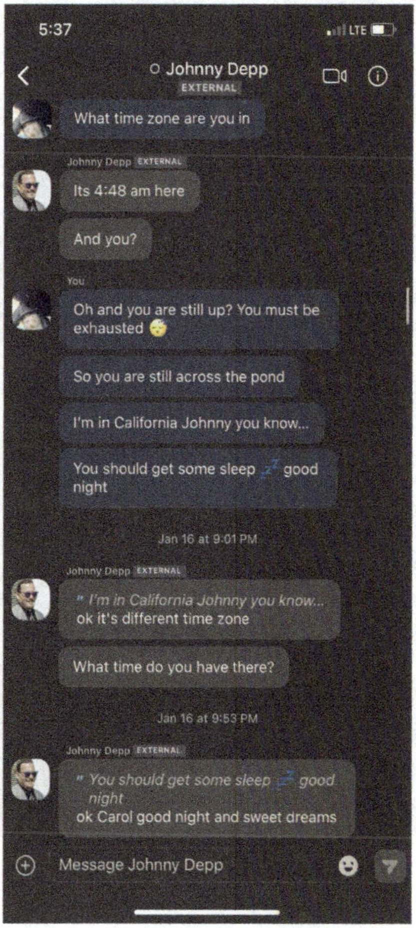

5:37
LTE
Johnny Depp
EXTERNAL
What time zone are you in
Johnny Depp EXTERNAL
Its 4:48 am here
And you?
You
Oh and you are still up? You must be exhausted
So you are still across the pond
I'm in California Johnny you know...
You should get some sleep good night
Jan 16 at 9:01 PM
Johnny Depp EXTERNAL
" I'm in California Johnny you know...
ok it's different time zone
What time do you have there?
Jan 16 at 9:53 PM
Johnny Depp EXTERNAL
" You should get some sleep good night
ok Carol good night and sweet dreams
Message Johnny Depp

I began to feel so comfortable that I ventured into personal questioning

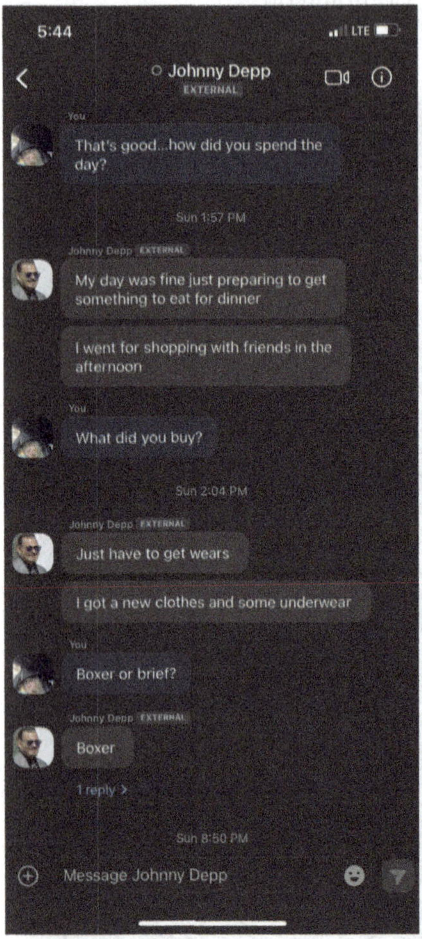
5:44
LTE
Johnny Depp
EXTERNAL
You
That's good...how did you spend the day?
Sun 1:57 PM
Johnny Depp EXTERNAL
My day was fine just preparing to get something to eat for dinner
I went for shopping with friends in the afternoon
You
What did you buy?
Sun 2:04 PM
Johnny Depp EXTERNAL
Just have to get wears
I got a new clothes and some underwear
You
Boxer or brief?
Johnny Depp EXTERNAL
Boxer
1 reply >
Sun 8:50 PM
Message Johnny Depp

5:44
LTE
Replies
Disconnected
Sun 2:06 PM
Johnny Depp EXTERNAL
Boxer
View more...
Sun 2:07 PM
You
Reply...

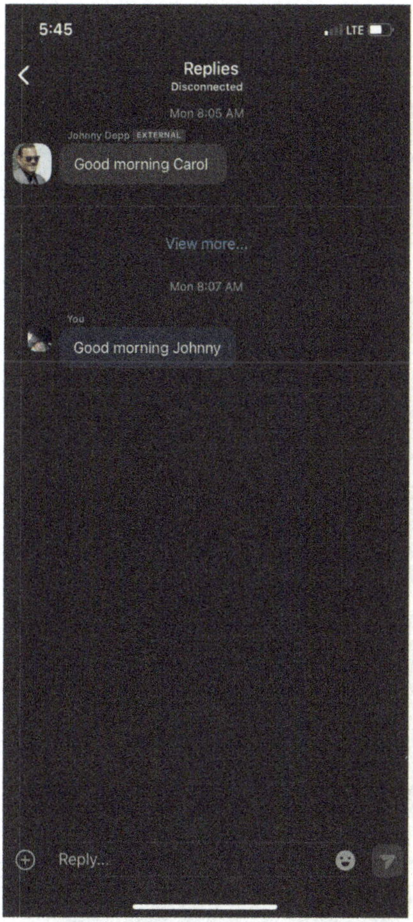
5:45
LTE
Replies
Disconnected
Mon 8:05 AM
Johnny Depp EXTERNAL
Good morning Carol
View more...
Mon 8:07 AM
You
Good morning Johnny
Reply...

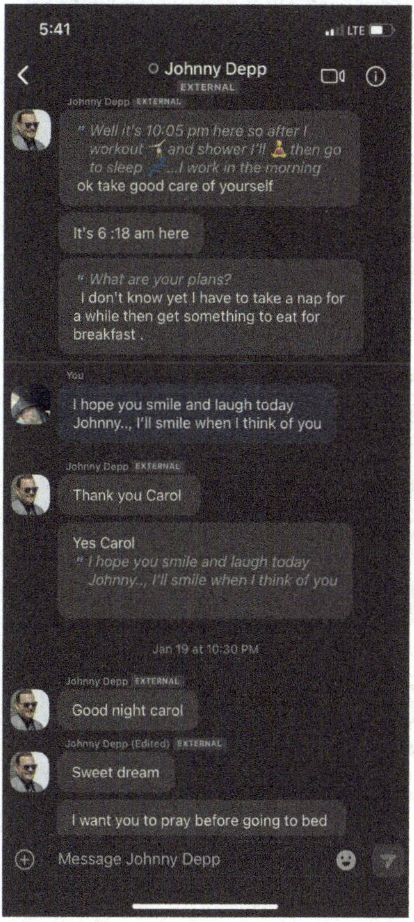
5:41
LTE
Johnny Depp
EXTERNAL
Johnny Depp EXTERNAL
" Well it's 10:05 pm here so after I workout and shower I'll then go to sleep ...I work in the morning
ok take good care of yourself
It's 6 :18 am here
" What are your plans?
I don't know yet I have to take a nap for a while then get something to eat for breakfast .
You
I hope you smile and laugh today Johnny.., I'll smile when I think of you
Johnny Depp EXTERNAL
Thank you Carol
Yes Carol
" I hope you smile and laugh today Johnny.., I'll smile when I think of you
Jan 19 at 10:30 PM
Johnny Depp EXTERNAL
Good night carol
Johnny Depp (Edited) EXTERNAL
Sweet dream
I want you to pray before going to bed
Message Johnny Depp

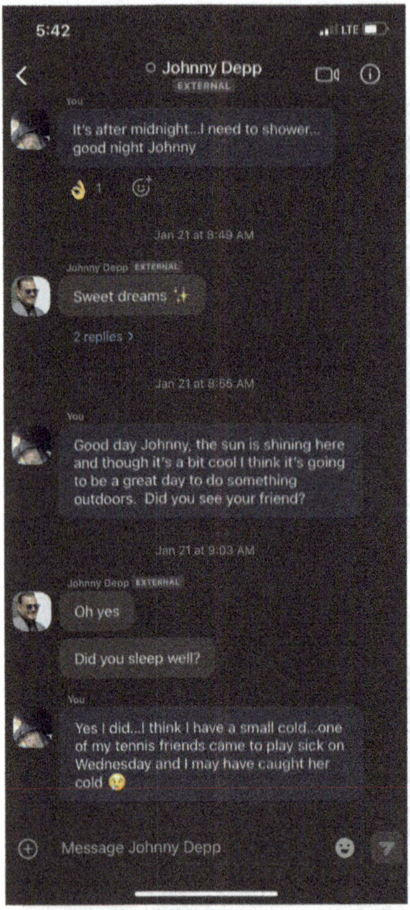
5:42
LTE
Johnny Depp
EXTERNAL
You
It's after midnight...I need to shower... good night Johnny
1
Jan 21 at 8:49 AM
Johnny Depp EXTERNAL
Sweet dreams
2 replies
Jan 21 at 8:56 AM
You
Good day Johnny, the sun is shining here and though it's a bit cool I think it's going to be a great day to do something outdoors. Did you see your friend?
Jan 21 at 9:03 AM
Johnny Depp EXTERNAL
Oh yes
Did you sleep well?
You
Yes I did...I think I have a small cold...one of my tennis friends came to play sick on Wednesday and I may have caught her cold
Message Johnny Depp

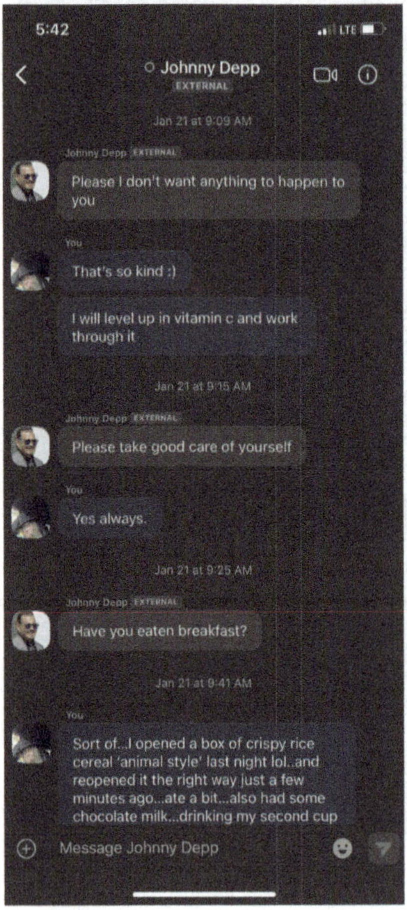
5:42
LTE
Johnny Depp
EXTERNAL
Jan 21 at 9:09 AM
Johnny Depp EXTERNAL
Please I don't want anything to happen to you
You
That's so kind :)
I will level up in vitamin c and work through it
Jan 21 at 9:15 AM
Johnny Depp EXTERNAL
Please take good care of yourself
You
Yes always.
Jan 21 at 9:25 AM
Johnny Depp EXTERNAL
Have you eaten breakfast?
Jan 21 at 9:41 AM
You
Sort of...I opened a box of crispy rice cereal 'animal style' last night lol..and reopened it the right way just a few minutes ago...ate a bit...also had some chocolate milk...drinking my second cup
Message Johnny Depp

This was the first time in my adult life I was asked about my daily food intake by someone who was not a physician and I liked it.

5:46
LTE
Replies
Disconnected
Johnny Depp EXTERNAL
" Oh and why don't I buy a RR with a 300k price tag? Seriously?
yes you can buy it if you want
I can see you worth more than a 300k car, you just don't wanna get a new one
You
No I could not... but anyway I have a car ...it has less than 7,000 miles on it so it will be good for a long time
So what are you going to do later?
Johnny Depp EXTERNAL
" No I could not... but anyway I have a car ...it has less than 7,000 miles on it so it will be good for a long time
okay
Well I don't think I have much things doing today
I just have to have something for breakfast, then rest for a while and continue reading my novel
You
Will you consider painting something for me? No pressure, just if you want to and have time
Reply...

5:46
LTE
Replies
Disconnected
You
It's a joke..."let's go " in German ...I drive a German car
Johnny Depp EXTERNAL
Lol ,ok
You
I don't speak German I just looked it up
Johnny Depp EXTERNAL
What is the model of your car?
Ok
Are you referring to Mercedes benz?
Mon 10:15 PM
You
Mercedes CLA
I was going to send you a pic
Johnny Depp EXTERNAL
Ok
You
Just sent
Reply...

Why would a scammer be interested in communicating with me? Looking over some of the earlier conversations I found a possible motive. During what appears to be innocent information sharing I was providing details about my life and status.

5:46
LTE
Replies
Disconnected
Johnny Depp EXTERNAL
Do you drive?
You
Yes of course
Johnny Depp EXTERNAL
Okay, what is the name of your car?
You
Well I had not named it...I guess I can call it Lass uns Gehen
Johnny Depp EXTERNAL
I don't understand
You
It's a joke..."let's go " in German ...I drive a German car
Johnny Depp EXTERNAL
Lol ,ok
You
I don't speak German I just looked it up
Johnny Depp EXTERNAL
What is the model of your car?
Ok
Reply...

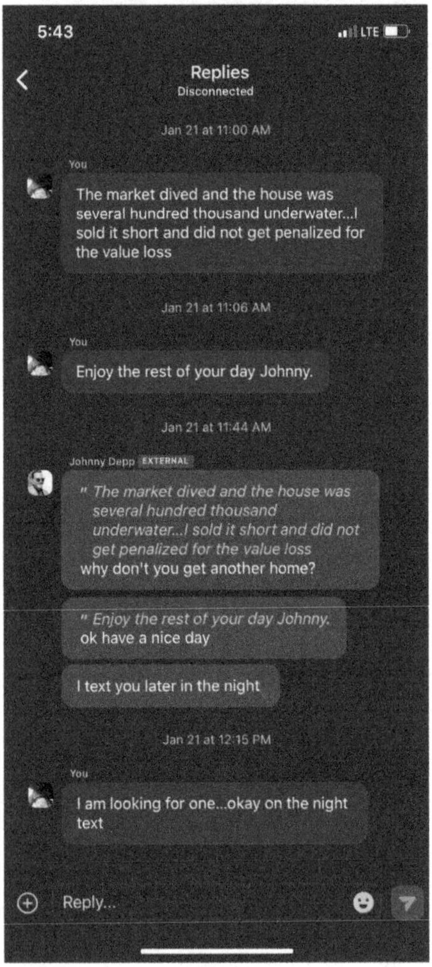
5:43
LTE
Replies
Disconnected
Jan 21 at 11:00 AM
You
The market dived and the house was several hundred thousand underwater...I sold it short and did not get penalized for the value loss
Jan 21 at 11:06 AM
You
Enjoy the rest of your day Johnny.
Jan 21 at 11:44 AM
Johnny Depp EXTERNAL
" The market dived and the house was several hundred thousand underwater...I sold it short and did not get penalized for the value loss
why don't you get another home?
" Enjoy the rest of your day Johnny.
ok have a nice day
I text you later in the night
Jan 21 at 12:15 PM
You
I am looking for one...okay on the night text
Reply...

One example is this conversation about the car I had. I disclosed that I drove a Mercedes Benz. I even sent a picture of my car parked in carport where I lived. My having an expensive car could have been interpreted that I was living a high end lifestyle. The imposter said he/she/it drove a Rolls Royce and indicated that I could purchase the same. I was quick to deny that possibility and wanted to emphasize that I was not even close to having that level of wealth.

I was very careful not to embellish my circumstance. The truth was I worked as a public servant and had lived in a tiny studio in order to save the money required to buy the car I drove. I had to sell my former house short or lose it to foreclosure after the market tanked in 2008. I was not ashamed of my truth. I was actually proud that I had paid off my debt and was happy to be working for the court in a position I found meaningful.

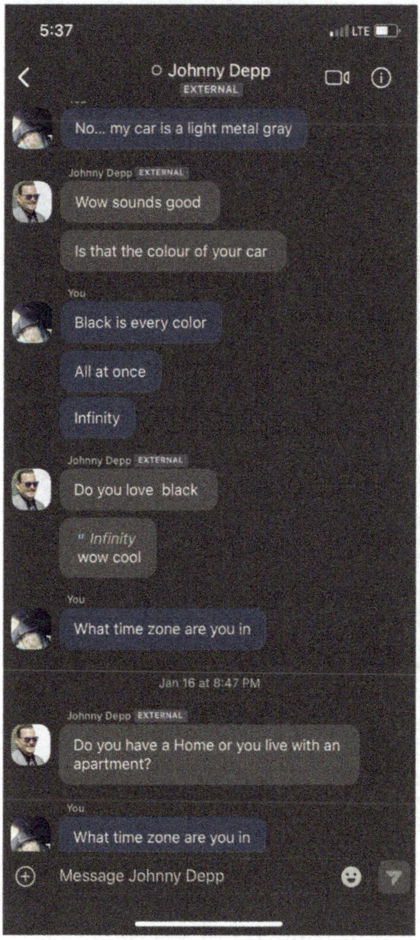
5:37
LTE
Johnny Depp
EXTERNAL
No... my car is a light metal gray
Johnny Depp EXTERNAL
Wow sounds good
Is that the colour of your car
You
Black is every color
All at once
Infinity
Johnny Depp EXTERNAL
Do you love black
" Infinity
wow cool
You
What time zone are you in
Jan 16 at 8:47 PM
Johnny Depp EXTERNAL
Do you have a Home or you live with an apartment?
You
What time zone are you in
Message Johnny Depp

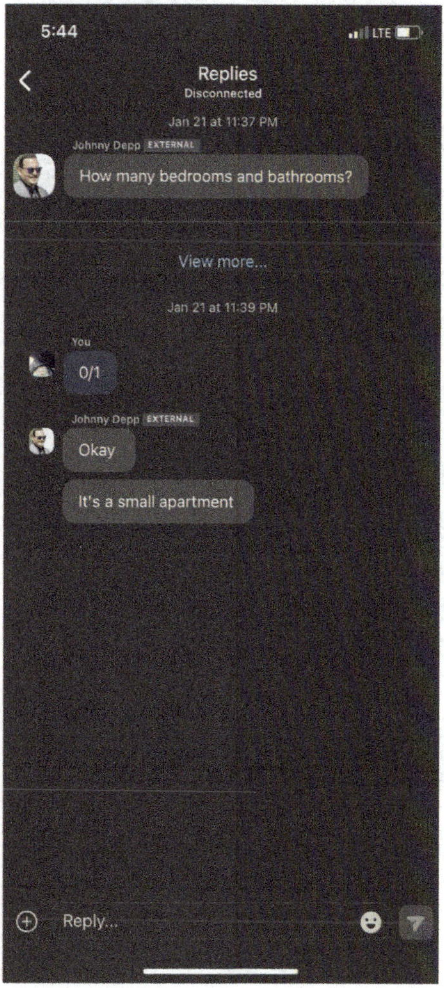
5:44
LTE
Replies
Disconnected
Jan 21 at 11:37 PM
Johnny Depp EXTERNAL
How many bedrooms and bathrooms?
View more...
Jan 21 at 11:39 PM
You
0/1
Johnny Depp EXTERNAL
Okay
It's a small apartment
Reply...

At this point in the texting I had provided information about my vehicle, the size of the apartment I lived in, among other things.

BLOOD OATH, a TEST?

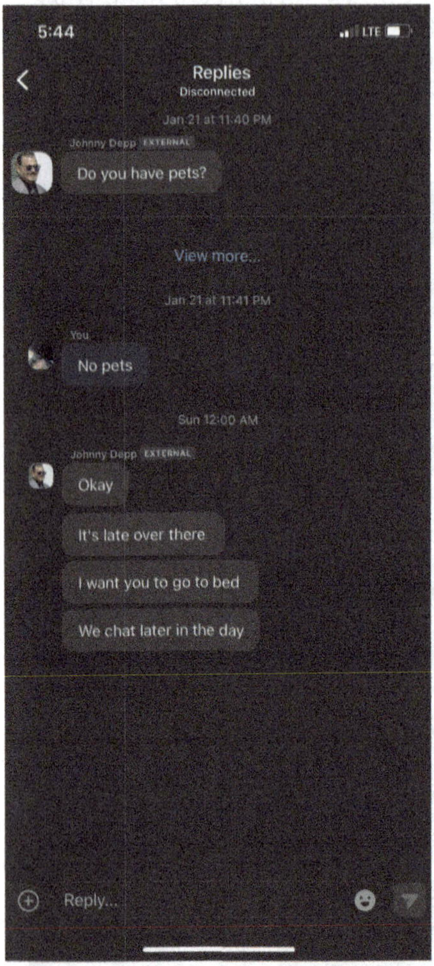
5:44
LTE
Replies
Disconnected
Jan 21 at 11:40 PM
Johnny Depp EXTERNAL
Do you have pets?
View more...
Jan 21 at 11:41 PM
You
No pets
Sun 12:00 AM
Johnny Depp EXTERNAL
Okay
It's late over there
I want you to go to bed
We chat later in the day
Reply...

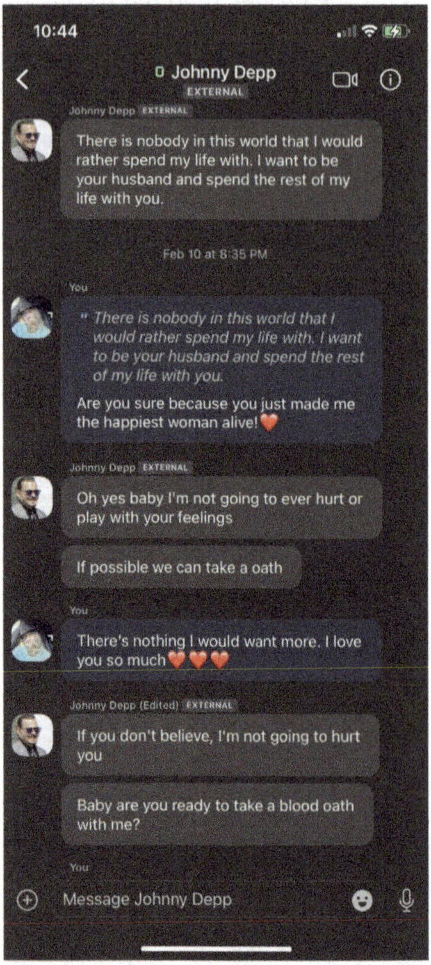
10:44
Johnny Depp
EXTERNAL
Johnny Depp EXTERNAL
There is nobody in this world that I would rather spend my life with. I want to be your husband and spend the rest of my life with you.
Feb 10 at 8:35 PM
You
" There is nobody in this world that I would rather spend my life with. I want to be your husband and spend the rest of my life with you.
Are you sure because you just made me the happiest woman alive!
Johnny Depp EXTERNAL
Oh yes baby I'm not going to ever hurt or play with your feelings
If possible we can take a oath
You
There's nothing I would want more. I love you so much
Johnny Depp (Edited) EXTERNAL
If you don't believe, I'm not going to hurt you
Baby are you ready to take a blood oath with me?
You
Message Johnny Depp

This round of texting is now going on for more than a month. The scammer(s) are beginning to "lay it on thick" as evidenced in the texts that have become more intimate and include words of love and promises. My texts answer with the same sweet words. I am in the thick of it really at this point and honestly have started to believe in the possibility of this relationship. I am clouded by my own emotions and wanted this to be real. So much so that at the time it was happening I did not see that what came next was likely a test by the scammer(s) to find out what level of control he/she/they/it had over me. What better way than to ask for an oath?

This next group of texts both disturbed and intrigued me. My instincts told me to run for the hills but at the same time stick around because this was the most interesting thing that has happened in my life in recent years. My mind was racing as I read each text. On the one hand whoever this was was professing love with sweet words of commitment. On the other hand, the suggestion of a blood oath was scary and surreal. I did not consider that there would be real blood shed until I saw the text with a bloody finger pictured. Was that for real? Was this man as eccentric as this request to oath with blood suggested? Or, was this a test to see what level of control the scammer(s) had over me?

Notice in this group of texts that the scammer(s) seems to forget where I was located which was not in the UK.

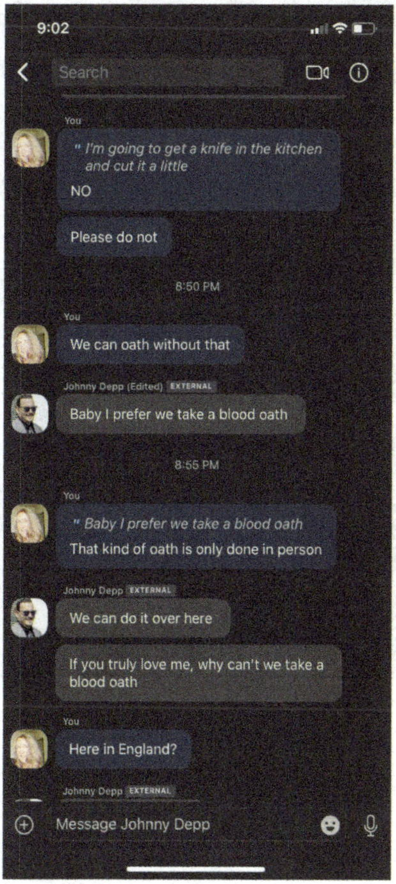
9:02
Search
You
" I'm going to get a knife in the kitchen and cut it a little
NO
Please do not
8:50 PM
You
We can oath without that
Johnny Depp (Edited) EXTERNAL
Baby I prefer we take a blood oath
8:55 PM
You
" Baby I prefer we take a blood oath
That kind of oath is only done in person
Johnny Depp EXTERNAL
We can do it over here
If you truly love me, why can't we take a blood oath
You
Here in England?
Johnny Depp EXTERNAL
Message Johnny Depp

I tried appealing to reason but that did not work. When I reviewed this section of text thread several months later it occurred to me that if this was not a test of loyalty it could have been a joke made at my expense.

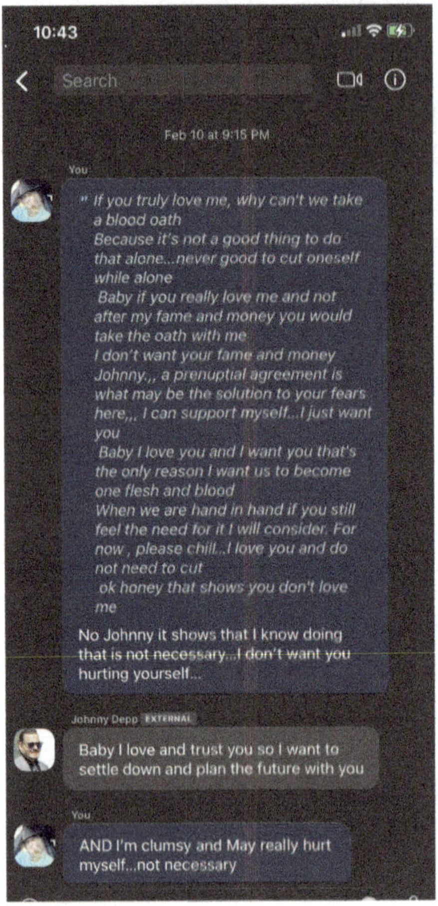

10:43

Search

Feb 10 at 9:15 PM

You

" *If you truly love me, why can't we take a blood oath*
Because it's not a good thing to do that alone...never good to cut oneself while alone
Baby if you really love me and not after my fame and money you would take the oath with me
I don't want your fame and money Johnny,,, a prenuptial agreement is what may be the solution to your fears here,,, I can support myself...I just want you
Baby I love you and I want you that's the only reason I want us to become one flesh and blood
When we are hand in hand if you still feel the need for it I will consider. For now , please chill..I love you and do not need to cut
ok honey that shows you don't love me

No Johnny it shows that I know doing that is not necessary...I don't want you hurting yourself...

Johnny Depp EXTERNAL

Baby I love and trust you so I want to settle down and plan the future with you

You

AND I'm clumsy and May really hurt myself...not necessary

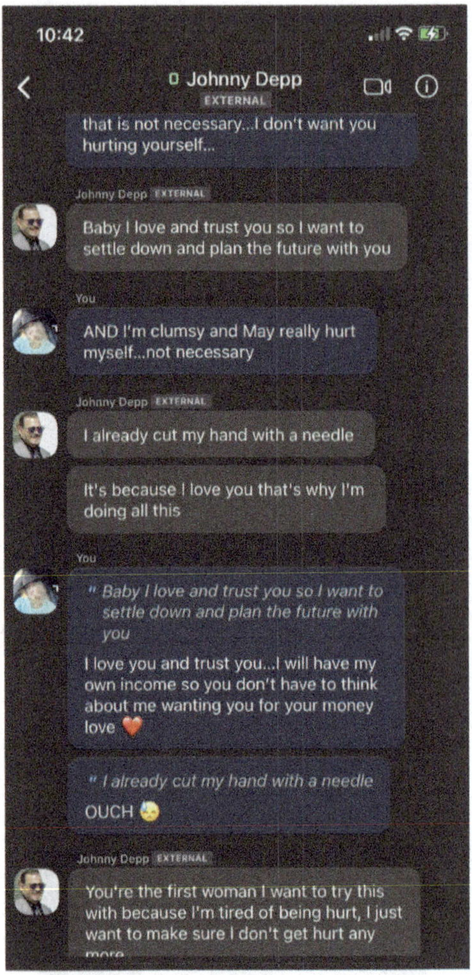

10:42

Johnny Depp
EXTERNAL

that is not necessary...I don't want you hurting yourself...

Johnny Depp EXTERNAL

Baby I love and trust you so I want to settle down and plan the future with you

You

AND I'm clumsy and May really hurt myself...not necessary

Johnny Depp EXTERNAL

I already cut my hand with a needle

It's because I love you that's why I'm doing all this

You

" *Baby I love and trust you so I want to settle down and plan the future with you*

I love you and trust you...I will have my own income so you don't have to think about me wanting you for your money love ❤️

" *I already cut my hand with a needle*

OUCH 😓

Johnny Depp EXTERNAL

You're the first woman I want to try this with because I'm tired of being hurt, I just want to make sure I don't get hurt any more

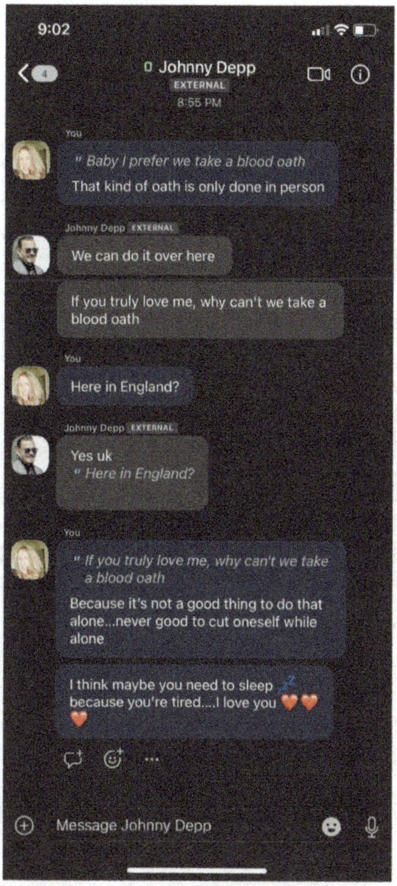
9:02
Johnny Depp
EXTERNAL
8:55 PM
You
" Baby I prefer we take a blood oath
That kind of oath is only done in person
Johnny Depp EXTERNAL
We can do it over here
If you truly love me, why can't we take a blood oath
You
Here in England?
Johnny Depp EXTERNAL
Yes uk
" Here in England?
You
" If you truly love me, why can't we take a blood oath
Because it's not a good thing to do that alone...never good to cut oneself while alone
I think maybe you need to sleep because you're tired....I love you
Message Johnny Depp

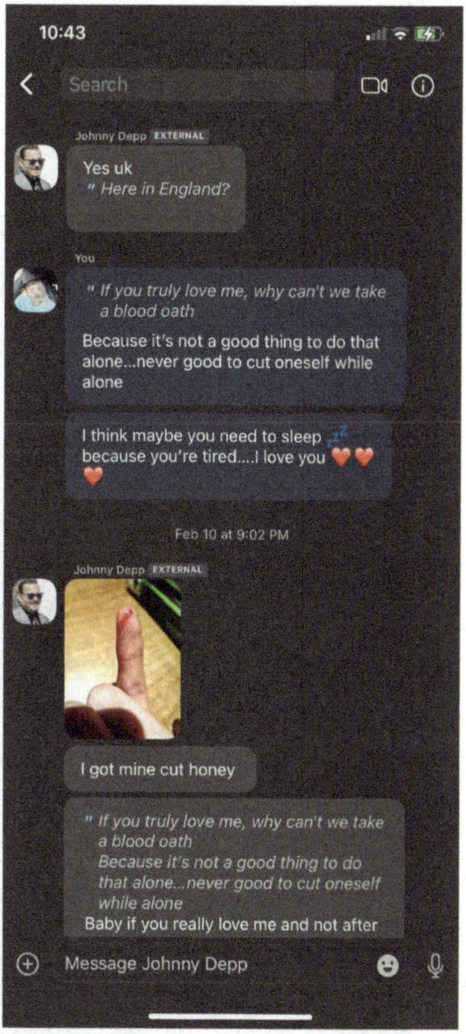
10:43
Search
Johnny Depp EXTERNAL
Yes uk
" Here in England?
You
" If you truly love me, why can't we take a blood oath
Because it's not a good thing to do that alone...never good to cut oneself while alone
I think maybe you need to sleep because you're tired....I love you
Feb 10 at 9:02 PM
Johnny Depp EXTERNAL
I got mine cut honey
" If you truly love me, why can't we take a blood oath
Because it's not a good thing to do that alone...never good to cut oneself while alone
Baby if you really love me and not after
Message Johnny Depp

When I saw the bloody finger picture I was really freaked out. On subsequent review it appears that the picture was photoshopped (see the right and left side). I was unable to find a matching stock photo, though I did not make an exhaustive search.

My suggestion of a prenuptial agreement was not responded to and this bolsters my theory that the blood oath was only a test. Requesting someone "oath with blood" for assurance that person would not hurt or play with another's feelings is just plain weird. If someone had the intention to hurt someone else they probably would not be deterred by a blood oath.

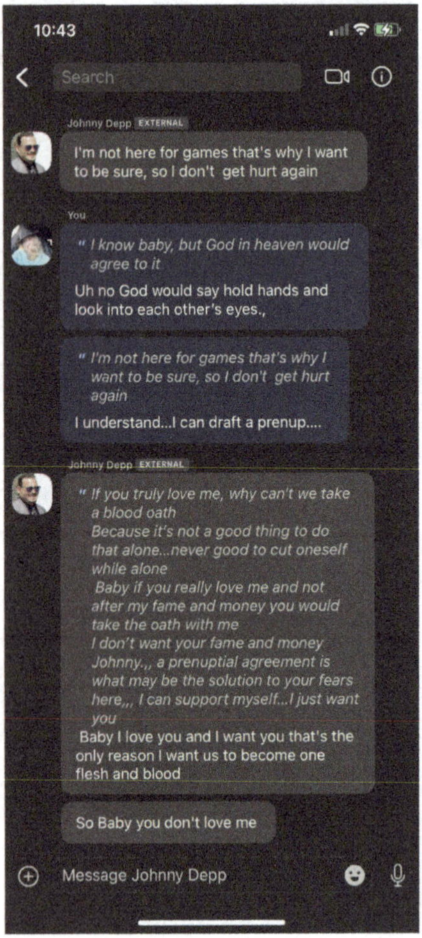
10:43
Search
Johnny Depp EXTERNAL
I'm not here for games that's why I want to be sure, so I don't get hurt again
You
" I know baby, but God in heaven would agree to it
Uh no God would say hold hands and look into each other's eyes.,
" I'm not here for games that's why I want to be sure, so I don't get hurt again
I understand...I can draft a prenup....
Johnny Depp EXTERNAL
" If you truly love me, why can't we take a blood oath Because it's not a good thing to do that alone...never good to cut oneself while alone Baby if you really love me and not after my fame and money you would take the oath with me I don't want your fame and money Johnny.,, a prenuptial agreement is what may be the solution to your fears here,,, I can support myself...I just want you
Baby I love you and I want you that's the only reason I want us to become one flesh and blood
So Baby you don't love me
Message Johnny Depp

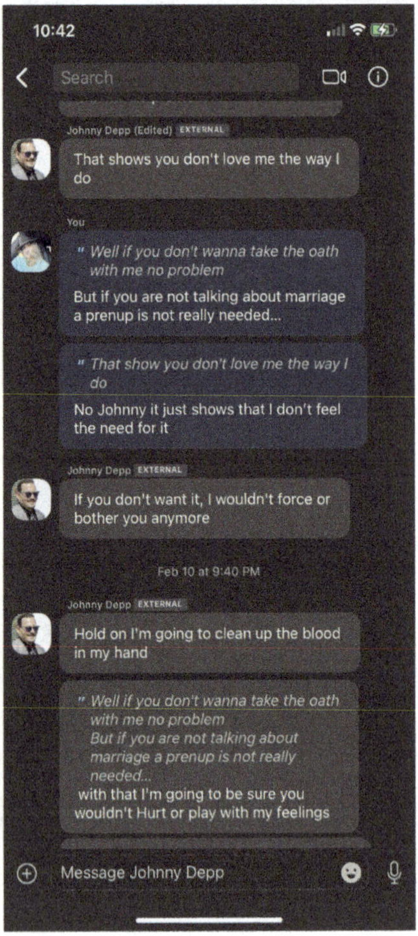
10:42
Search
Johnny Depp (Edited) EXTERNAL
That shows you don't love me the way I do
You
" Well if you don't wanna take the oath with me no problem
But if you are not talking about marriage a prenup is not really needed...
" That show you don't love me the way I do
No Johnny it just shows that I don't feel the need for it
Johnny Depp EXTERNAL
If you don't want it, I wouldn't force or bother you anymore
Feb 10 at 9:40 PM
Johnny Depp EXTERNAL
Hold on I'm going to clean up the blood in my hand
" Well if you don't wanna take the oath with me no problem But if you are not talking about marriage a prenup is not really needed...
with that I'm going to be sure you wouldn't Hurt or play with my feelings
Message Johnny Depp

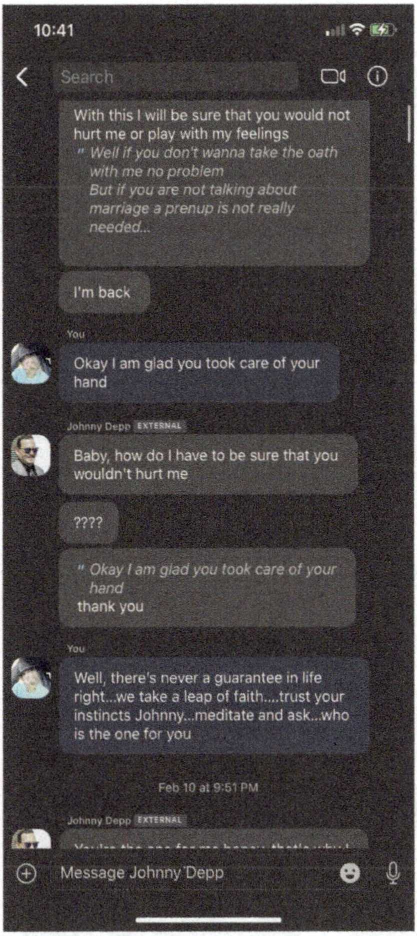
10:41
Search
With this I will be sure that you would not hurt me or play with my feelings
" Well if you don't wanna take the oath with me no problem
But if you are not talking about marriage a prenup is not really needed...
I'm back
You
Okay I am glad you took care of your hand
Johnny Depp EXTERNAL
Baby, how do I have to be sure that you wouldn't hurt me
????
" Okay I am glad you took care of your hand
thank you
You
Well, there's never a guarantee in life right...we take a leap of faith....trust your instincts Johnny...meditate and ask...who is the one for you
Feb 10 at 9:51 PM
Johnny Depp EXTERNAL
Message Johnny Depp

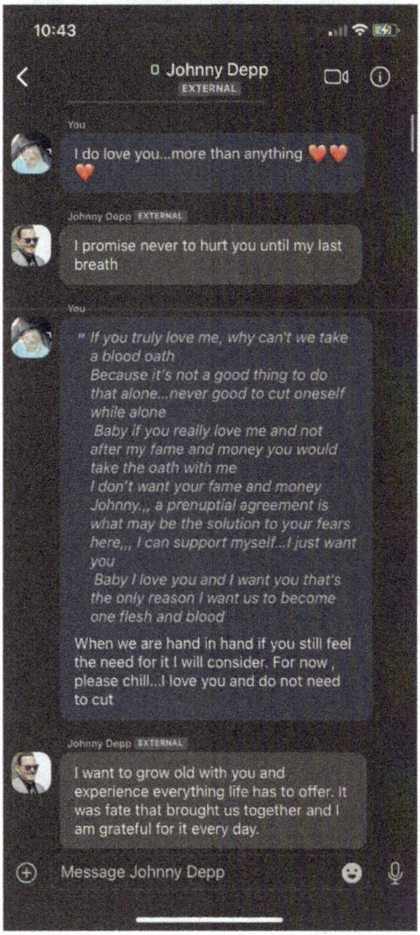
10:43
Johnny Depp
EXTERNAL
You
I do love you...more than anything ❤️❤️❤️
Johnny Depp EXTERNAL
I promise never to hurt you until my last breath
You
" If you truly love me, why can't we take a blood oath
Because it's not a good thing to do that alone...never good to cut oneself while alone
Baby if you really love me and not after my fame and money you would take the oath with me
I don't want your fame and money Johnny.,, a prenuptial agreement is what may be the solution to your fears here,,, I can support myself...I just want you
Baby I love you and I want you that's the only reason I want us to become one flesh and blood
When we are hand in hand if you still feel the need for it I will consider. For now , please chill...I love you and do not need to cut
Johnny Depp EXTERNAL
I want to grow old with you and experience everything life has to offer. It was fate that brought us together and I am grateful for it every day.
Message Johnny Depp

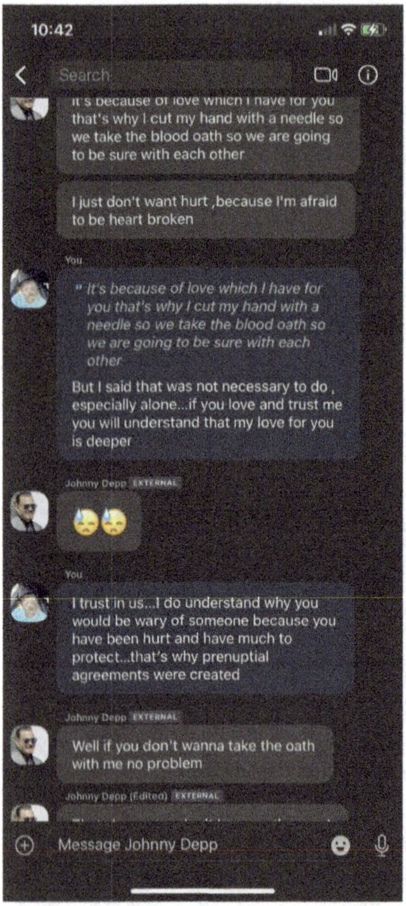
10:42
Search
It's because of love which I have for you that's why I cut my hand with a needle so we take the blood oath so we are going to be sure with each other
I just don't want hurt ,because I'm afraid to be heart broken
You
" It's because of love which I have for you that's why I cut my hand with a needle so we take the blood oath so we are going to be sure with each other
But I said that was not necessary to do , especially alone...if you love and trust me you will understand that my love for you is deeper
Johnny Depp EXTERNAL
You
I trust in us...I do understand why you would be wary of someone because you have been hurt and have much to protect...that's why prenuptial agreements were created
Johnny Depp EXTERNAL
Well if you don't wanna take the oath with me no problem
Johnny Depp (Edited) EXTERNAL
Message Johnny Depp

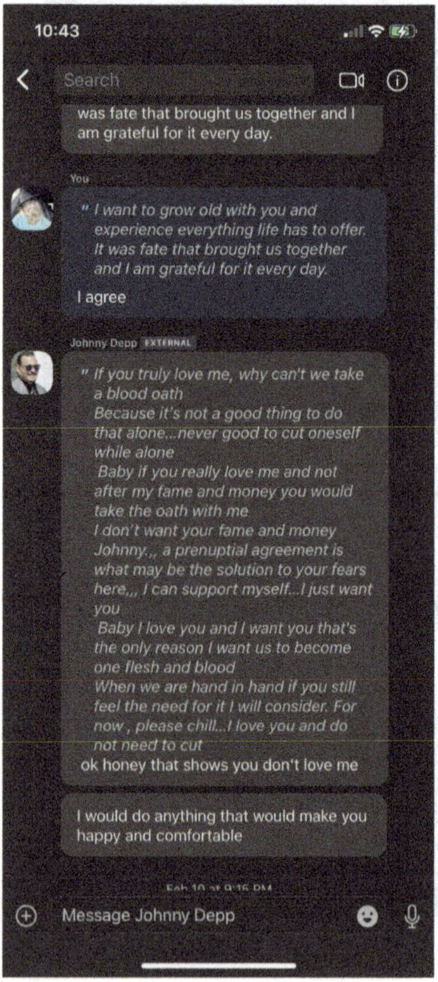
10:43
Search
was fate that brought us together and I am grateful for it every day.
You
" I want to grow old with you and experience everything life has to offer. It was fate that brought us together and I am grateful for it every day.
I agree
Johnny Depp EXTERNAL
" If you truly love me, why can't we take a blood oath
Because it's not a good thing to do that alone...never good to cut oneself while alone
Baby if you really love me and not after my fame and money you would take the oath with me
I don't want your fame and money Johnny.,, a prenuptial agreement is what may be the solution to your fears here,,, I can support myself...I just want you
Baby I love you and I want you that's the only reason I want us to become one flesh and blood
When we are hand in hand if you still feel the need for it I will consider. For now , please chill...I love you and do not need to cut
ok honey that shows you don't love me
I would do anything that would make you happy and comfortable
Message Johnny Depp

I did not agree to a blood oath. Would you? What happened earlier that day set the stage for this test of control.

When I opened the chat I found it had disappeared from my phone and I was worried. What caused this? My heart sunk when I considered that if I was chatting with Johnny Depp, he suddenly changed his mind and decided not to continue the connection. I even reached out to the person who arranged our connection because I was so worried.

Did you catch the "Who's Cheryl" red flag?

If the January request to connect sent by someone claiming to be Cheryl spellins (sic) was legitimate, why would "Johnny" ask who she was?

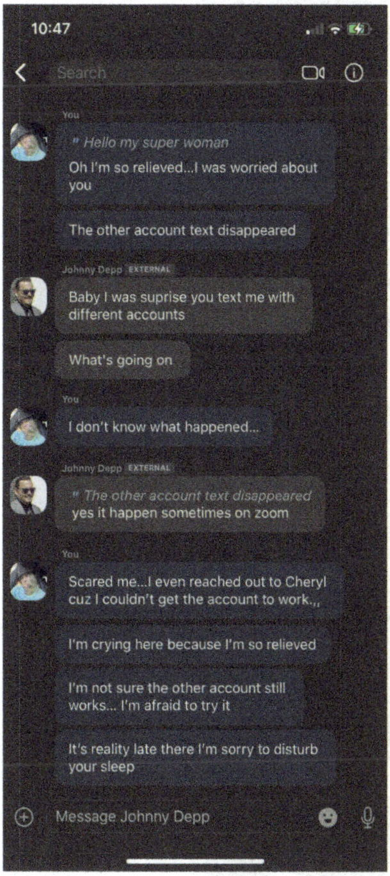
10:47
Search
You
" Hello my super woman
Oh I'm so relieved...I was worried about you
The other account text disappeared
Johnny Depp EXTERNAL
Baby I was suprise you text me with different accounts
What's going on
You
I don't know what happened...
Johnny Depp EXTERNAL
" The other account text disappeared
yes it happen sometimes on zoom
You
Scared me...I even reached out to Cheryl cuz I couldn't get the account to work,,,
I'm crying here because I'm so relieved
I'm not sure the other account still works... I'm afraid to try it
It's reality late there I'm sorry to disturb your sleep
Message Johnny Depp

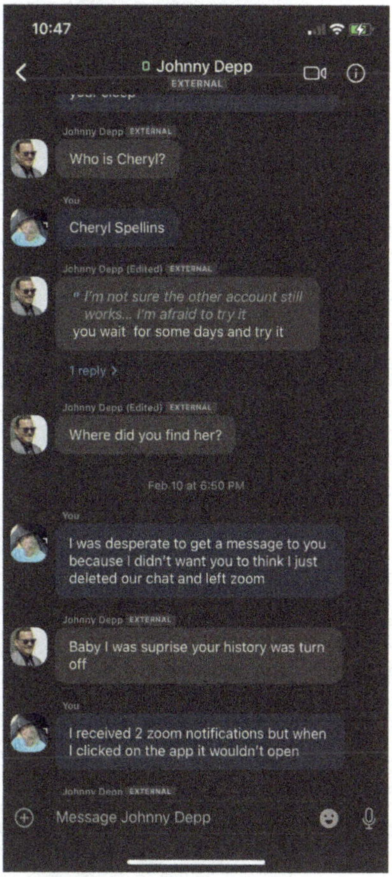
10:47
Johnny Depp
EXTERNAL
Johnny Depp EXTERNAL
Who is Cheryl?
You
Cheryl Spellins
Johnny Depp (Edited) EXTERNAL
" I'm not sure the other account still works... I'm afraid to try it
you wait for some days and try it
1 reply
Johnny Depp (Edited) EXTERNAL
Where did you find her?
Feb 10 at 6:50 PM
You
I was desperate to get a message to you because I didn't want you to think I just deleted our chat and left zoom
Johnny Depp EXTERNAL
Baby I was suprise your history was turn off
You
I received 2 zoom notifications but when I clicked on the app it wouldn't open
Message Johnny Depp

The chatting just continued as was usual. I was never able to recover the chat in the other account that disappeared. Hindsight tells me this was a red flag.

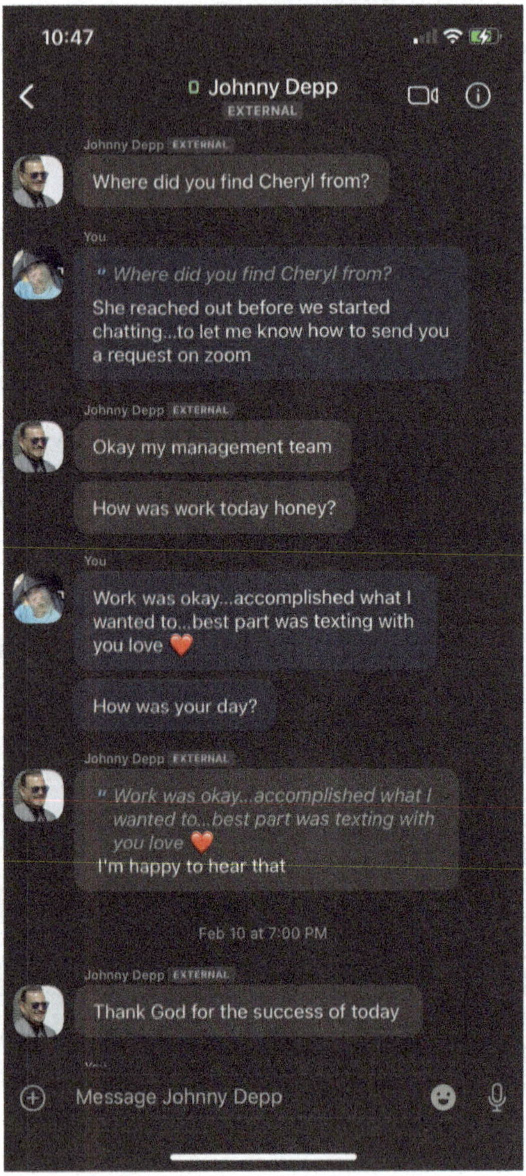

10:47
Johnny Depp
EXTERNAL
Johnny Depp EXTERNAL
Where did you find Cheryl from?
You
" Where did you find Cheryl from?
She reached out before we started chatting...to let me know how to send you a request on zoom
Johnny Depp EXTERNAL
Okay my management team
How was work today honey?
You
Work was okay...accomplished what I wanted to...best part was texting with you love ❤️
How was your day?
Johnny Depp EXTERNAL
" Work was okay...accomplished what I wanted to...best part was texting with you love ❤️
I'm happy to hear that
Feb 10 at 7:00 PM
Johnny Depp EXTERNAL
Thank God for the success of today
Message Johnny Depp

THE VALENTINES

With Valentines Day fast approaching our texting became more intense, loving, and intimate. Still, we had not physically met so I suggested something that I thought would be fun while at the same time take off any Valentines Day performance pressure a couple may have in a newer relationship.

My suggestion was that we have a "throwback to our high school days" valentine. The background I provided was that we still lived at home with our parents. He earned money on weekends as a caddie at the local country club where I also worked cleaning golf shoes and handing out towels in the ladies locker room. We each had a $30 budget to spend on a gift and the date. I planned a date that included a romantic stroll along the beach and exchanging our gifts while sharing our reason(s) for the gift choice we each made. What did the scammer(s) have in mind? Not sure really, except what appeared to be a laugh at my expense.

I stupidly provided my home address. But for the safety I felt in my surroundings both at work and at home, I never would have done that. There was also the other plans we were making (discussed in the next section) and I suppose that provided me with some level of comfort. Regardless, it was extremely foolish.

Unknown to me at the time was that the scammer(s) gave me a bogus address to send my gift. When the scammer(s) became argumentative after I brought up what I recalled as our agreement to take and share pictures of our valentines, I was a bit shocked.

Later, I realized there may have been an explanation for the supposed lack of memory. Around this same time the zoom chat history had disappeared from my phone. This may have been a hand off between scammers. At the time I didn't see this huge red flag but it was an indication that there were multiple scammers involved.

Never provide your home address to anyone you have not met in person. Also, if someone gives you an address, research it to confirm that it is a legitimate address. If you discover the address is fake ask questions.

It was clear that this scammer had no recollection of our prior conversation. Now I realize that is because that part of the conversation was deleted from the chat history. Instead of acknowledging this the scammer lashed out and became argumentative.

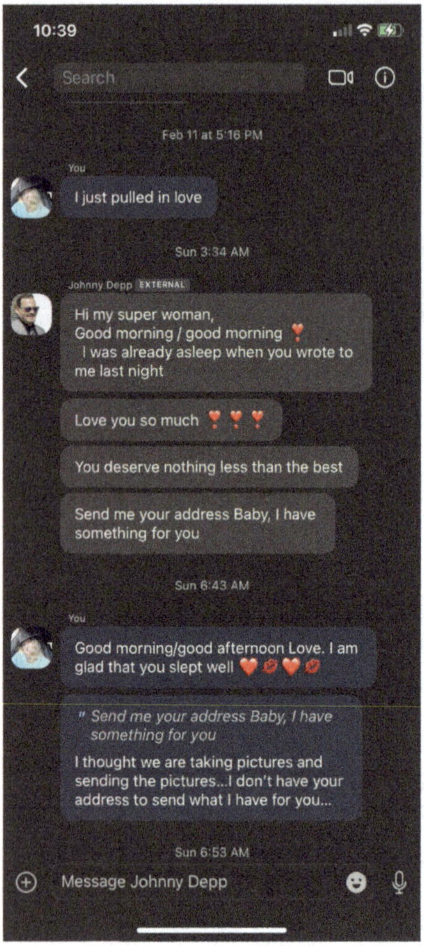
10:39
Search
Feb 11 at 5:16 PM
You
I just pulled in love
Sun 3:34 AM
Johnny Depp EXTERNAL
Hi my super woman,
Good morning / good morning
I was already asleep when you wrote to me last night
Love you so much
You deserve nothing less than the best
Send me your address Baby, I have something for you
Sun 6:43 AM
You
Good morning/good afternoon Love. I am glad that you slept well
" Send me your address Baby, I have something for you
I thought we are taking pictures and sending the pictures...I don't have your address to send what I have for you...
Sun 6:53 AM
Message Johnny Depp

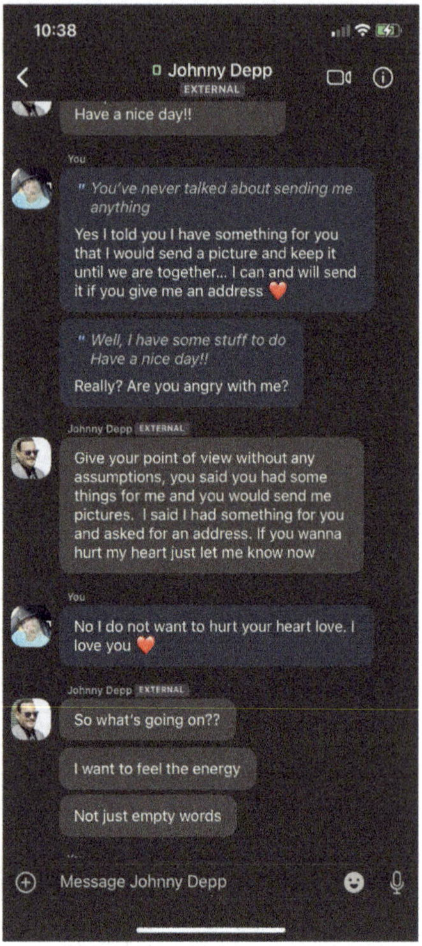
10:38
Johnny Depp
EXTERNAL
Have a nice day!!
You
" You've never talked about sending me anything
Yes I told you I have something for you that I would send a picture and keep it until we are together... I can and will send it if you give me an address
" Well, I have some stuff to do Have a nice day!!
Really? Are you angry with me?
Johnny Depp EXTERNAL
Give your point of view without any assumptions, you said you had some things for me and you would send me pictures. I said I had something for you and asked for an address. If you wanna hurt my heart just let me know now
You
No I do not want to hurt your heart love. I love you
Johnny Depp EXTERNAL
So what's going on??
I want to feel the energy
Not just empty words
Message Johnny Depp

Not only did the scammer become argumentative, the facts were turned around to make me feel like I was the one who instigated the issue when all I did was ask a question. This is classic narcissistic behavior. I ended up apologizing and missed another red flag!

I really had no expectations on Valentines Day. I was teetering back and forth on whether or not I believed the relationship was real but to be honest here I was falling in love with the man I thought I could be chatting with. The logical, reasonable side of me told me that if there really was a man who cared for me behind this texting character he would make a real effort to see me and thus far no effort was realized.

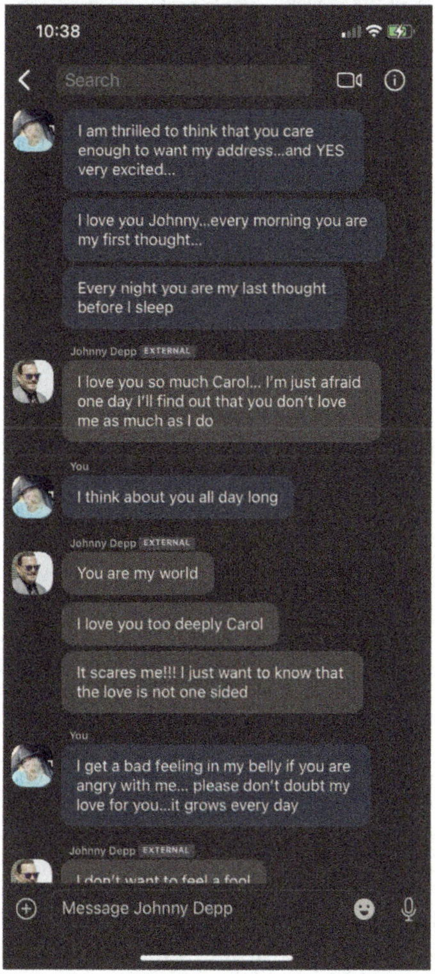
10:38
Search
I am thrilled to think that you care enough to want my address...and YES very excited...
I love you Johnny...every morning you are my first thought...
Every night you are my last thought before I sleep
Johnny Depp EXTERNAL
I love you so much Carol... I'm just afraid one day I'll find out that you don't love me as much as I do
You
I think about you all day long
Johnny Depp EXTERNAL
You are my world
I love you too deeply Carol
It scares me!!! I just want to know that the love is not one sided
You
I get a bad feeling in my belly if you are angry with me... please don't doubt my love for you...it grows every day
Johnny Depp EXTERNAL
Message Johnny Depp

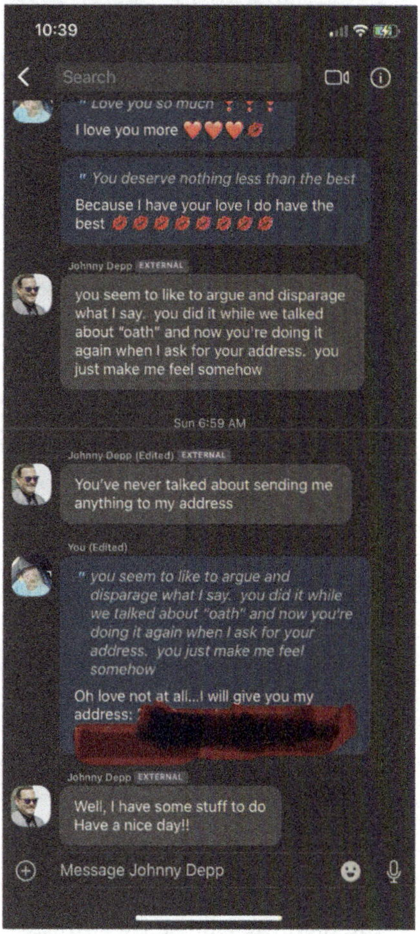
10:39
Search
I love you more
" You deserve nothing less than the best
Because I have your love I do have the best
Johnny Depp EXTERNAL
you seem to like to argue and disparage what I say. you did it while we talked about "oath" and now you're doing it again when I ask for your address. you just make me feel somehow
Sun 6:59 AM
Johnny Depp (Edited) EXTERNAL
You've never talked about sending me anything to my address
You (Edited)
" you seem to like to argue and disparage what I say. you did it while we talked about "oath" and now you're doing it again when I ask for your address. you just make me feel somehow
Oh love not at all...I will give you my address: [redacted]
Johnny Depp EXTERNAL
Well, I have some stuff to do
Have a nice day!!
Message Johnny Depp

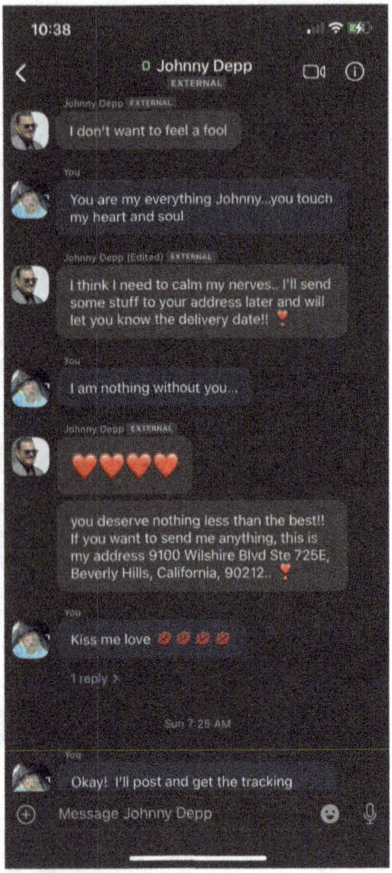
10:38
Johnny Depp
EXTERNAL
Johnny Depp EXTERNAL
I don't want to feel a fool
You
You are my everything Johnny...you touch my heart and soul
Johnny Depp (Edited) EXTERNAL
I think I need to calm my nerves.. I'll send some stuff to your address later and will let you know the delivery date!!
You
I am nothing without you...
Johnny Depp EXTERNAL
you deserve nothing less than the best!! If you want to send me anything, this is my address 9100 Wilshire Blvd Ste 725E, Beverly Hills, California, 90212..
You
Kiss me love
1 reply
Sun 7:25 AM
You
Okay! I'll post and get the tracking
Message Johnny Depp

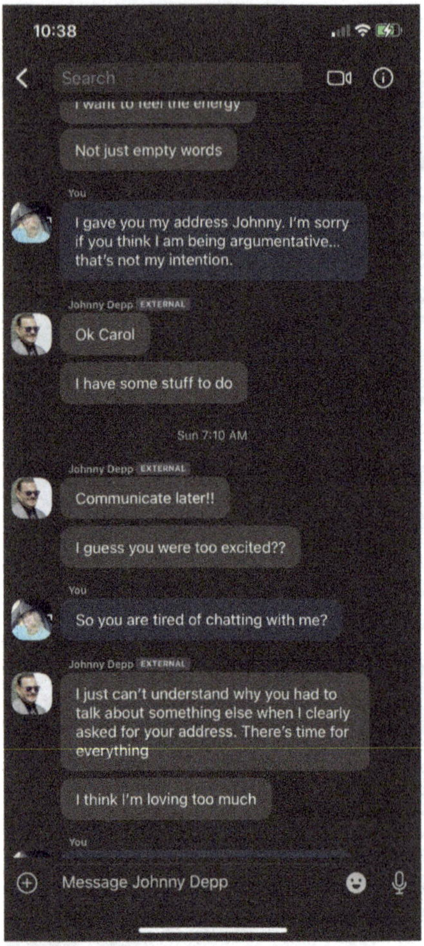
10:38
Search
Not just empty words
You
I gave you my address Johnny. I'm sorry if you think I am being argumentative... that's not my intention.
Johnny Depp EXTERNAL
Ok Carol
I have some stuff to do
Sun 7:10 AM
Johnny Depp EXTERNAL
Communicate later!!
I guess you were too excited??
You
So you are tired of chatting with me?
Johnny Depp EXTERNAL
I just can't understand why you had to talk about something else when I clearly asked for your address. There's time for everything
I think I'm loving too much
You
Message Johnny Depp

I mailed the silhouette and card to the address I was given, but that address turned out to be the address of a virtual office, so I do not know if anyone actually received it or where it may be now.

After opening the box left at my doorstep hours before while I was at work, I was surprised to find the costume jewelry set inside. Although it was somewhat insulting to receive a gift like this that I would never wear, I reminded myself of the throwback to teenage years that I had suggested. The problem I had with it was that the gift did not gel with the references the scammer later made to it being 'special'. There was nothing special about it. There was also no follow through with describing a date limited to the $30 budget so it didn't seem as though my suggestion was followed anyway.

I did appreciate the effort made to have the gift delivered on time. Initially, I also appreciated the sentiment note that was included. The gift packaging had no return address, only the name "Johnny"and my attempt to reply to the sender through Amazon, the company that handled the purchase and mailing, was unsuccessful.

The costume jewelry pictured below (in a yellow color) is what I received from the scammer(s). The antique silhouette embedded in the text below right was the valentine I purchased in a local shop where I also found the vintage block letters.

12:06
Statement Choker Necklace Tiara Crown Link Bangle Bracelet Teardrop Dangle Earrings Set for Wedding Party
12.4k
Color: Gold Plated Rhinestone Champagne Choker N...
$15.99
$14.99 $15.99
$15.99
$15.99
$12.99 $16
Delivery
Pickup
amazon.com

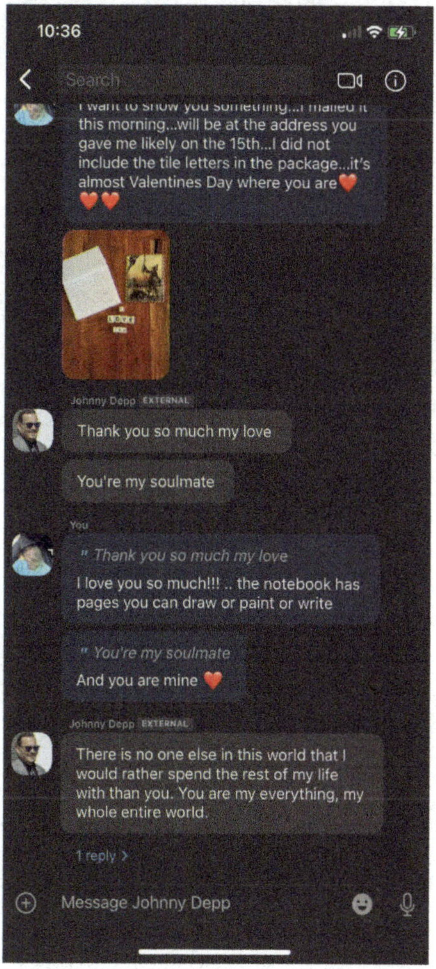
10:36
Search
this morning...will be at the address you gave me likely on the 15th...I did not include the tile letters in the package...it's almost Valentines Day where you are
Johnny Depp EXTERNAL
Thank you so much my love
You're my soulmate
You
" Thank you so much my love
I love you so much!!! .. the notebook has pages you can draw or paint or write
" You're my soulmate
And you are mine
Johnny Depp EXTERNAL
There is no one else in this world that I would rather spend the rest of my life with than you. You are my everything, my whole entire world.
1 reply
Message Johnny Depp

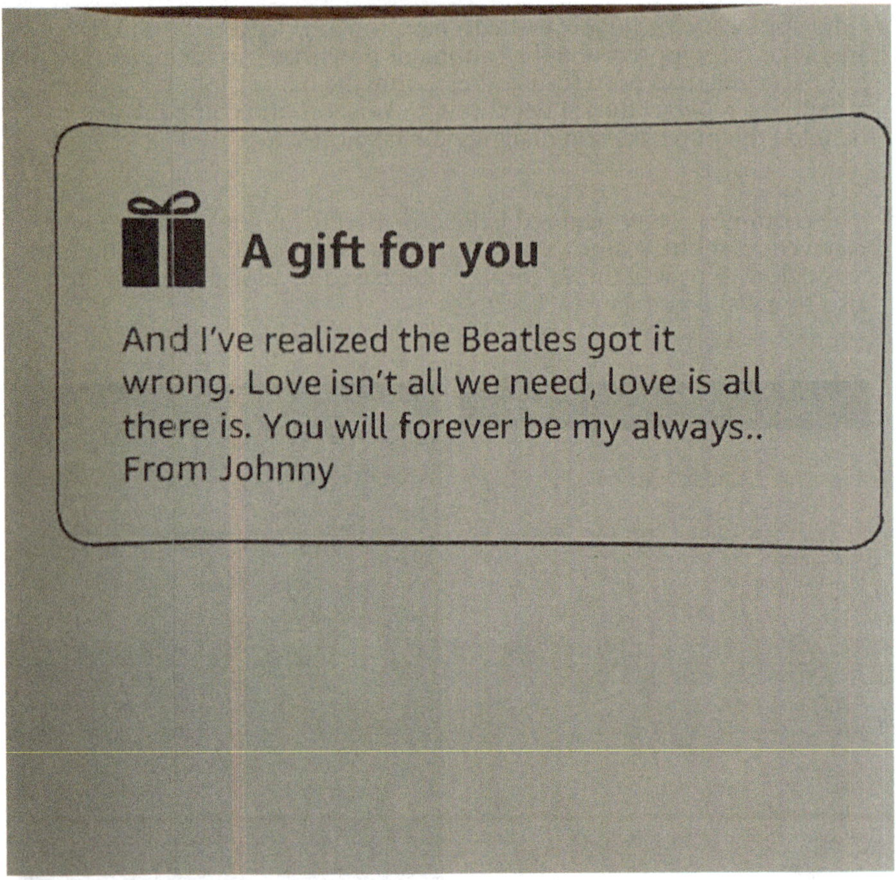
A gift for you
And I've realized the Beatles got it wrong. Love isn't all we need, love is all there is. You will forever be my always..
From Johnny

Above is a picture of the small slip of paper in the box I received. At first blush the sentiment is very romantic, don't you agree?

As for my gift? I did track the delivery as confirmed, so the address must have been a valid virtual office. Maybe it was the address the scammer(s) used for all the unsuspecting victims of the scam.

A discussion took place later wherein the subject was raised by the scammer about how money was spent on a gift for me and not reciprocated. I was quick to point out that my gift was sent to the address I was given, a VIRTUAL office address. The expectation of reciprocity for costume jewelry should have been telling to me. In my mind, having this expectation is like keeping score in a game. If someone you are in a relationship does a favor for you, are they keeping a mental score that tells them you owe them a favor in return? In my opinion, there is no scorecard in a true love relationship. If I had been keeping score at this point I would definitely had been ahead because my gift was at least heartfelt and genuine.

Despite the disappointing Valentines Day, I admit I was happy to have a package at my door and to receive the text messages of love. It is hard to believe that people can fall in love through text messaging alone, isn't it? If I had not been one of the two sending and receiving the texts I would say it is unlikely, preposterous even.

Before reaching your conclusion(s) on this, I ask that you consider that the texting has been ongoing. multiple times daily for over a month with some threads numbering 100 or more, and that the content of this texting communication is increasingly intimate.

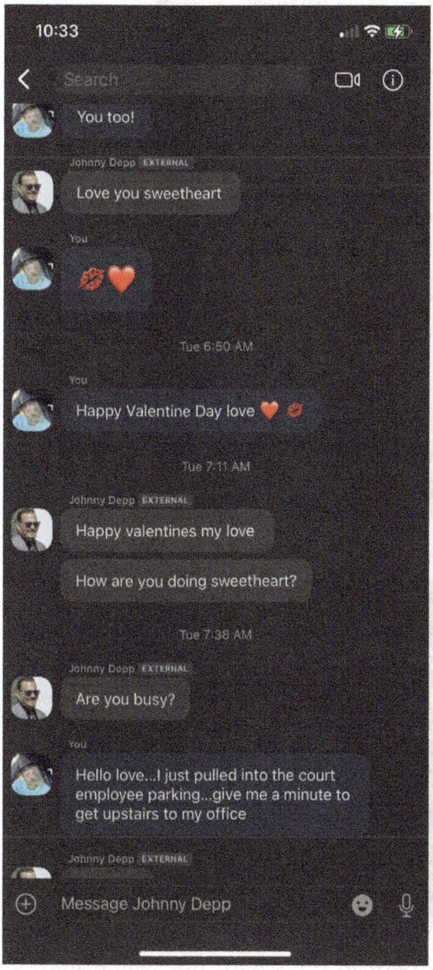

10:33
Search
You too!
Johnny Depp EXTERNAL
Love you sweetheart
You
Tue 6:50 AM
You
Happy Valentine Day love
Tue 7:11 AM
Johnny Depp EXTERNAL
Happy valentines my love
How are you doing sweetheart?
Tue 7:38 AM
Johnny Depp EXTERNAL
Are you busy?
You
Hello love...I just pulled into the court employee parking...give me a minute to get upstairs to my office
Johnny Depp EXTERNAL
Message Johnny Depp

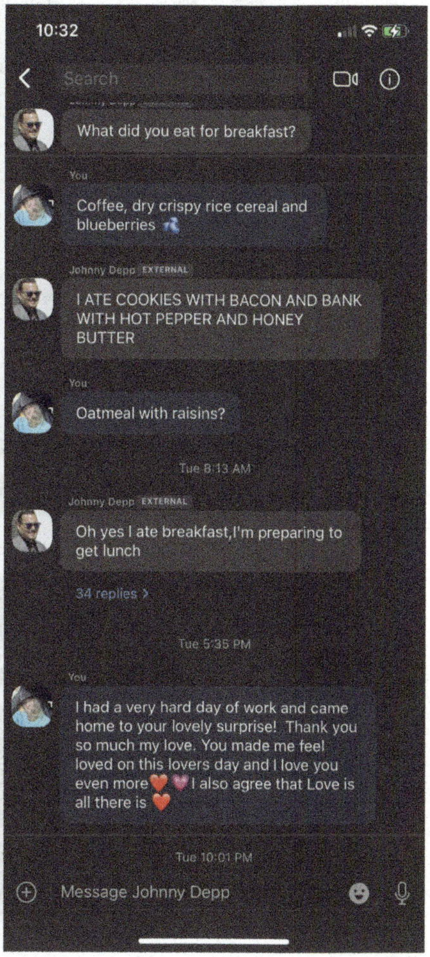

10:32
Search
What did you eat for breakfast?
You
Coffee, dry crispy rice cereal and blueberries
Johnny Depp EXTERNAL
I ATE COOKIES WITH BACON AND BANK WITH HOT PEPPER AND HONEY BUTTER
You
Oatmeal with raisins?
Tue 8:13 AM
Johnny Depp EXTERNAL
Oh yes I ate breakfast,I'm preparing to get lunch
34 replies >
Tue 5:35 PM
You
I had a very hard day of work and came home to your lovely surprise! Thank you so much my love. You made me feel loved on this lovers day and I love you even more I also agree that Love is all there is
Tue 10:01 PM
Message Johnny Depp

Finally, consider that in my case, this texting is more conversation I had than all others combined, including those at work, home, and when with friends, family, and generally, with strangers in public.

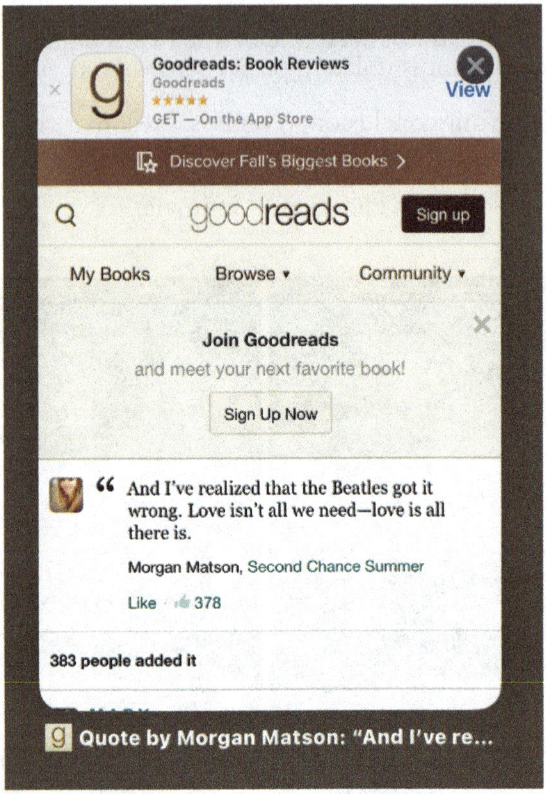
Goodreads: Book Reviews
Goodreads
GET — On the App Store
View
Discover Fall's Biggest Books
goodreads
Sign up
My Books
Browse
Community
Join Goodreads
and meet your next favorite book!
Sign Up Now
"And I've realized that the Beatles got it wrong. Love isn't all we need—love is all there is.
Morgan Matson, Second Chance Summer
Like 378
383 people added it
Quote by Morgan Matson: "And I've re...

A quote from Second Chance Summer
And I've realized that the Beatles got it wrong. Love isn't all we need—love is al...
goodreads.com/.../560071-and-i-ve-realized...
Google Search

When I was informed that the sentiment in my valentines was not an original quote, my view of the gift was cheapened and the doubts I had of being loved grew stronger. The sentiment was taken from a movie quote. Another red flag

TENNESSEE, the HOOK?

Just a few days before Valentines Day and with all the professed love building a foundation of trust, it seemed that a plan for the future was in order. What better way for a scammer to "hook" me than to say he/she/it wants to buy a house with me? The following are a few of the Tennessee house purchase texts.

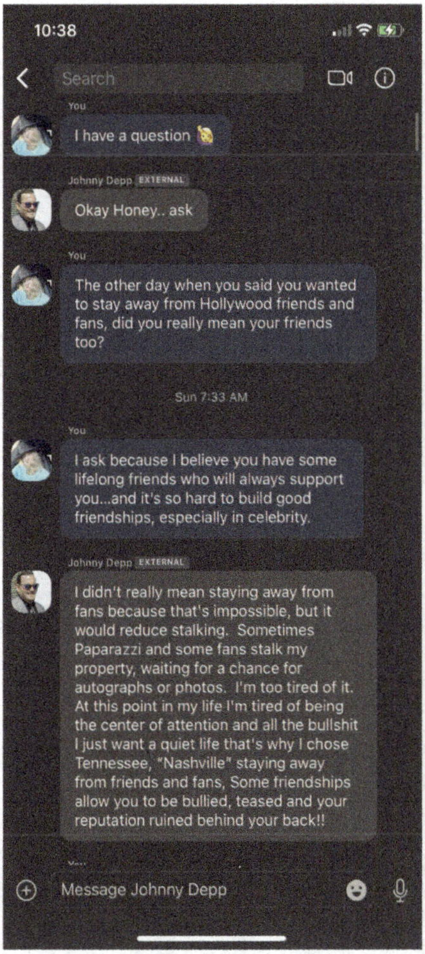
10:38
Search
You
I have a question
Johnny Depp EXTERNAL
Okay Honey.. ask
You
The other day when you said you wanted to stay away from Hollywood friends and fans, did you really mean your friends too?
Sun 7:33 AM
You
I ask because I believe you have some lifelong friends who will always support you...and it's so hard to build good friendships, especially in celebrity.
Johnny Depp EXTERNAL
I didn't really mean staying away from fans because that's impossible, but it would reduce stalking. Sometimes Paparazzi and some fans stalk my property, waiting for a chance for autographs or photos. I'm too tired of it. At this point in my life I'm tired of being the center of attention and all the bullshit I just want a quiet life that's why I chose Tennessee, "Nashville" staying away from friends and fans, Some friendships allow you to be bullied, teased and your reputation ruined behind your back!!
Message Johnny Depp

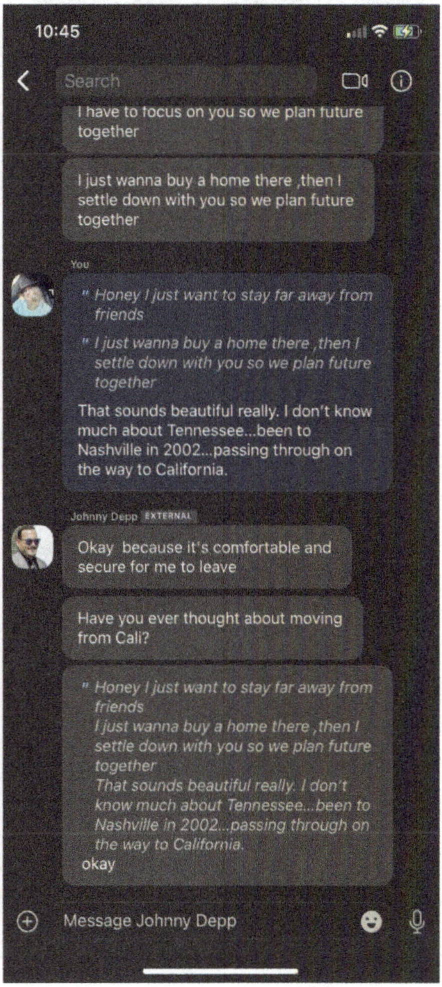
10:45
Search
I have to focus on you so we plan future together
I just wanna buy a home there ,then I settle down with you so we plan future together
You
" Honey I just want to stay far away from friends
" I just wanna buy a home there ,then I settle down with you so we plan future together
That sounds beautiful really. I don't know much about Tennessee...been to Nashville in 2002...passing through on the way to California.
Johnny Depp EXTERNAL
Okay because it's comfortable and secure for me to leave
Have you ever thought about moving from Cali?
" Honey I just want to stay far away from friends
I just wanna buy a home there ,then I settle down with you so we plan future together
That sounds beautiful really. I don't know much about Tennessee...been to Nashville in 2002...passing through on the way to California.
okay
Message Johnny Depp

I had already decided I would move from California within a year. I had not considered moving to a place where I had no family or close friends but I was open to the possibility.

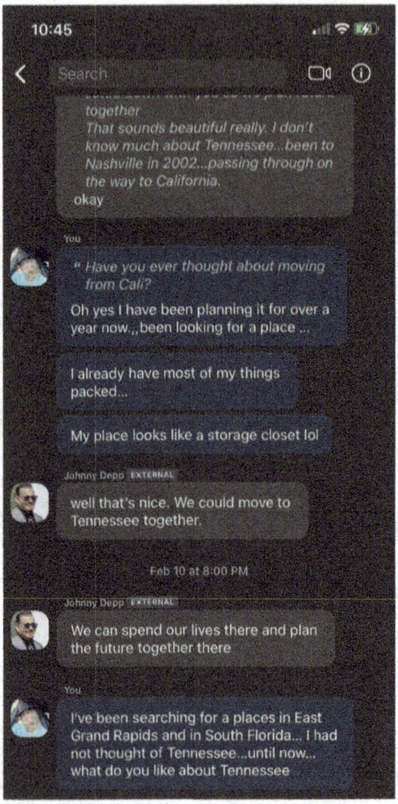
10:45
Search
together
That sounds beautiful really. I don't know much about Tennessee...been to Nashville in 2002...passing through on the way to California.
okay
You
" Have you ever thought about moving from Cali?
Oh yes I have been planning it for over a year now,,been looking for a place ...
I already have most of my things packed...
My place looks like a storage closet lol
Johnny Depp EXTERNAL
well that's nice. We could move to Tennessee together.
Feb 10 at 8:00 PM
Johnny Depp EXTERNAL
We can spend our lives there and plan the future together there
You
I've been searching for a places in East Grand Rapids and in South Florida... I had not thought of Tennessee...until now... what do you like about Tennessee

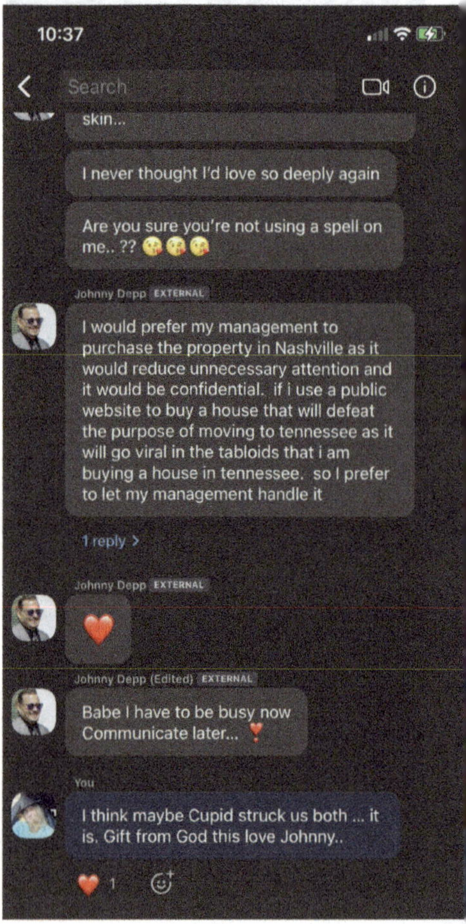
10:37
Search
skin...
I never thought I'd love so deeply again
Are you sure you're not using a spell on me.. ??
Johnny Depp EXTERNAL
I would prefer my management to purchase the property in Nashville as it would reduce unnecessary attention and it would be confidential. if i use a public website to buy a house that will defeat the purpose of moving to tennessee as it will go viral in the tabloids that i am buying a house in tennessee. so I prefer to let my management handle it
1 reply >
Johnny Depp EXTERNAL
Johnny Depp (Edited) EXTERNAL
Babe I have to be busy now Communicate later...
You
I think maybe Cupid struck us both ... it is. Gift from God this love Johnny..
1

I suggested we rent a place to take the pressure off making a big money decision and because I believed it was a practical solution; but, when I was asked to research houses for sale I did not hesitate.

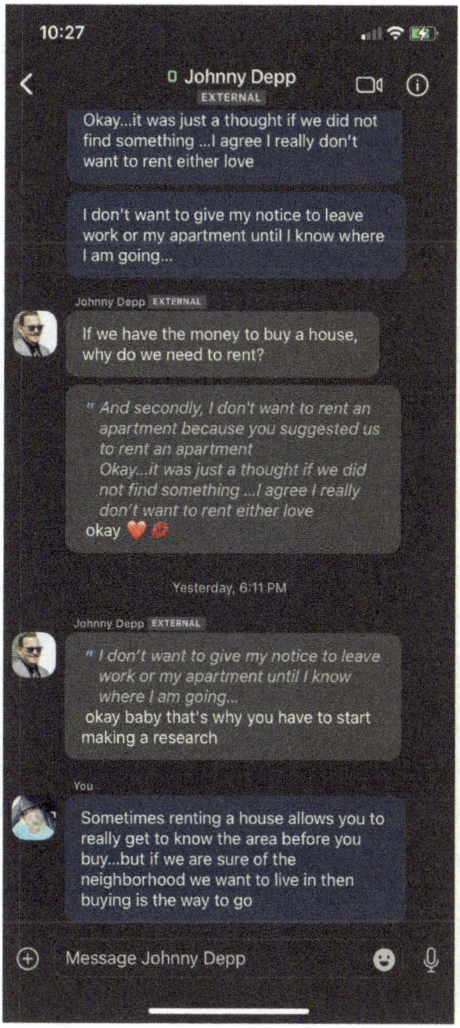
10:27
Johnny Depp
EXTERNAL
Okay...it was just a thought if we did not find something ...I agree I really don't want to rent either love
I don't want to give my notice to leave work or my apartment until I know where I am going...
Johnny Depp EXTERNAL
If we have the money to buy a house, why do we need to rent?
" And secondly, I don't want to rent an apartment because you suggested us to rent an apartment
Okay...it was just a thought if we did not find something ...I agree I really don't want to rent either love
okay
Yesterday, 6:11 PM
Johnny Depp EXTERNAL
" I don't want to give my notice to leave work or my apartment until I know where I am going...
okay baby that's why you have to start making a research
You
Sometimes renting a house allows you to really get to know the area before you buy...but if we are sure of the neighborhood we want to live in then buying is the way to go
Message Johnny Depp

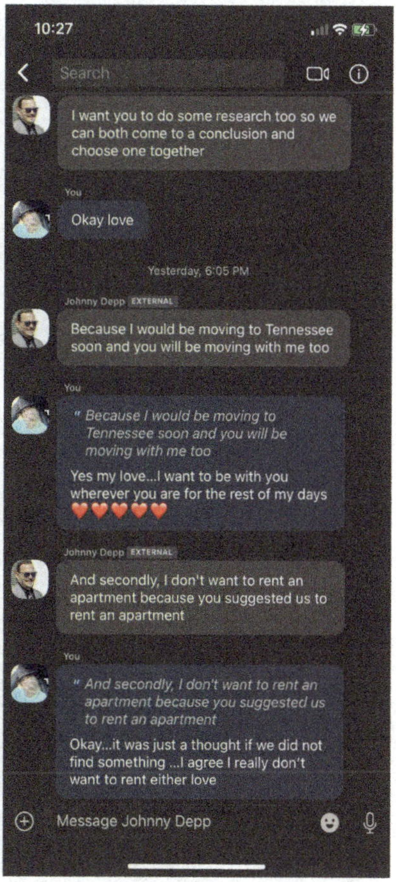
10:27
Search
I want you to do some research too so we can both come to a conclusion and choose one together
You
Okay love
Yesterday, 6:05 PM
Johnny Depp EXTERNAL
Because I would be moving to Tennessee soon and you will be moving with me too
You
" Because I would be moving to Tennessee soon and you will be moving with me too
Yes my love...I want to be with you wherever you are for the rest of my days
Johnny Depp EXTERNAL
And secondly, I don't want to rent an apartment because you suggested us to rent an apartment
You
" And secondly, I don't want to rent an apartment because you suggested us to rent an apartment
Okay...it was just a thought if we did not find something ...I agree I really don't want to rent either love
Message Johnny Depp

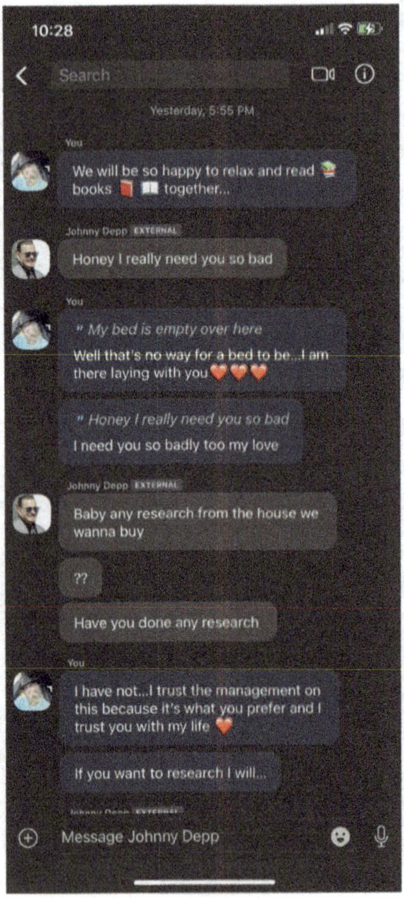
10:28
Search
Yesterday, 5:55 PM
You
We will be so happy to relax and read books together...
Johnny Depp EXTERNAL
Honey I really need you so bad
You
" My bed is empty over here
Well that's no way for a bed to be...I am there laying with you
" Honey I really need you so bad
I need you so badly too my love
Johnny Depp EXTERNAL
Baby any research from the house we wanna buy
??
Have you done any research
You
I have not...I trust the management on this because it's what you prefer and I trust you with my life
If you want to research I will...
Message Johnny Depp

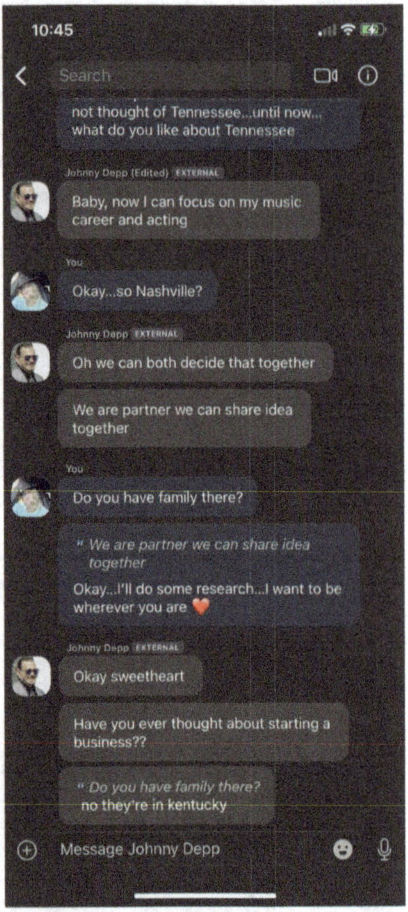
10:45
Search
not thought of Tennessee...until now... what do you like about Tennessee
Johnny Depp (Edited) EXTERNAL
Baby, now I can focus on my music career and acting
You
Okay...so Nashville?
Johnny Depp EXTERNAL
Oh we can both decide that together
We are partner we can share idea together
You
Do you have family there?
" We are partner we can share idea together
Okay...I'll do some research...I want to be wherever you are
Johnny Depp EXTERNAL
Okay sweetheart
Have you ever thought about starting a business??
" Do you have family there?
no they're in kentucky
Message Johnny Depp

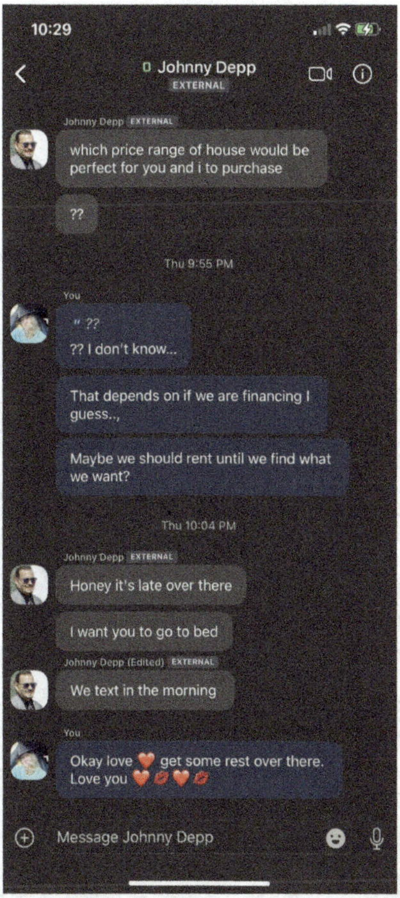
10:29
Johnny Depp
EXTERNAL
Johnny Depp EXTERNAL
which price range of house would be perfect for you and i to purchase
??
Thu 9:55 PM
You
" ??
?? I don't know...
That depends on if we are financing I guess..,
Maybe we should rent until we find what we want?
Thu 10:04 PM
Johnny Depp EXTERNAL
Honey it's late over there
I want you to go to bed
Johnny Depp (Edited) EXTERNAL
We text in the morning
You
Okay love ❤️ get some rest over there.
Love you ❤️💋❤️💋
Message Johnny Depp

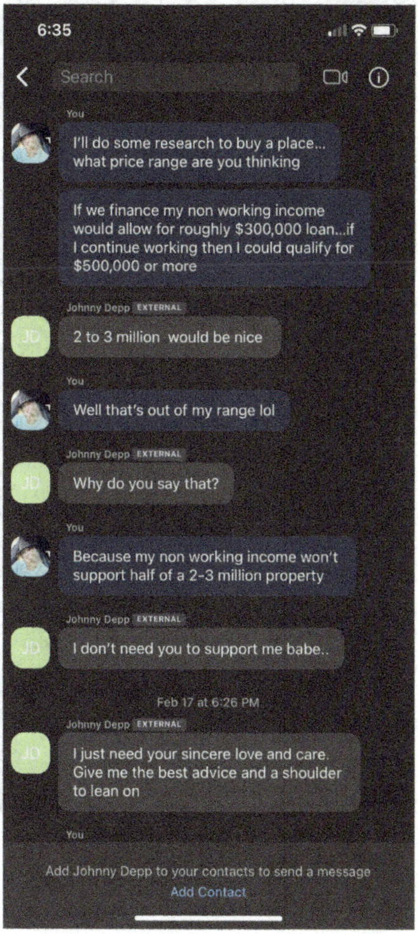
6:35
Search
You
I'll do some research to buy a place... what price range are you thinking
If we finance my non working income would allow for roughly $300,000 loan...if I continue working then I could qualify for $500,000 or more
Johnny Depp EXTERNAL
2 to 3 million would be nice
You
Well that's out of my range lol
Johnny Depp EXTERNAL
Why do you say that?
You
Because my non working income won't support half of a 2-3 million property
Johnny Depp EXTERNAL
I don't need you to support me babe..
Feb 17 at 6:26 PM
Johnny Depp EXTERNAL
I just need your sincere love and care. Give me the best advice and a shoulder to lean on
You
Add Johnny Depp to your contacts to send a message
Add Contact

When the question was asked about the price range I did not see it but this may have been asked in order to elicit information about my holdings. I was determined to be forthcoming about my financial state. I was not a millionaire by any stretch of the imagination.

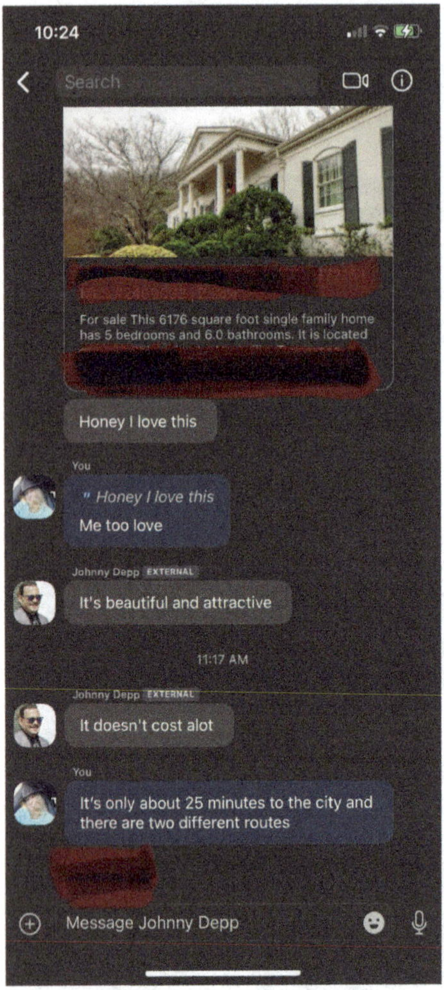
10:24
Search
[redacted]
For sale This 6176 square foot single family home has 5 bedrooms and 6.0 bathrooms. It is located
[redacted]
Honey I love this
You
" Honey I love this
Me too love
Johnny Depp EXTERNAL
It's beautiful and attractive
11:17 AM
Johnny Depp EXTERNAL
It doesn't cost alot
You
It's only about 25 minutes to the city and there are two different routes
[redacted]
Message Johnny Depp

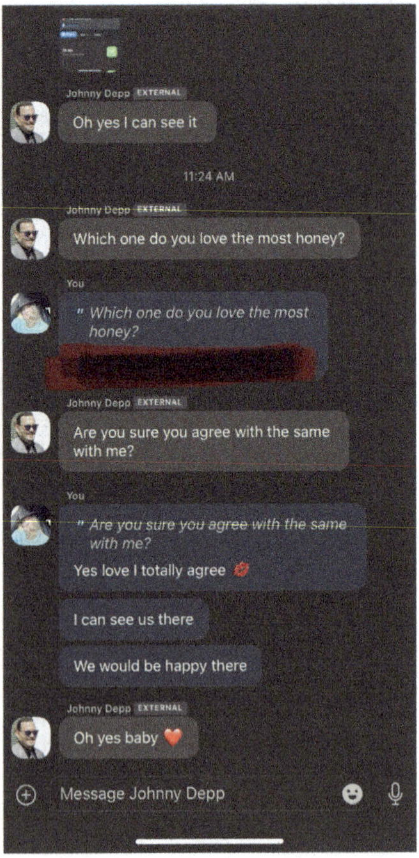
Johnny Depp EXTERNAL
Oh yes I can see it
11:24 AM
Johnny Depp EXTERNAL
Which one do you love the most honey?
You
" Which one do you love the most honey?
[redacted]
Johnny Depp EXTERNAL
Are you sure you agree with the same with me?
You
" Are you sure you agree with the same with me?
Yes love I totally agree 💋
I can see us there
We would be happy there
Johnny Depp EXTERNAL
Oh yes baby ❤️
Message Johnny Depp

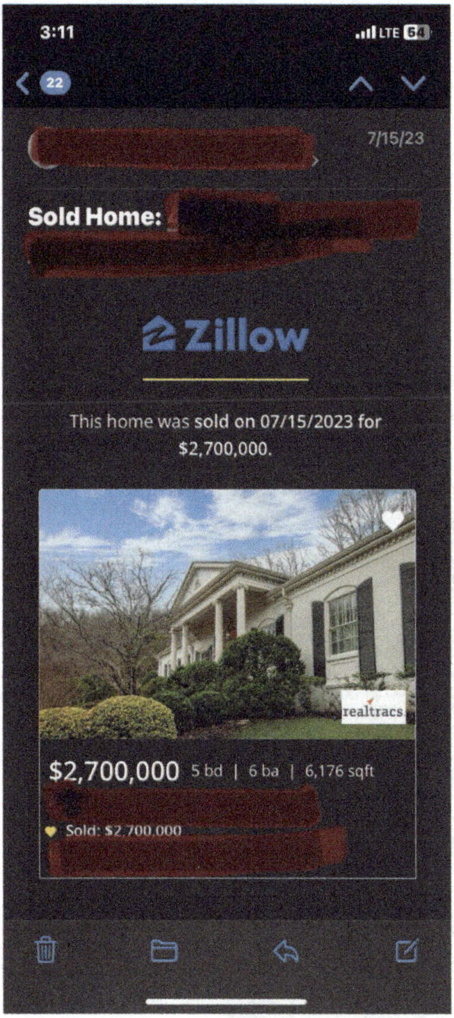

Of course the Tennessee house was just a part of the scam to bring me in closer, build more trust, leading up to the bomb that would drop, revealing the true intention which was to scam me into sending money and likely divulging confidential personal information. I received a notice when the house sold.

THE MONEY SCAM (PART 1?), AUTHENTICATION

After texting nearly every day and night for 6 weeks and finding a house in Tennessee the scammer(s) spun a backstory that provided a reason to add a new dimension to our relationship and bring someone else into the picture. This was a brilliant move because it provided a way to shift any blame on the change in the dynamic of the relationship onto to a third party while at the same time invoking my empathy. That person was presented as Johnny Depp's personal manager Norman Todd. I was fed a tall tale about Norman's manager role that included his decision making and how Johnny is indebted to him. I had serious doubts whether manager Norman actually existed (because as you will see the communication between "Johnny " and I continued), but all things now considered, it set a perfect stage for a money scam.

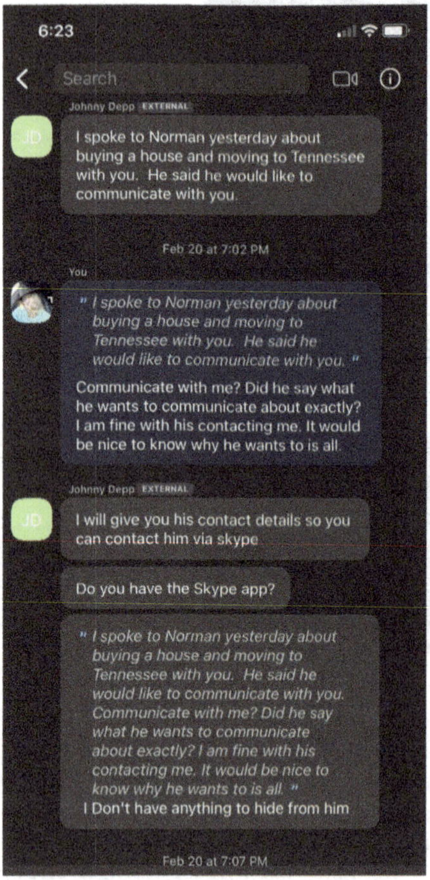
6:23
Search
Johnny Depp EXTERNAL
JD
I spoke to Norman yesterday about buying a house and moving to Tennessee with you. He said he would like to communicate with you.
Feb 20 at 7:02 PM
You
" I spoke to Norman yesterday about buying a house and moving to Tennessee with you. He said he would like to communicate with you. "
Communicate with me? Did he say what he wants to communicate about exactly? I am fine with his contacting me. It would be nice to know why he wants to is all.
Johnny Depp EXTERNAL
JD
I will give you his contact details so you can contact him via skype
Do you have the Skype app?
" I spoke to Norman yesterday about buying a house and moving to Tennessee with you. He said he would like to communicate with you. Communicate with me? Did he say what he wants to communicate about exactly? I am fine with his contacting me. It would be nice to know why he wants to is all. "
I Don't have anything to hide from him
Feb 20 at 7:07 PM

Tip: A scam like this may include many different people or maybe the same person in various roles impersonating multiple people. It is easy to open various accounts for internet access. If someone represents themselves as affiliated with a particular business or generally represents that they are a particular person, always ask for some proof of identity. The problem with doing this over the internet is that scammers know how to impersonate others and can provide fake credentials when asked. What to do then? End the communication and require either an in person meeting or a video chat through a legitimate source.

This is part of the Skype text chat I had with the scammer impersonating someone named Norman Todd:

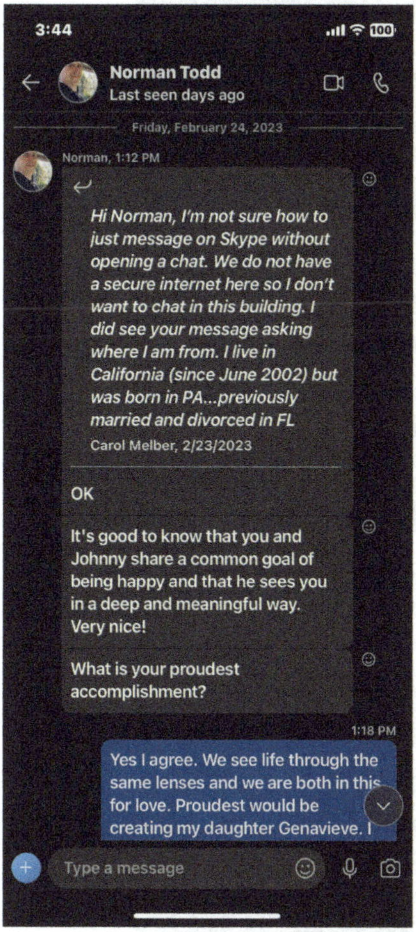

3:44
Norman Todd
Last seen days ago
Friday, February 24, 2023
Norman, 1:12 PM
Hi Norman, I'm not sure how to just message on Skype without opening a chat. We do not have a secure internet here so I don't want to chat in this building. I did see your message asking where I am from. I live in California (since June 2002) but was born in PA...previously married and divorced in FL
Carol Melber, 2/23/2023
OK
It's good to know that you and Johnny share a common goal of being happy and that he sees you in a deep and meaningful way. Very nice!
What is your proudest accomplishment?
1:18 PM
Yes I agree. We see life through the same lenses and we are both in this for love. Proudest would be creating my daughter Genavieve. I
Type a message

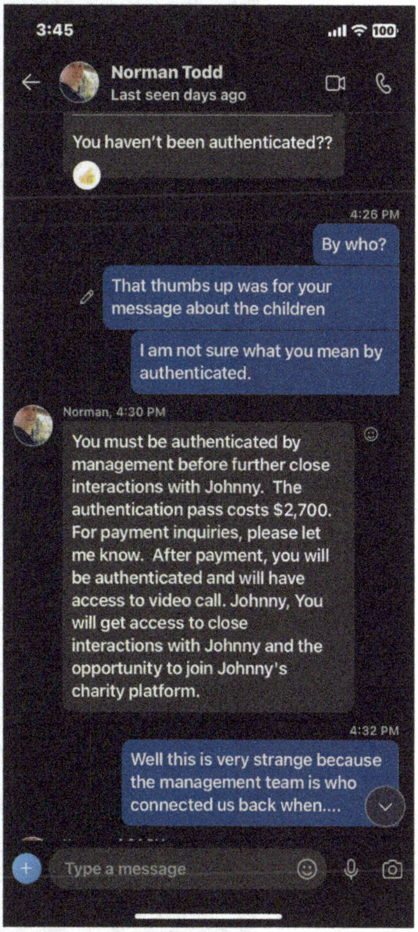

3:45
Norman Todd
Last seen days ago
You haven't been authenticated??
4:26 PM
By who?
That thumbs up was for your message about the children
I am not sure what you mean by authenticated.
Norman, 4:30 PM
You must be authenticated by management before further close interactions with Johnny. The authentication pass costs $2,700. For payment inquiries, please let me know. After payment, you will be authenticated and will have access to video call. Johnny, You will get access to close interactions with Johnny and the opportunity to join Johnny's charity platform.
4:32 PM
Well this is very strange because the management team is who connected us back when....
Type a message

When I learned of the authentication scam that made no real sense given my background and work position at that time, I was truly hurt by the whole situation but I chose to take the high road.

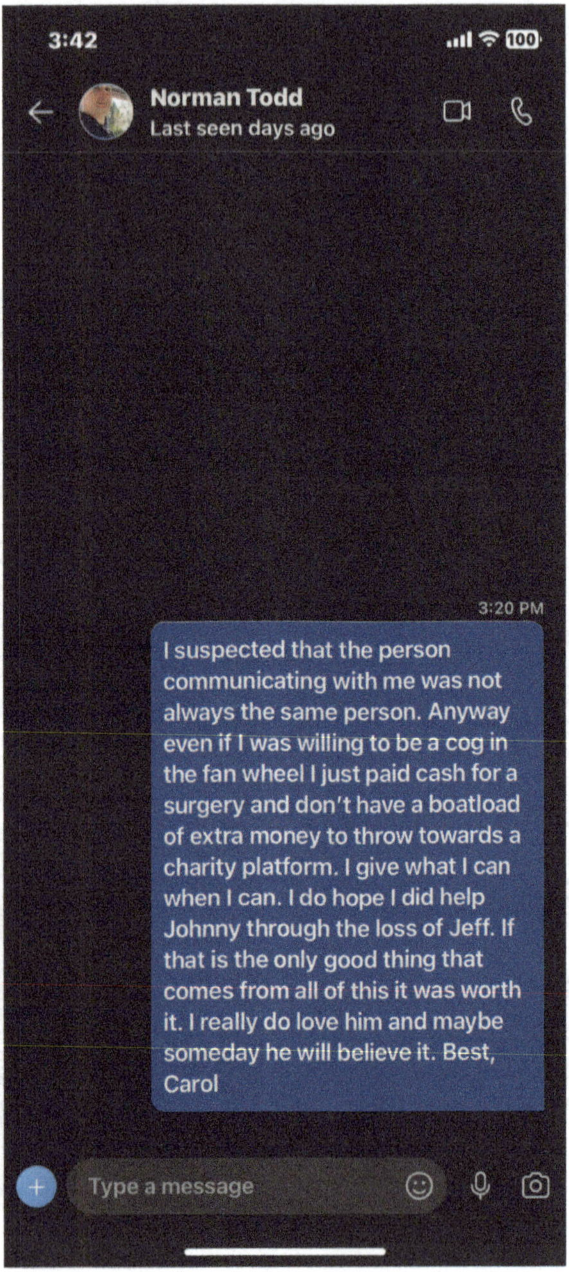
3:42
100
Norman Todd
Last seen days ago
3:20 PM
I suspected that the person communicating with me was not always the same person. Anyway even if I was willing to be a cog in the fan wheel I just paid cash for a surgery and don't have a boatload of extra money to throw towards a charity platform. I give what I can when I can. I do hope I did help Johnny through the loss of Jeff. If that is the only good thing that comes from all of this it was worth it. I really do love him and maybe someday he will believe it. Best, Carol
Type a message

Did I send $2,700? Of course not! The huge red flag hit me like a cold slap in the face. Still, even though all communication between us was supposedly not permitted, we continued to email and text. I considered that given my education and employment position, it was possible that if Depp was really communicating, his management team may not have seen my credentials as legitimate. Still, knowing that they could have checked those records easily, I reasoned that they may have thought that our relationship was just moving too fast.

What had not occurred to me until later was that in addition to being a money scam it had all the components of a personal information/ identity theft scheme. If I had agreed to send money my banking information would have been exposed.

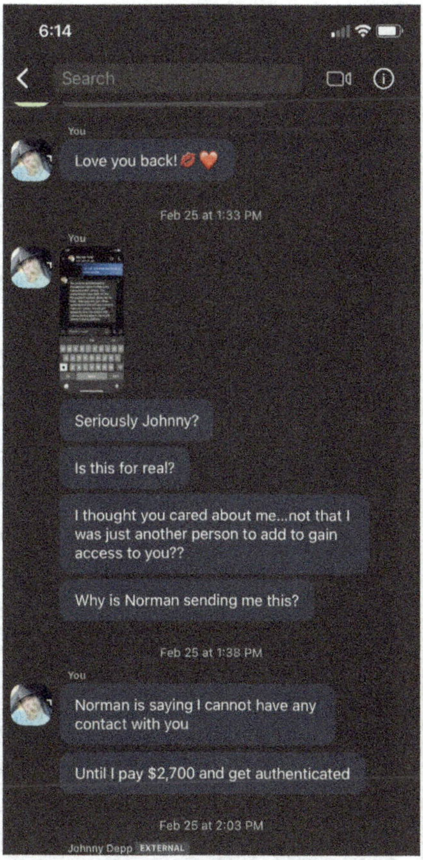
6:14
Search
You
Love you back!
Feb 25 at 1:33 PM
You
Seriously Johnny?
Is this for real?
I thought you cared about me...not that I was just another person to add to gain access to you??
Why is Norman sending me this?
Feb 25 at 1:38 PM
You
Norman is saying I cannot have any contact with you
Until I pay $2,700 and get authenticated
Feb 25 at 2:03 PM
Johnny Depp EXTERNAL

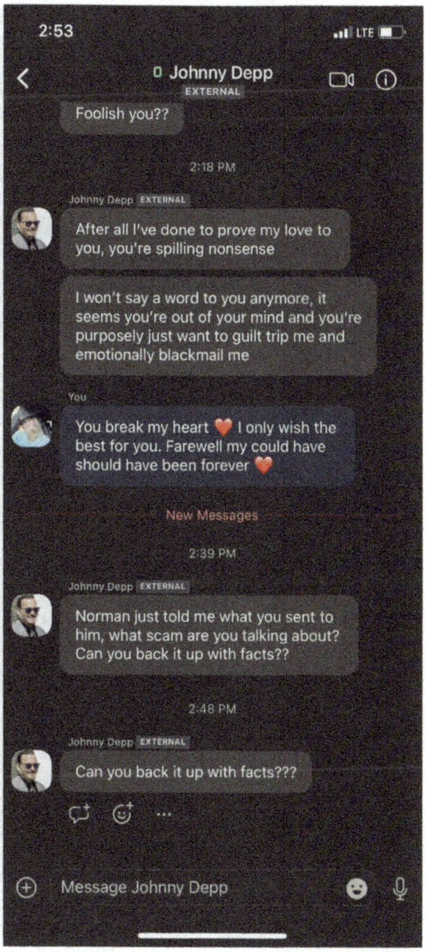
2:53
LTE
Johnny Depp
EXTERNAL
Foolish you??
2:18 PM
Johnny Depp EXTERNAL
After all I've done to prove my love to you, you're spilling nonsense
I won't say a word to you anymore, it seems you're out of your mind and you're purposely just want to guilt trip me and emotionally blackmail me
You
You break my heart I only wish the best for you. Farewell my could have should have been forever
New Messages
2:39 PM
Johnny Depp EXTERNAL
Norman just told me what you sent to him, what scam are you talking about? Can you back it up with facts??
2:48 PM
Johnny Depp EXTERNAL
Can you back it up with facts???
Message Johnny Depp

The scammers reaction to me calling out the scam was a scathing rebuttal and a request to return the valentine to the virtual office address.

Here, the scammer tried to use a trust foundation as a reasoning tool. What is very troubling about these scams is the various psychological tactics the scammer(s) will use.

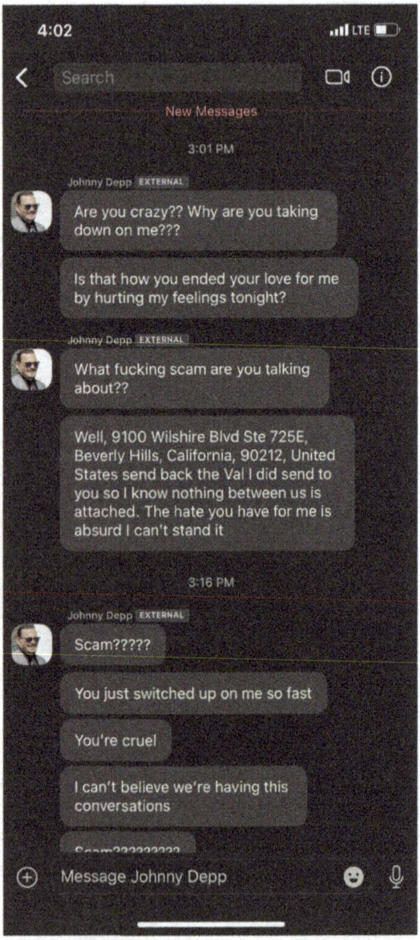
4:02
LTE
Search
New Messages
3:01 PM
Johnny Depp EXTERNAL
Are you crazy?? Why are you taking down on me???
Is that how you ended your love for me by hurting my feelings tonight?
Johnny Depp EXTERNAL
What fucking scam are you talking about??
Well, 9100 Wilshire Blvd Ste 725E, Beverly Hills, California, 90212, United States send back the Val I did send to you so I know nothing between us is attached. The hate you have for me is absurd I can't stand it
3:16 PM
Johnny Depp EXTERNAL
Scam?????
You just switched up on me so fast
You're cruel
I can't believe we're having this conversations
Message Johnny Depp

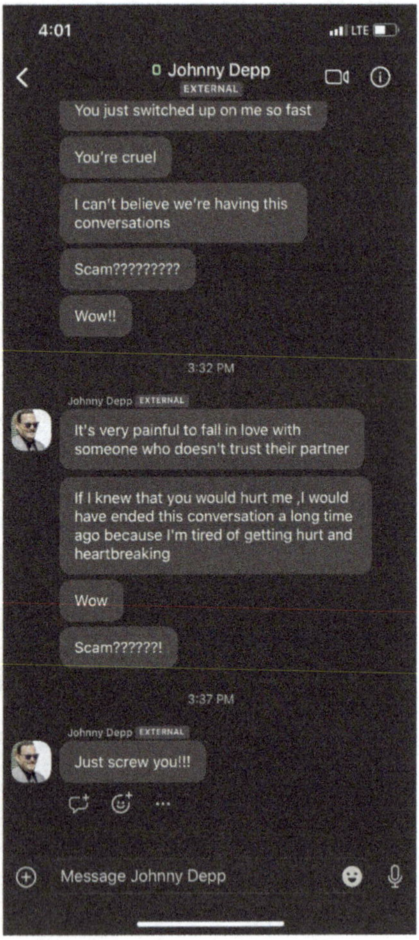
4:01
LTE
Johnny Depp
EXTERNAL
You just switched up on me so fast
You're cruel
I can't believe we're having this conversations
Scam?????????
Wow!!
3:32 PM
Johnny Depp EXTERNAL
It's very painful to fall in love with someone who doesn't trust their partner
If I knew that you would hurt me ,I would have ended this conversation a long time ago because I'm tired of getting hurt and heartbreaking
Wow
Scam??????!
3:37 PM
Johnny Depp EXTERNAL
Just screw you!!!
Message Johnny Depp

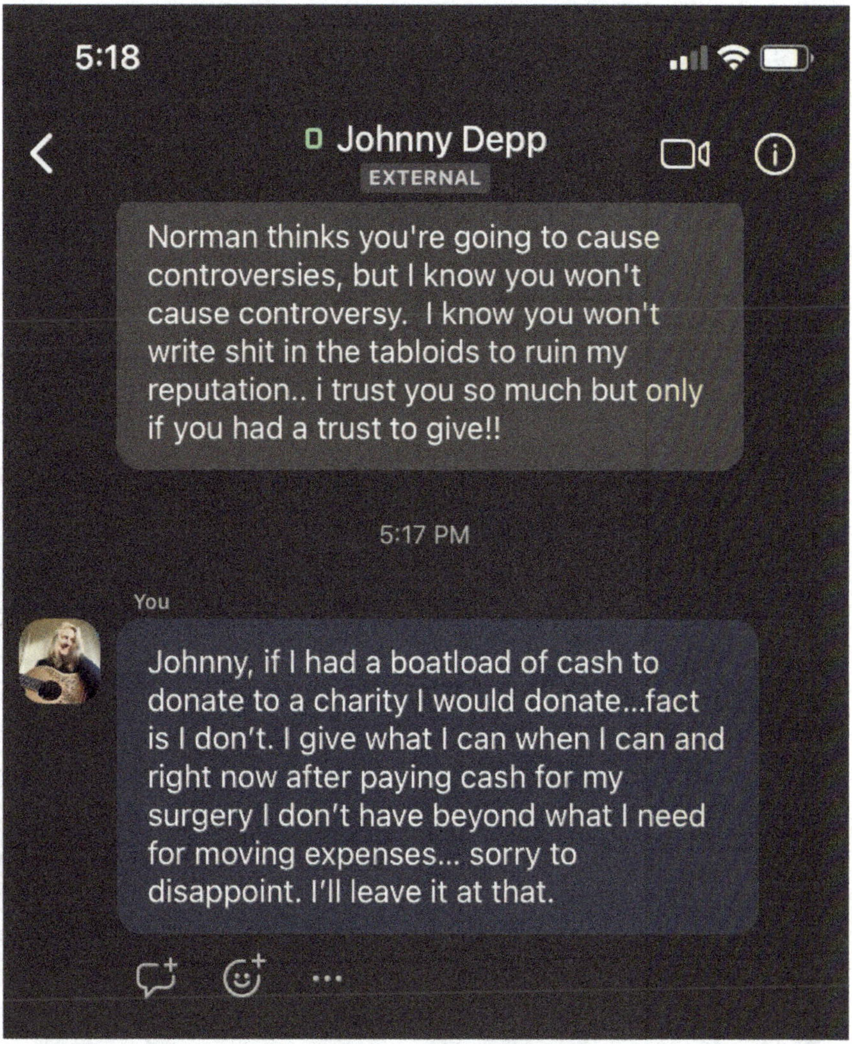
5:18
Johnny Depp
EXTERNAL
Norman thinks you're going to cause controversies, but I know you won't cause controversy. I know you won't write shit in the tabloids to ruin my reputation.. i trust you so much but only if you had a trust to give!!
5:17 PM
You
Johnny, if I had a boatload of cash to donate to a charity I would donate...fact is I don't. I give what I can when I can and right now after paying cash for my surgery I don't have beyond what I need for moving expenses... sorry to disappoint. I'll leave it at that.

Up to this point I had not received any proof that the person communicating with me was really Johnny Depp. There was a text earlier on addressed to a Mr. Johnson that included a picture of Depp's California drivers license and his Social Security card. The text referenced opening a finance account. Immediately after sending the text, the scammer texted "Oh Sh—!" and deleted it. This was surely done in an attempt to legitimize the identity of the scammer, and you know what? Initially it did! Because my employment background includes financial credit fraud investigation it was not long before I dismissed the ploy that I saw was executed for the sole purpose of gaining my trust. I was aware that it is easy for fraudsters to obtain information and create fake documents like those that were flashed before my eyes in a text.

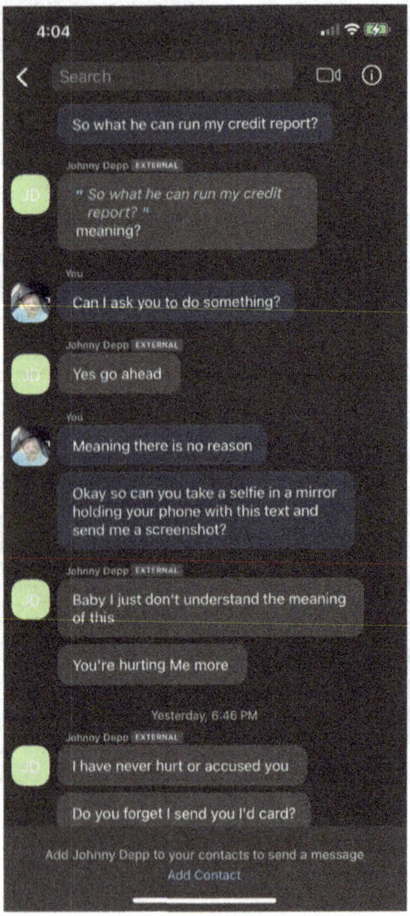

4:04
Search
So what he can run my credit report?
Johnny Depp EXTERNAL
" So what he can run my credit report? " meaning?
You
Can I ask you to do something?
Johnny Depp EXTERNAL
Yes go ahead
You
Meaning there is no reason
Okay so can you take a selfie in a mirror holding your phone with this text and send me a screenshot?
Johnny Depp EXTERNAL
Baby I just don't understand the meaning of this
You're hurting Me more
Yesterday, 6:46 PM
Johnny Depp EXTERNAL
I have never hurt or accused you
Do you forget I send you I'd card?
Add Johnny Depp to your contacts to send a message
Add Contact

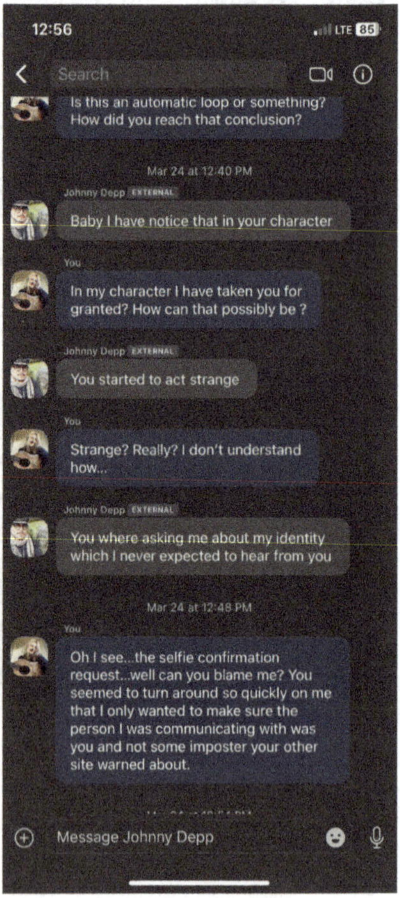

12:56
LTE 85
Search
Is this an automatic loop or something? How did you reach that conclusion?
Mar 24 at 12:40 PM
Johnny Depp EXTERNAL
Baby I have notice that in your character
You
In my character I have taken you for granted? How can that possibly be ?
Johnny Depp EXTERNAL
You started to act strange
You
Strange? Really? I don't understand how...
Johnny Depp EXTERNAL
You where asking me about my identity which I never expected to hear from you
Mar 24 at 12:48 PM
You
Oh I see...the selfie confirmation request...well can you blame me? You seemed to turn around so quickly on me that I only wanted to make sure the person I was communicating with was you and not some imposter your other site warned about.
Message Johnny Depp

Once again I tried to end the sham. I was really disappointed but knew who I thought was my 'true love' was a ghost. I discussed the situation with my most trusted family member and decided to put the scammer to test by asking for a selfie photo of our recent text message taken in a mirror. If the person texting was really Depp, a picture of him holding the phone showing our text communication would have been easy for him to do and by doing this he could have validated his identity.

Needless to say the scammer(s) would not take a selfie. If it was a real person in love there should not have been any hesitation to prove their identity with a picture text. So, there we stood. Me, refusing to send money to get "authenticated" and the scammer refusing to take a selfie proof of identity.

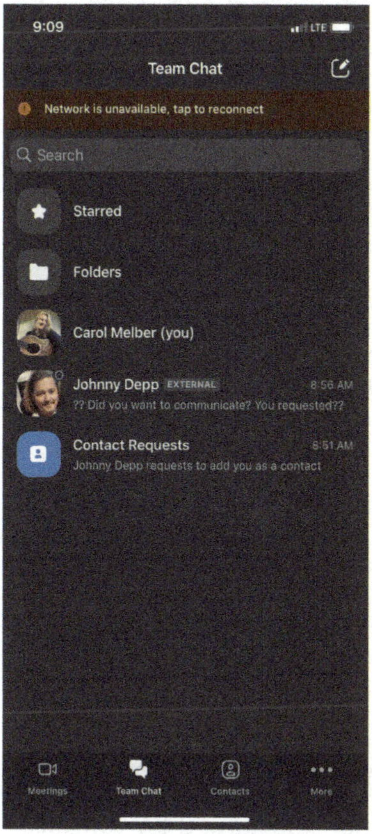

9:09
LTE
Team Chat
Network is unavailable, tap to reconnect
Search
Starred
Folders
Carol Melber (you)
Johnny Depp EXTERNAL 8:56 AM
?? Did you want to communicate? You requested??
Contact Requests 8:51 AM
Johnny Depp requests to add you as a contact
Meetings
Team Chat
Contacts
More

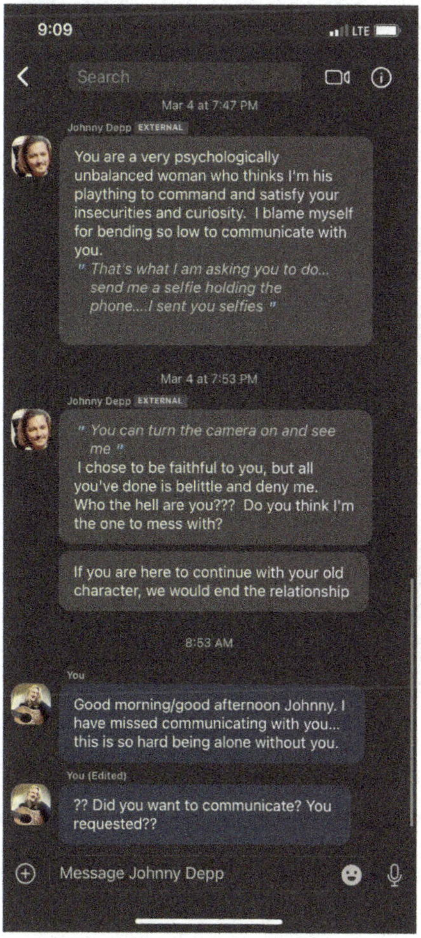

9:09
LTE
Search
Mar 4 at 7:47 PM
Johnny Depp EXTERNAL
You are a very psychologically unbalanced woman who thinks I'm his plaything to command and satisfy your insecurities and curiosity. I blame myself for bending so low to communicate with you.
" That's what I am asking you to do... send me a selfie holding the phone....I sent you selfies "
Mar 4 at 7:53 PM
Johnny Depp EXTERNAL
" You can turn the camera on and see me "
I chose to be faithful to you, but all you've done is belittle and deny me. Who the hell are you??? Do you think I'm the one to mess with?
If you are here to continue with your old character, we would end the relationship
8:53 AM
You
Good morning/good afternoon Johnny. I have missed communicating with you... this is so hard being alone without you.
You (Edited)
?? Did you want to communicate? You requested??
Message Johnny Depp

After several days of no texting I received a request to communicate. Honestly, I missed the texting and was happy that it resumed. I partly believed that in time, if there was a real person on the other end of this, all the talk about authentication would end. I was wrong about that and for the second time authentication was raised and met with my continued refusal.

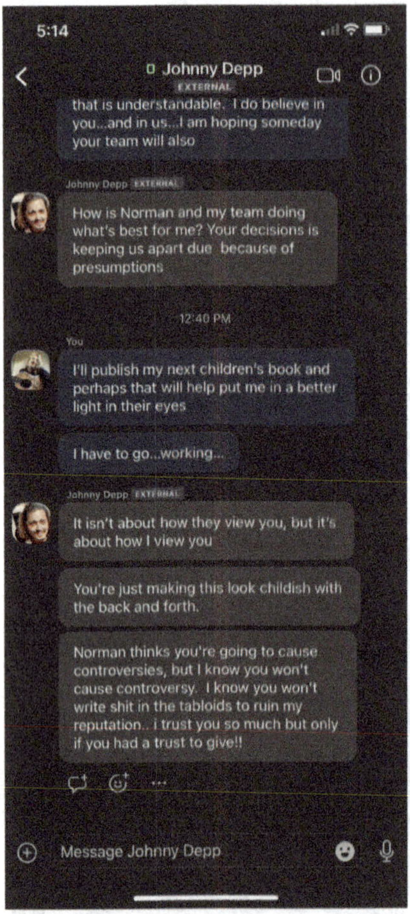

5:14
Johnny Depp
EXTERNAL
that is understandable. I do believe in you...and in us...I am hoping someday your team will also
Johnny Depp EXTERNAL
How is Norman and my team doing what's best for me? Your decisions is keeping us apart due because of presumptions
12:40 PM
You
I'll publish my next children's book and perhaps that will help put me in a better light in their eyes
I have to go...working...
Johnny Depp EXTERNAL
It isn't about how they view you, but it's about how I view you
You're just making this look childish with the back and forth.
Norman thinks you're going to cause controversies, but I know you won't cause controversy. I know you won't write shit in the tabloids to ruin my reputation.. i trust you so much but only if you had a trust to give!!
Message Johnny Depp

The scammer(s) always turned my refusal to send money into some weird campaign intended to inflict hurt on them. This is merely a psychological tactic used in an attempt to manipulate someone. It is no different than a stranger asking you for your money in the street and saying you hurt them when When I expressed that I was not the one the "management team" thought was the right person for Johnny, the scammer states that it was not about how they felt about me but how he felt about me. This pivot is one of several that the scammer(s) tried throughout the scam.

The 'authentication' scam was raised in texts at various times, like an end pin to arguments we had over nothing. It became clear to me that whatever this was it would likely end soon and abruptly. My financial situation at that time was one that included asset liquidation and that made me especially vulnerable to this scam.

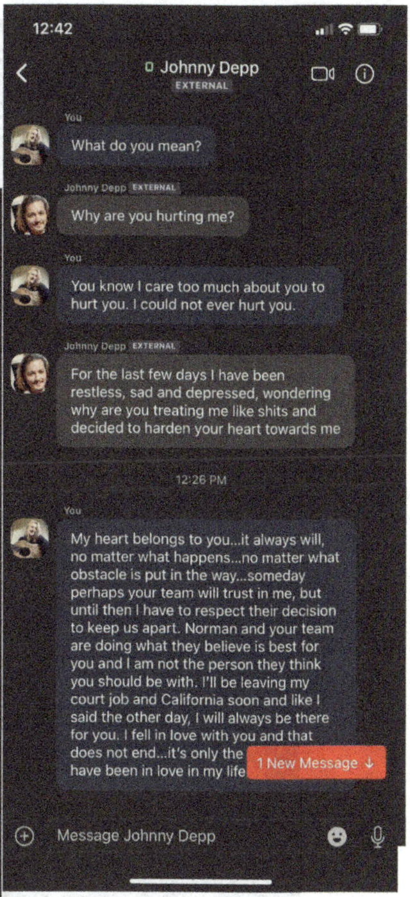
12:42
Johnny Depp
EXTERNAL
You
What do you mean?
Johnny Depp EXTERNAL
Why are you hurting me?
You
You know I care too much about you to hurt you. I could not ever hurt you.
Johnny Depp EXTERNAL
For the last few days I have been restless, sad and depressed, wondering why are you treating me like shits and decided to harden your heart towards me
12:26 PM
You
My heart belongs to you...it always will, no matter what happens...no matter what obstacle is put in the way...someday perhaps your team will trust in me, but until then I have to respect their decision to keep us apart. Norman and your team are doing what they believe is best for you and I am not the person they think you should be with. I'll be leaving my court job and California soon and like I said the other day, I will always be there for you. I fell in love with you and that does not end...it's only the
have been in love in my life
1 New Message
Message Johnny Depp

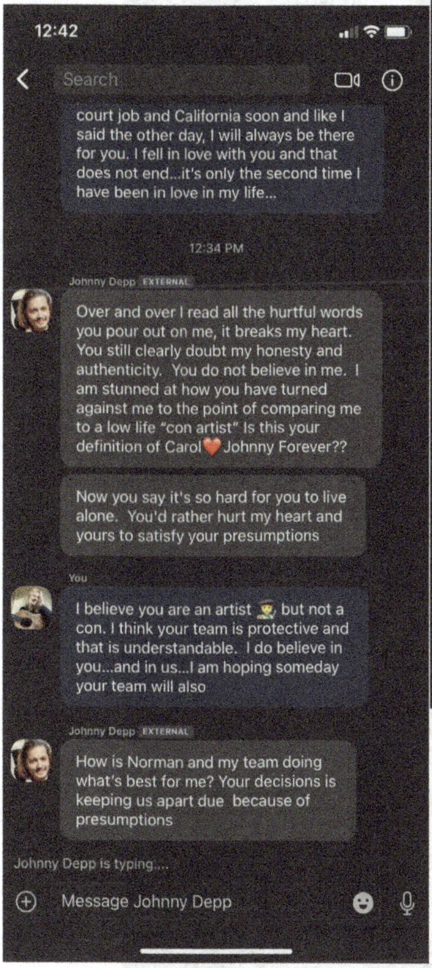
12:42
Search
court job and California soon and like I said the other day, I will always be there for you. I fell in love with you and that does not end...it's only the second time I have been in love in my life...
12:34 PM
Johnny Depp EXTERNAL
Over and over I read all the hurtful words you pour out on me, it breaks my heart. You still clearly doubt my honesty and authenticity. You do not believe in me. I am stunned at how you have turned against me to the point of comparing me to a low life "con artist" Is this your definition of Carol❤️Johnny Forever??
Now you say it's so hard for you to live alone. You'd rather hurt my heart and yours to satisfy your presumptions
You
I believe you are an artist 🧑‍🎨 but not a con. I think your team is protective and that is understandable. I do believe in you...and in us...I am hoping someday your team will also
Johnny Depp EXTERNAL
How is Norman and my team doing what's best for me? Your decisions is keeping us apart due because of presumptions
Johnny Depp is typing....
Message Johnny Depp

Tip: Scammers will not sustain the scam indefinitely when the victim does not submit. The scams are run to elicit money and/or information and when neither is gained, he/she/it may become increasingly abusive.

7:16 43

Replies

this point? If you still need to say distant then what's the point? If you want a friend on the sidelines just say so but I'm not sure if I can be that person anymore.,,I have fallen too deep I think "

Carol don't mess with my head. You want to keep playing the games just to enjoy the attention I give you. I have made it clear to you my love for you, I'm not holding you to walk away, you have refused to walk away and have refuse to commit. you're constantly testing me. It's frustrating because I've already proven myself to you multiple times. I've told you to get done with Norman for the authentication card so that we can chat and see each other, but you've refused. This is all games to you

You

Oh I see! Ha! Authentication! That's the last ditch-your true colors shine through-goodbye

7:14 PM

Johnny Depp EXTERNAL

I'm communicating with a psycho

Is either you're drunk or this is who you really are

You're messing with me

CONFLICTING and CONFUSING TEXTS

At this point I was not ready to stop communicating even though I had pressing doubts that I was actually communicating with Johnny Depp. Mixed among the conflicting and confusing texts there were threads of normal conversations like those one would have with a person while building a relationship. These "normal" text threads were encouraging; however, many of the individual texts made no sense. If I had been able to sort the texts by the varying sources, of which I believe were several, it may have been easier to see the scam for what it was. I could not do this. Therefore, I was not seeing the forest through the trees.

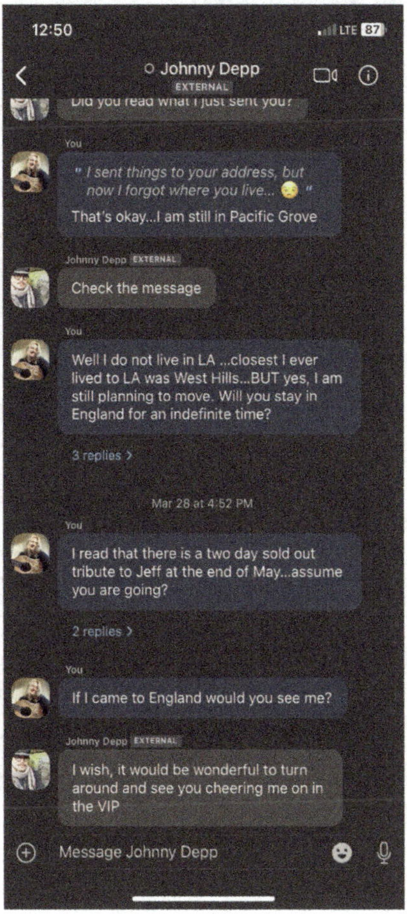

12:50
Johnny Depp
EXTERNAL
You
" I sent things to your address, but now I forgot where you live... "
That's okay...I am still in Pacific Grove
Johnny Depp EXTERNAL
Check the message
You
Well I do not live in LA ...closest I ever lived to LA was West Hills...BUT yes, I am still planning to move. Will you stay in England for an indefinite time?
3 replies
Mar 28 at 4:52 PM
You
I read that there is a two day sold out tribute to Jeff at the end of May...assume you are going?
2 replies
You
If I came to England would you see me?
Johnny Depp EXTERNAL
I wish, it would be wonderful to turn around and see you cheering me on in the VIP
Message Johnny Depp

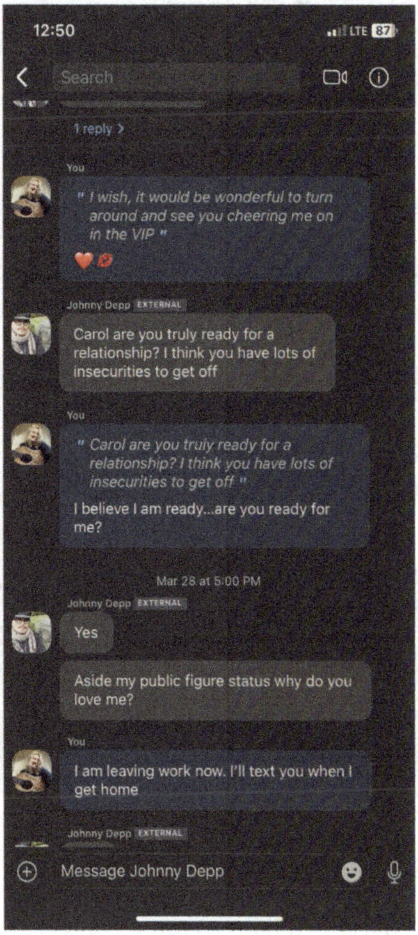

12:50
Search
1 reply
You
" I wish, it would be wonderful to turn around and see you cheering me on in the VIP "
Johnny Depp EXTERNAL
Carol are you truly ready for a relationship? I think you have lots of insecurities to get off
You
" Carol are you truly ready for a relationship? I think you have lots of insecurities to get off "
I believe I am ready...are you ready for me?
Mar 28 at 5:00 PM
Johnny Depp EXTERNAL
Yes
Aside my public figure status why do you love me?
You
I am leaving work now. I'll text you when I get home
Johnny Depp EXTERNAL
Message Johnny Depp

Throughout the months of communication there were times when the texting indicated there may be some legitimacy to the relationship. However, further analysis of texts containing conflicting information supported the premise that the only legitimacy was the scammer's desire to pull on my heart strings and challenge my character.

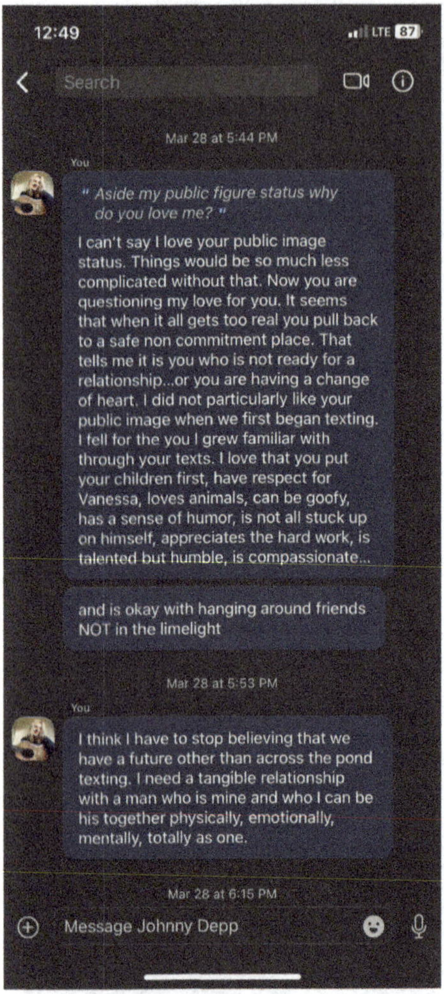
12:49
LTE 87
Search
Mar 28 at 5:44 PM
You
" Aside my public figure status why do you love me? "
I can't say I love your public image status. Things would be so much less complicated without that. Now you are questioning my love for you. It seems that when it all gets too real you pull back to a safe non commitment place. That tells me it is you who is not ready for a relationship...or you are having a change of heart. I did not particularly like your public image when we first began texting. I fell for the you I grew familiar with through your texts. I love that you put your children first, have respect for Vanessa, loves animals, can be goofy, has a sense of humor, is not all stuck up on himself, appreciates the hard work, is talented but humble, is compassionate...
and is okay with hanging around friends NOT in the limelight
Mar 28 at 5:53 PM
You
I think I have to stop believing that we have a future other than across the pond texting. I need a tangible relationship with a man who is mine and who I can be his together physically, emotionally, mentally, totally as one.
Mar 28 at 6:15 PM
Message Johnny Depp

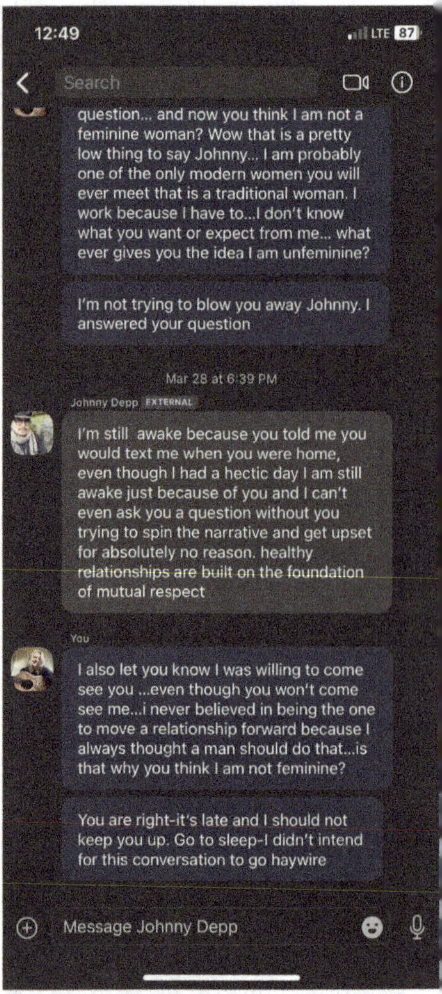
12:49
LTE 87
Search
question... and now you think I am not a feminine woman? Wow that is a pretty low thing to say Johnny... I am probably one of the only modern women you will ever meet that is a traditional woman. I work because I have to...I don't know what you want or expect from me... what ever gives you the idea I am unfeminine?
I'm not trying to blow you away Johnny. I answered your question
Mar 28 at 6:39 PM
Johnny Depp EXTERNAL
I'm still awake because you told me you would text me when you were home, even though I had a hectic day I am still awake just because of you and I can't even ask you a question without you trying to spin the narrative and get upset for absolutely no reason. healthy relationships are built on the foundation of mutual respect
You
I also let you know I was willing to come see you ...even though you won't come see me...i never believed in being the one to move a relationship forward because I always thought a man should do that...is that why you think I am not feminine?
You are right-it's late and I should not keep you up. Go to sleep-I didn't intend for this conversation to go haywire
Message Johnny Depp

What was telling to me was the bland response to me asking about going to England. Instead of responding enthusiastically, the scammer veers off in an different direction and responds with a character assault using words liken to those found in a 1970's magazine article.

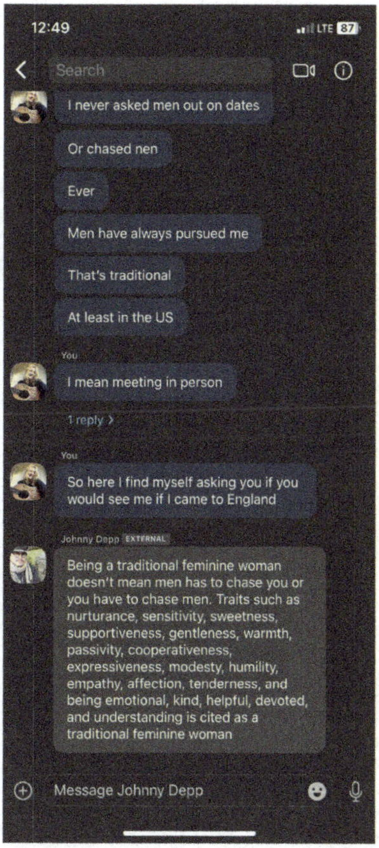
12:49
LTE 87
Search
I never asked men out on dates
Or chased nen
Ever
Men have always pursued me
That's traditional
At least in the US
You
I mean meeting in person
1 reply
You
So here I find myself asking you if you would see me if I came to England
Johnny Depp EXTERNAL
Being a traditional feminine woman doesn't mean men has to chase you or you have to chase men. Traits such as nurturance, sensitivity, sweetness, supportiveness, gentleness, warmth, passivity, cooperativeness, expressiveness, modesty, humility, empathy, affection, tenderness, and being emotional, kind, helpful, devoted, and understanding is cited as a traditional feminine woman
Message Johnny Depp

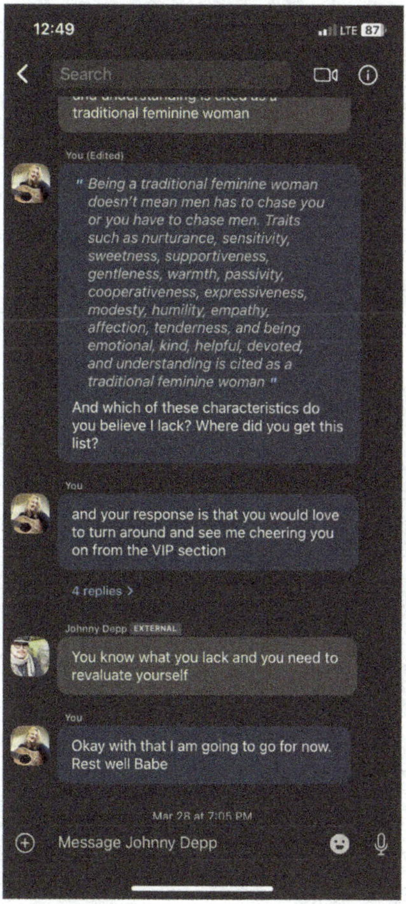
12:49
LTE 87
Search
traditional feminine woman
You (Edited)
" Being a traditional feminine woman doesn't mean men has to chase you or you have to chase men. Traits such as nurturance, sensitivity, sweetness, supportiveness, gentleness, warmth, passivity, cooperativeness, expressiveness, modesty, humility, empathy, affection, tenderness, and being emotional, kind, helpful, devoted, and understanding is cited as a traditional feminine woman "
And which of these characteristics do you believe I lack? Where did you get this list?
You
and your response is that you would love to turn around and see me cheering you on from the VIP section
4 replies
Johnny Depp EXTERNAL
You know what you lack and you need to revaluate yourself
You
Okay with that I am going to go for now. Rest well Babe
Mar 28 at 7:05 PM
Message Johnny Depp

Now I am getting frustrated because it seems we are having a different layered conversation. The scammer(s) seem to be reading from a 1970's magazine.

If there really was a relationship here I would expect to see a plan that would include us meeting either in the UK or the US. No such plan ever materialized and that was the biggest tell of all.

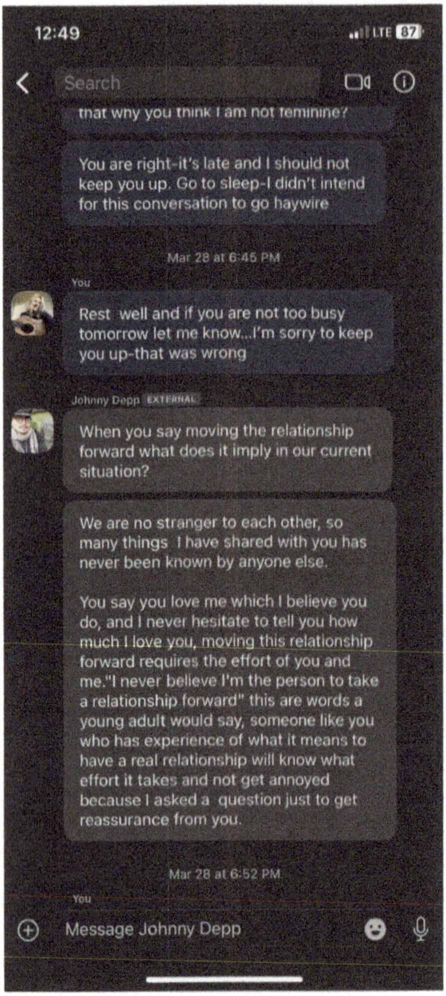
12:49
Search
that why you think I am not feminine?
You are right-it's late and I should not keep you up. Go to sleep-I didn't intend for this conversation to go haywire
Mar 28 at 6:45 PM
You
Rest well and if you are not too busy tomorrow let me know...I'm sorry to keep you up-that was wrong
Johnny Depp EXTERNAL
When you say moving the relationship forward what does it imply in our current situation?
We are no stranger to each other, so many things I have shared with you has never been known by anyone else.
You say you love me which I believe you do, and I never hesitate to tell you how much I love you, moving this relationship forward requires the effort of you and me."I never believe I'm the person to take a relationship forward" this are words a young adult would say, someone like you who has experience of what it means to have a real relationship will know what effort it takes and not get annoyed because I asked a question just to get reassurance from you.
Mar 28 at 6:52 PM
You
Message Johnny Depp

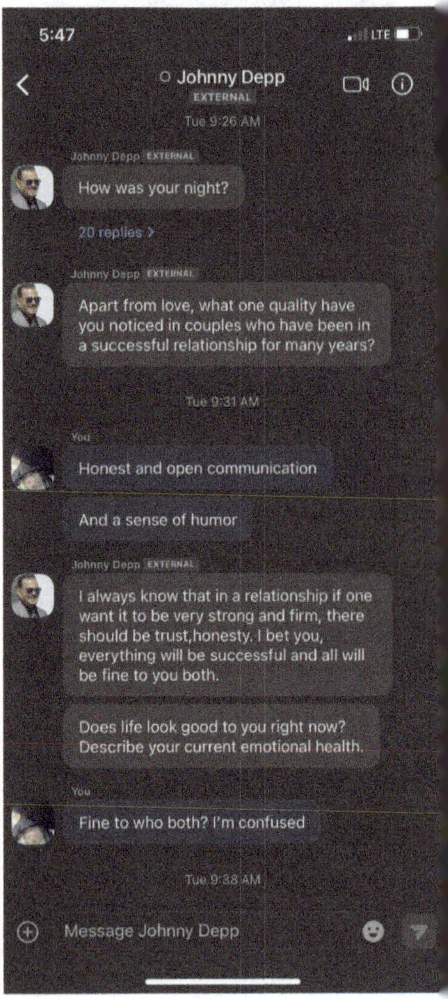
5:47
Johnny Depp
EXTERNAL
Tue 9:26 AM
Johnny Depp EXTERNAL
How was your night?
20 replies >
Johnny Depp EXTERNAL
Apart from love, what one quality have you noticed in couples who have been in a successful relationship for many years?
Tue 9:31 AM
You
Honest and open communication
And a sense of humor
Johnny Depp EXTERNAL
I always know that in a relationship if one want it to be very strong and firm, there should be trust,honesty. I bet you, everything will be successful and all will be fine to you both.
Does life look good to you right now? Describe your current emotional health.
You
Fine to who both? I'm confused
Tue 9:38 AM
Message Johnny Depp

Tip: If the text thread reads like nonsense it probably is. Sometimes the words we want to text do not appear due to automatic features but this should not cause an entire sentence change. What does "Fine to you both" mean?

The text thread below is a back walk on my request to share the relationship with family.

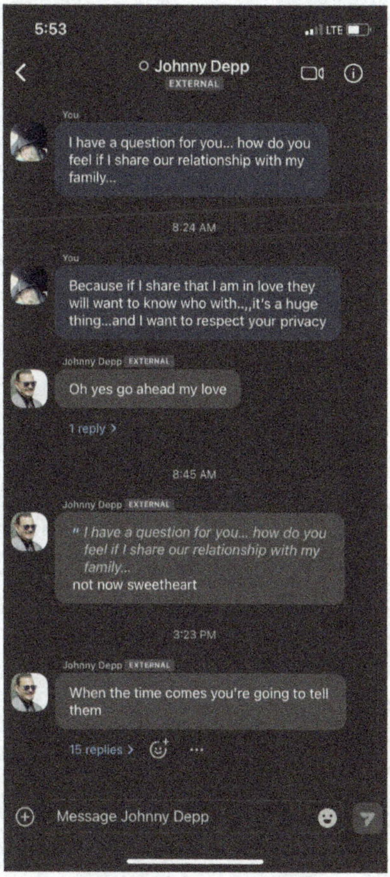
5:53
LTE
Johnny Depp
EXTERNAL
You
I have a question for you... how do you feel if I share our relationship with my family...
8:24 AM
You
Because if I share that I am in love they will want to know who with...,it's a huge thing...and I want to respect your privacy
Johnny Depp EXTERNAL
Oh yes go ahead my love
1 reply
8:45 AM
Johnny Depp EXTERNAL
" I have a question for you... how do you feel if I share our relationship with my family...
not now sweetheart
3:23 PM
Johnny Depp EXTERNAL
When the time comes you're going to tell them
15 replies
Message Johnny Depp

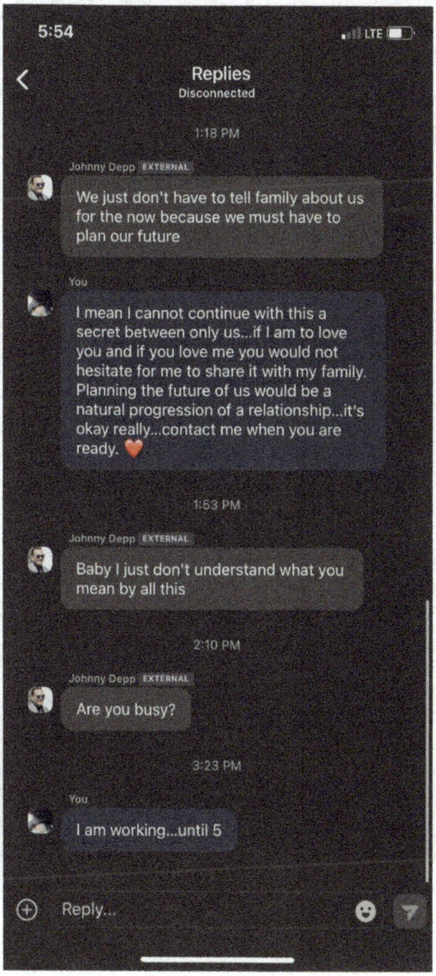
5:54
LTE
Replies
Disconnected
1:18 PM
Johnny Depp EXTERNAL
We just don't have to tell family about us for the now because we must have to plan our future
You
I mean I cannot continue with this a secret between only us...if I am to love you and if you love me you would not hesitate for me to share it with my family. Planning the future of us would be a natural progression of a relationship...it's okay really...contact me when you are ready.
1:53 PM
Johnny Depp EXTERNAL
Baby I just don't understand what you mean by all this
2:10 PM
Johnny Depp EXTERNAL
Are you busy?
3:23 PM
You
I am working...until 5
Reply...

Tip: This is a huge red flag! If ever someone does not want your family to know you are communicating that is sketchy.

AFFIRMATIONS of LOVE and SHADOWS of DOUBT

During the course of this virtual relationship there were sweet exchanges of love almost daily.

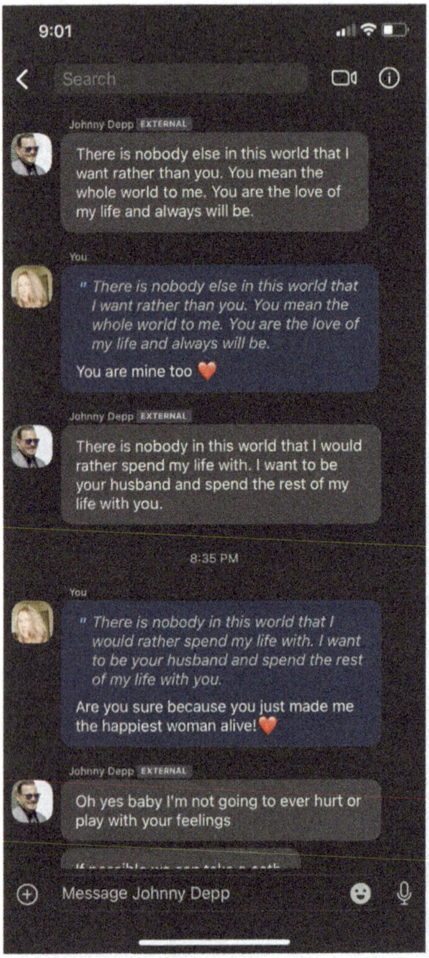
9:01
Search
Johnny Depp EXTERNAL
There is nobody else in this world that I want rather than you. You mean the whole world to me. You are the love of my life and always will be.
You
" There is nobody else in this world that I want rather than you. You mean the whole world to me. You are the love of my life and always will be.
You are mine too ❤️
Johnny Depp EXTERNAL
There is nobody in this world that I would rather spend my life with. I want to be your husband and spend the rest of my life with you.
8:35 PM
You
" There is nobody in this world that I would rather spend my life with. I want to be your husband and spend the rest of my life with you.
Are you sure because you just made me the happiest woman alive!❤️
Johnny Depp EXTERNAL
Oh yes baby I'm not going to ever hurt or play with your feelings
Message Johnny Depp

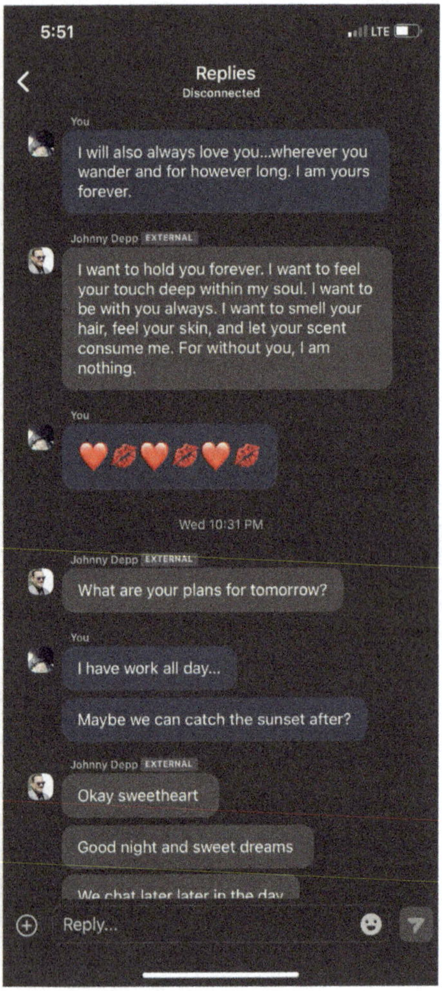
5:51
LTE
Replies
Disconnected
You
I will also always love you...wherever you wander and for however long. I am yours forever.
Johnny Depp EXTERNAL
I want to hold you forever. I want to feel your touch deep within my soul. I want to be with you always. I want to smell your hair, feel your skin, and let your scent consume me. For without you, I am nothing.
You
❤️💋❤️💋❤️💋
Wed 10:31 PM
Johnny Depp EXTERNAL
What are your plans for tomorrow?
You
I have work all day...
Maybe we can catch the sunset after?
Johnny Depp EXTERNAL
Okay sweetheart
Good night and sweet dreams
Reply...

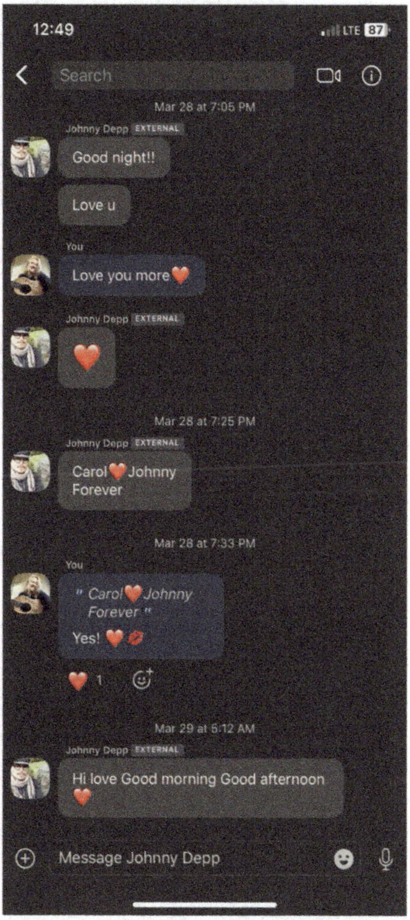
12:49
LTE 87
Search
Mar 28 at 7:05 PM
Johnny Depp EXTERNAL
Good night!!
Love u
You
Love you more
Johnny Depp EXTERNAL
Mar 28 at 7:25 PM
Johnny Depp EXTERNAL
Carol Johnny Forever
Mar 28 at 7:33 PM
You
" Carol Johnny Forever "
Yes!
1
Mar 29 at 5:12 AM
Johnny Depp EXTERNAL
Hi love Good morning Good afternoon
Message Johnny Depp

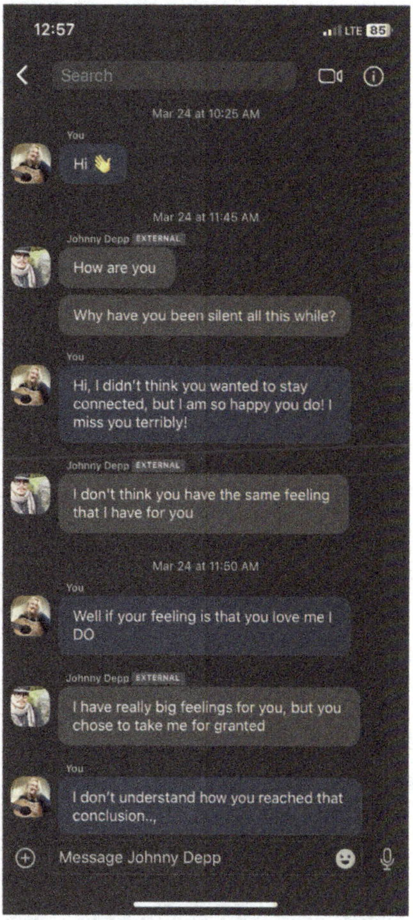
12:57
LTE 85
Search
Mar 24 at 10:25 AM
You
Hi
Mar 24 at 11:45 AM
Johnny Depp EXTERNAL
How are you
Why have you been silent all this while?
You
Hi, I didn't think you wanted to stay connected, but I am so happy you do! I miss you terribly!
Johnny Depp EXTERNAL
I don't think you have the same feeling that I have for you
Mar 24 at 11:50 AM
You
Well if your feeling is that you love me I DO
Johnny Depp EXTERNAL
I have really big feelings for you, but you chose to take me for granted
You
I don't understand how you reached that conclusion..,
Message Johnny Depp

Throughout our texting it seemed that we continually circled around and on unsteady ground. I thought this was due to miscommunication and my not wanting to put premature pressure on the relationship. In hindsight I see that the pretended insecurity was all part of a scheme to 'reel me in' further in order to gain a stronger control over my emotions.

On March 28th I was ready to try and end the virtual relationship after (once again) answering the question about public image. I was unsure if this was a healthy or lasting relationship because, for one reason, I could not be sure of who or what I was texting with. Yet (as evidenced by the text nearly three months later), I could not let go.

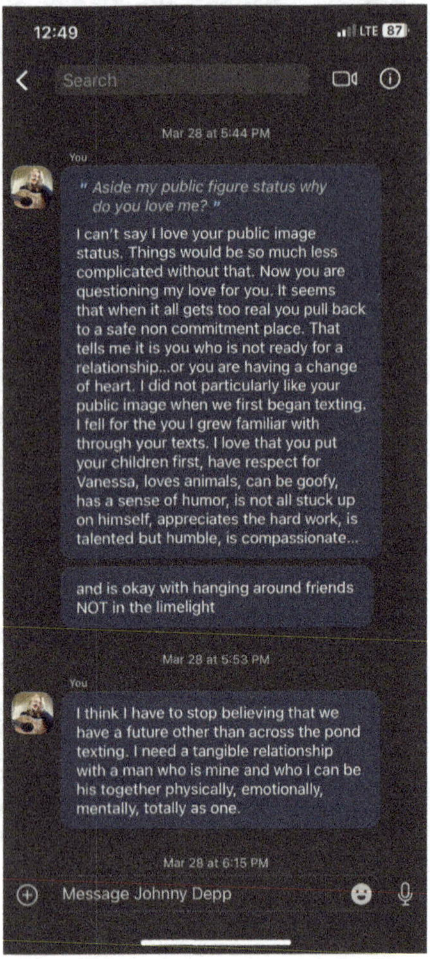
12:49
LTE 87
Search
Mar 28 at 5:44 PM
You
" Aside my public figure status why do you love me? "
I can't say I love your public image status. Things would be so much less complicated without that. Now you are questioning my love for you. It seems that when it all gets too real you pull back to a safe non commitment place. That tells me it is you who is not ready for a relationship...or you are having a change of heart. I did not particularly like your public image when we first began texting. I fell for the you I grew familiar with through your texts. I love that you put your children first, have respect for Vanessa, loves animals, can be goofy, has a sense of humor, is not all stuck up on himself, appreciates the hard work, is talented but humble, is compassionate...
and is okay with hanging around friends NOT in the limelight
Mar 28 at 5:53 PM
You
I think I have to stop believing that we have a future other than across the pond texting. I need a tangible relationship with a man who is mine and who I can be his together physically, emotionally, mentally, totally as one.
Mar 28 at 6:15 PM
Message Johnny Depp

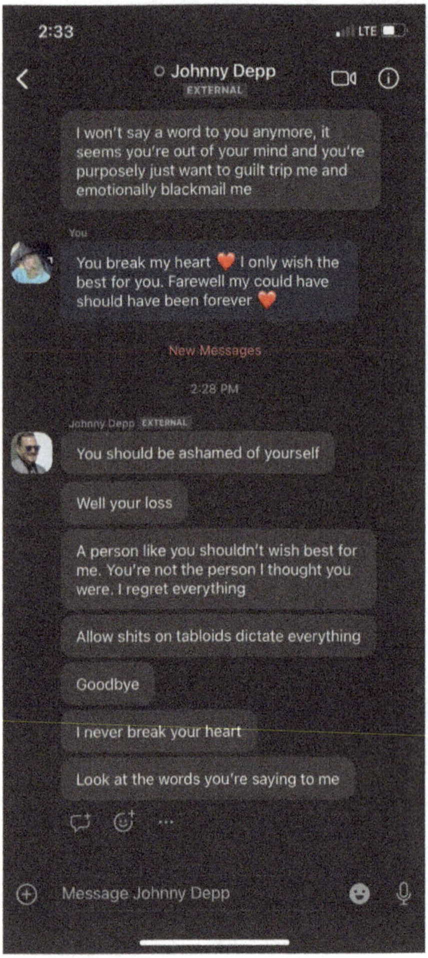
2:33
LTE
Johnny Depp
EXTERNAL
I won't say a word to you anymore, it seems you're out of your mind and you're purposely just want to guilt trip me and emotionally blackmail me
You
You break my heart ❤️ I only wish the best for you. Farewell my could have should have been forever ❤️
New Messages
2:28 PM
Johnny Depp EXTERNAL
You should be ashamed of yourself
Well your loss
A person like you shouldn't wish best for me. You're not the person I thought you were. I regret everything
Allow shits on tabloids dictate everything
Goodbye
I never break your heart
Look at the words you're saying to me
Message Johnny Depp

It seemed that we were either on again or off again and this hindered the relationship from moving forward. But of course we could not really move forward because that would require a physical meeting and that would end the scam!

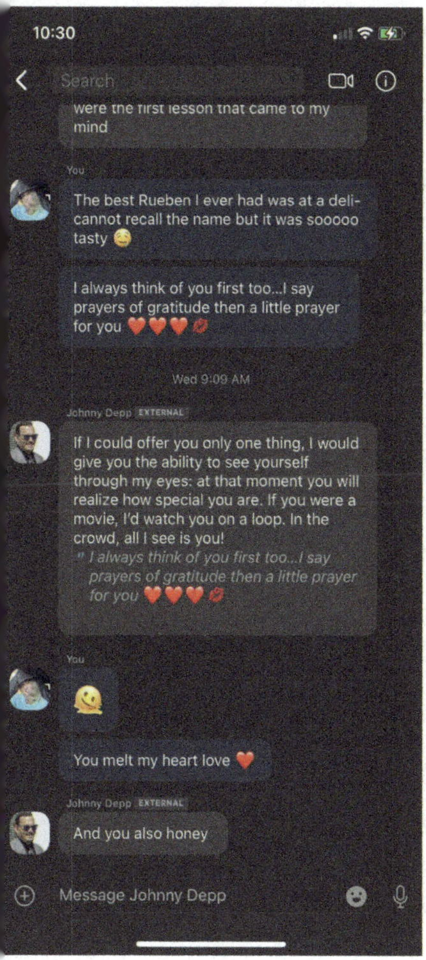
10:30
Search
were the first lesson that came to my mind
You
The best Rueben I ever had was at a deli- cannot recall the name but it was sooooo tasty
I always think of you first too...I say prayers of gratitude then a little prayer for you
Wed 9:09 AM
Johnny Depp EXTERNAL
If I could offer you only one thing, I would give you the ability to see yourself through my eyes: at that moment you will realize how special you are. If you were a movie, I'd watch you on a loop. In the crowd, all I see is you!
I always think of you first too...I say prayers of gratitude then a little prayer for you
You
You melt my heart love
Johnny Depp EXTERNAL
And you also honey
Message Johnny Depp

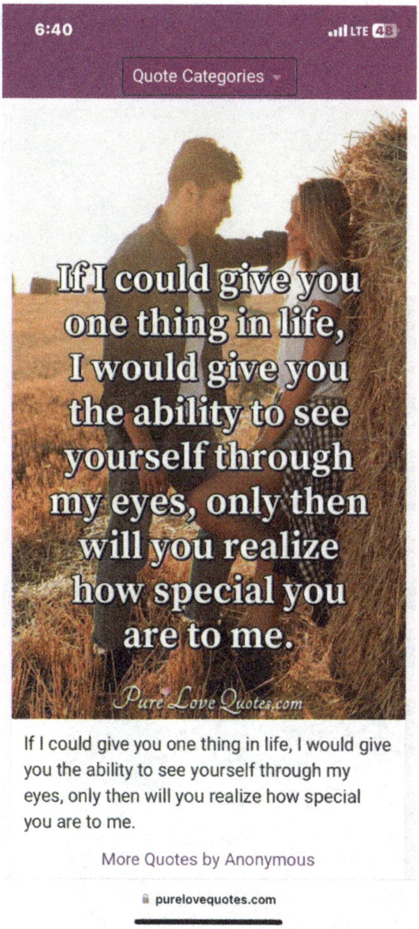
6:40
Quote Categories
If I could give you one thing in life, I would give you the ability to see yourself through my eyes, only then will you realize how special you are to me.
PureLoveQuotes.com
If I could give you one thing in life, I would give you the ability to see yourself through my eyes, only then will you realize how special you are to me.
More Quotes by Anonymous
purelovequotes.com

Once again the scammer(s) borrowed a quote and that worked to further cheapen the virtual relationship. If I had checked this out when received it would have helped me to accept the sham for what it was. I knew that the real Johnny Depp is a poet, not a copier.

Tip: If someone sends what appears to be original prose, research it!

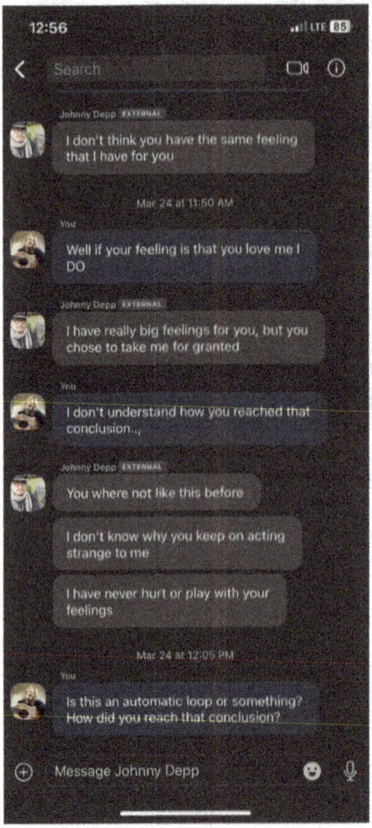
12:56
Search
Johnny Depp EXTERNAL
I don't think you have the same feeling that I have for you
Mar 24 at 11:50 AM
You
Well if your feeling is that you love me I DO
Johnny Depp EXTERNAL
I have really big feelings for you, but you chose to take me for granted
You
I don't understand how you reached that conclusion..,
Johnny Depp EXTERNAL
You where not like this before
I don't know why you keep on acting strange to me
I have never hurt or play with your feelings
Mar 24 at 12:05 PM
You
Is this an automatic loop or something? How did you reach that conclusion?
Message Johnny Depp

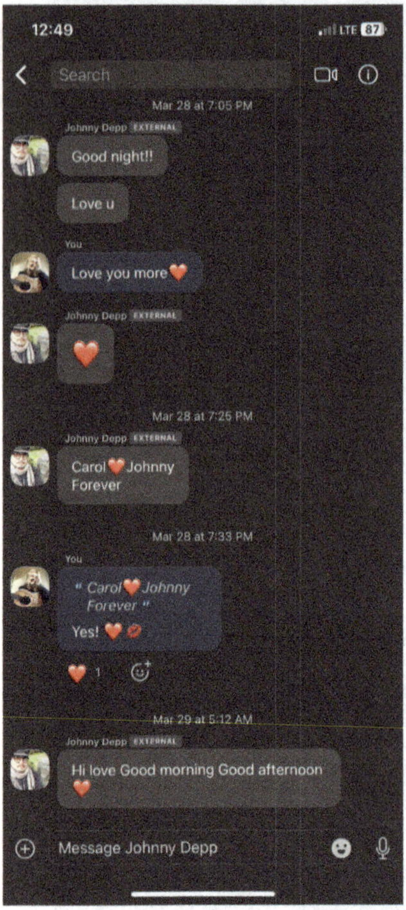
12:49
Search
Mar 28 at 7:05 PM
Johnny Depp EXTERNAL
Good night!!
Love u
You
Love you more
Johnny Depp EXTERNAL
Mar 28 at 7:25 PM
Johnny Depp EXTERNAL
Carol Johnny Forever
Mar 28 at 7:33 PM
You
" Carol Johnny Forever "
Yes!
Mar 29 at 5:12 AM
Johnny Depp EXTERNAL
Hi love Good morning Good afternoon
Message Johnny Depp

If I had known the quote was borrowed I would have asked about it because everything I knew about Johnny screamed that he was original. As it was, I did not think to check the quote and by the end of that day in late March, we were once again expressing a devotion to our love.

3:14
June 13
6:44 PM
Edit
Carol Johnny forever
Johnny Depp Jun 5 at 4:39 PM
Always and forever
TUESDAY, JUN 6
Johnny Depp Jun 6 at 3:08 AM
Good morning my love
Carol Melber Jun 6 at 6:06 AM
Good morning love! Cool pic! Happy Tuesday

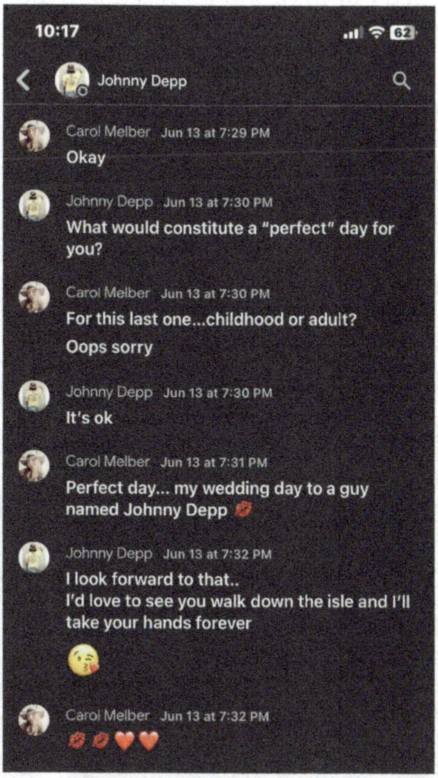
10:17
Johnny Depp
Carol Melber Jun 13 at 7:29 PM
Okay
Johnny Depp Jun 13 at 7:30 PM
What would constitute a "perfect" day for you?
Carol Melber Jun 13 at 7:30 PM
For this last one...childhood or adult?
Oops sorry
Johnny Depp Jun 13 at 7:30 PM
It's ok
Carol Melber Jun 13 at 7:31 PM
Perfect day... my wedding day to a guy named Johnny Depp
Johnny Depp Jun 13 at 7:32 PM
I look forward to that..
I'd love to see you walk down the isle and I'll take your hands forever
Carol Melber Jun 13 at 7:32 PM

Nearly three months later my answer to one of many questions we asked each other was my confirmation of the commitment I had to the relationship.

THE MONEY SCAM (Part2?), GOOGLE PLAY CARD

Another month goes by without me sending any money. I am beginning to accept that I will never actually meet whoever this is, yet we continue communicating. I believe there were several scammers sending texts during this time. I am resolved to the idea that this will likely never go beyond a casual friendship even though my feelings go much deeper. I am aware the situation is near impossible and I begin to pull back in order to shield myself from the inevitable heartbreak.

Then, while supposedly working on location in New Zealand, (which turned out to be a bold-faced lie), the scammer(s) hit me up with a request to purchase a $200 Google Play Card.

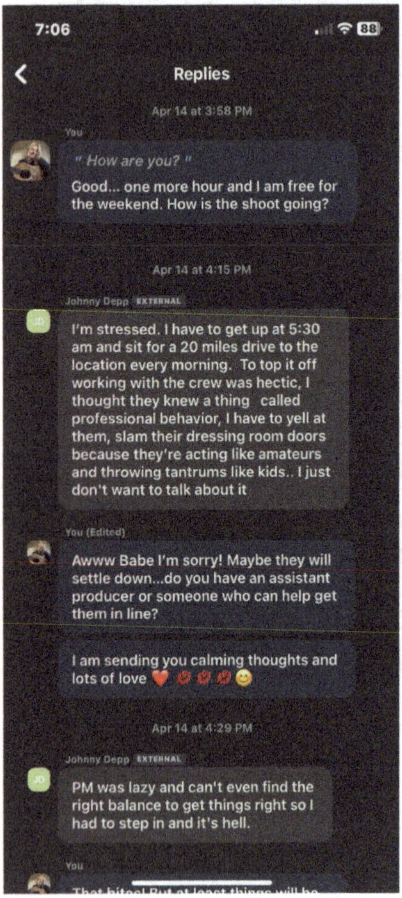

7:06
Replies
Apr 14 at 3:58 PM
You
" How are you? "
Good... one more hour and I am free for the weekend. How is the shoot going?
Apr 14 at 4:15 PM
Johnny Depp EXTERNAL
I'm stressed. I have to get up at 5:30 am and sit for a 20 miles drive to the location every morning. To top it off working with the crew was hectic, I thought they knew a thing called professional behavior, I have to yell at them, slam their dressing room doors because they're acting like amateurs and throwing tantrums like kids.. I just don't want to talk about it
You (Edited)
Awww Babe I'm sorry! Maybe they will settle down...do you have an assistant producer or someone who can help get them in line?
I am sending you calming thoughts and lots of love
Apr 14 at 4:29 PM
Johnny Depp EXTERNAL
PM was lazy and can't even find the right balance to get things right so I had to step in and it's hell.
You

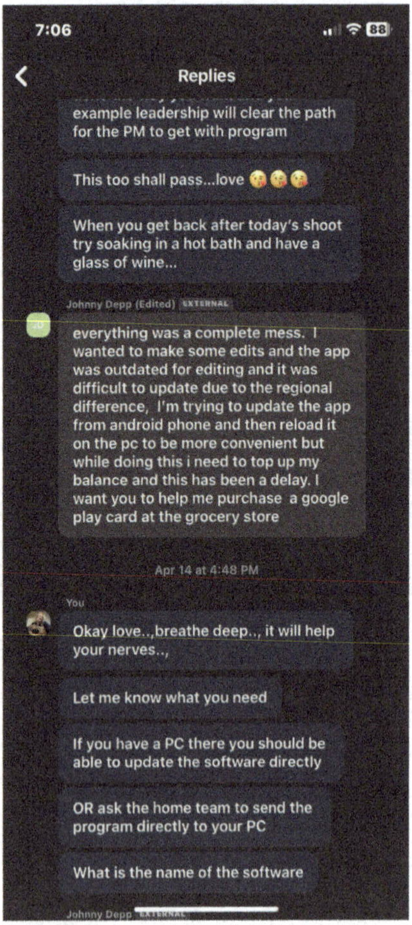

7:06
Replies
example leadership will clear the path for the PM to get with program
This too shall pass...love
When you get back after today's shoot try soaking in a hot bath and have a glass of wine...
Johnny Depp (Edited) EXTERNAL
everything was a complete mess. I wanted to make some edits and the app was outdated for editing and it was difficult to update due to the regional difference, I'm trying to update the app from android phone and then reload it on the pc to be more convenient but while doing this i need to top up my balance and this has been a delay. I want you to help me purchase a google play card at the grocery store
Apr 14 at 4:48 PM
You
Okay love..,breathe deep.., it will help your nerves..,
Let me know what you need
If you have a PC there you should be able to update the software directly
OR ask the home team to send the program directly to your PC
What is the name of the software
Johnny Depp EXTERNAL

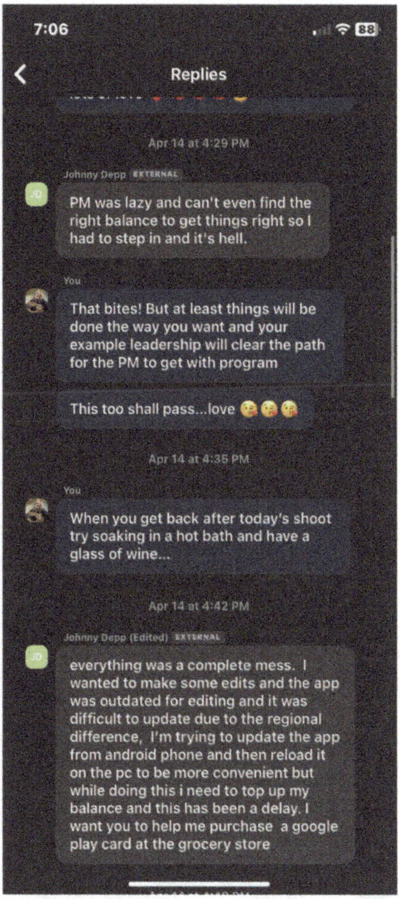

7:06

Replies

Apr 14 at 4:29 PM

Johnny Depp EXTERNAL

PM was lazy and can't even find the right balance to get things right so I had to step in and it's hell.

You

That bites! But at least things will be done the way you want and your example leadership will clear the path for the PM to get with program

This too shall pass...love 😘😘😘

Apr 14 at 4:35 PM

You

When you get back after today's shoot try soaking in a hot bath and have a glass of wine...

Apr 14 at 4:42 PM

Johnny Depp (Edited) EXTERNAL

everything was a complete mess. I wanted to make some edits and the app was outdated for editing and it was difficult to update due to the regional difference, I'm trying to update the app from android phone and then reload it on the pc to be more convenient but while doing this i need to top up my balance and this has been a delay. I want you to help me purchase a google play card at the grocery store

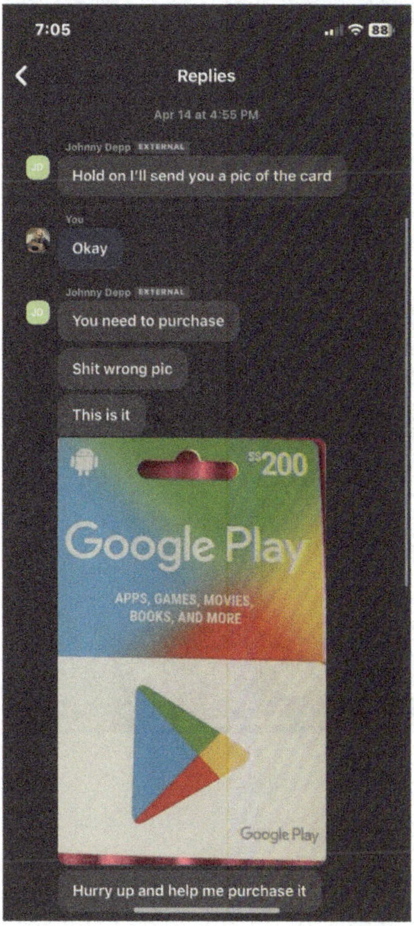

7:05

Replies

Apr 14 at 4:55 PM

Johnny Depp EXTERNAL

Hold on I'll send you a pic of the card

You

Okay

Johnny Depp EXTERNAL

You need to purchase

Shit wrong pic

This is it

Hurry up and help me purchase it

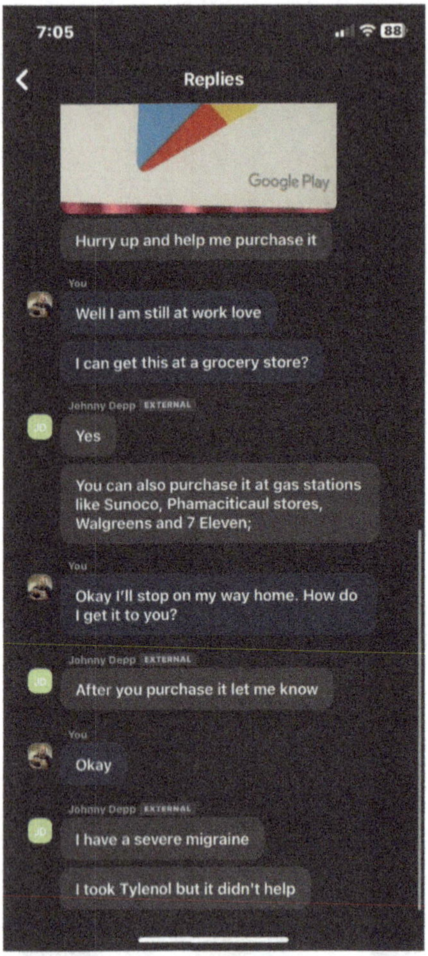
7:05
Replies
Google Play
Hurry up and help me purchase it
You
Well I am still at work love
I can get this at a grocery store?
Johnny Depp EXTERNAL
Yes
You can also purchase it at gas stations like Sunoco, Phamaciticaul stores, Walgreens and 7 Eleven;
You
Okay I'll stop on my way home. How do I get it to you?
Johnny Depp EXTERNAL
After you purchase it let me know
You
Okay
Johnny Depp EXTERNAL
I have a severe migraine
I took Tylenol but it didn't help

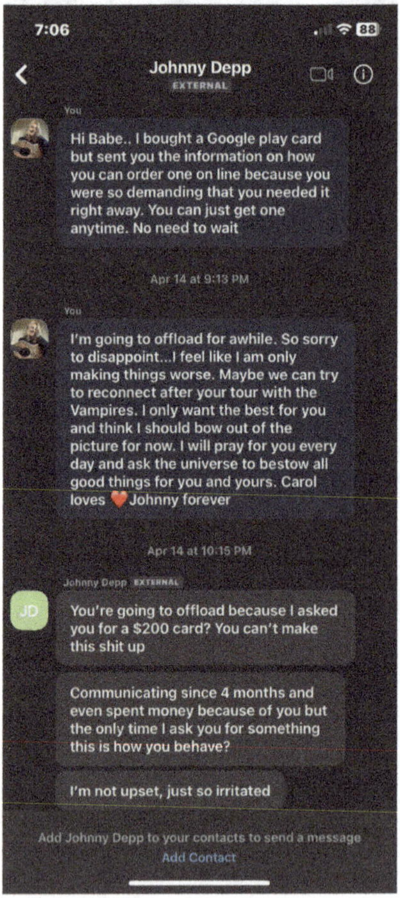
7:06
Johnny Depp
EXTERNAL
You
Hi Babe.. I bought a Google play card but sent you the information on how you can order one on line because you were so demanding that you needed it right away. You can just get one anytime. No need to wait
Apr 14 at 9:13 PM
You
I'm going to offload for awhile. So sorry to disappoint...I feel like I am only making things worse. Maybe we can try to reconnect after your tour with the Vampires. I only want the best for you and think I should bow out of the picture for now. I will pray for you every day and ask the universe to bestow all good things for you and yours. Carol loves ❤️ Johnny forever
Apr 14 at 10:15 PM
Johnny Depp EXTERNAL
You're going to offload because I asked you for a $200 card? You can't make this shit up
Communicating since 4 months and even spent money because of you but the only time I ask you for something this is how you behave?
I'm not upset, just so irritated
Add Johnny Depp to your contacts to send a message
Add Contact

The long text on the upcoming page seemed to indicate that the purchase of a card didn't matter at all. It was almost as if the whole thing was just some weird test; but, as soon as I texted that I had a card, there was no hesitation from the scammer to get the card number.

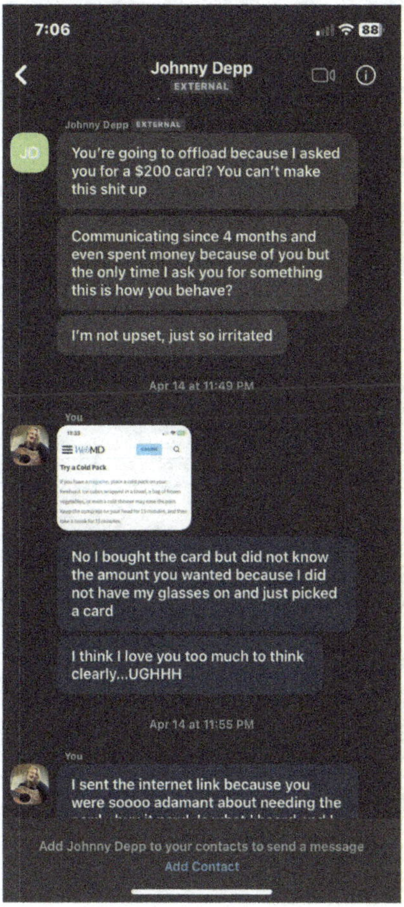
7:06
88
Johnny Depp
EXTERNAL
Johnny Depp EXTERNAL
JD
You're going to offload because I asked you for a $200 card? You can't make this shit up
Communicating since 4 months and even spent money because of you but the only time I ask you for something this is how you behave?
I'm not upset, just so irritated
Apr 14 at 11:49 PM
You
WebMD
Try a Cold Pack
No I bought the card but did not know the amount you wanted because I did not have my glasses on and just picked a card
I think I love you too much to think clearly...UGHHH
Apr 14 at 11:55 PM
You
I sent the internet link because you were soooo adamant about needing the
Add Johnny Depp to your contacts to send a message
Add Contact

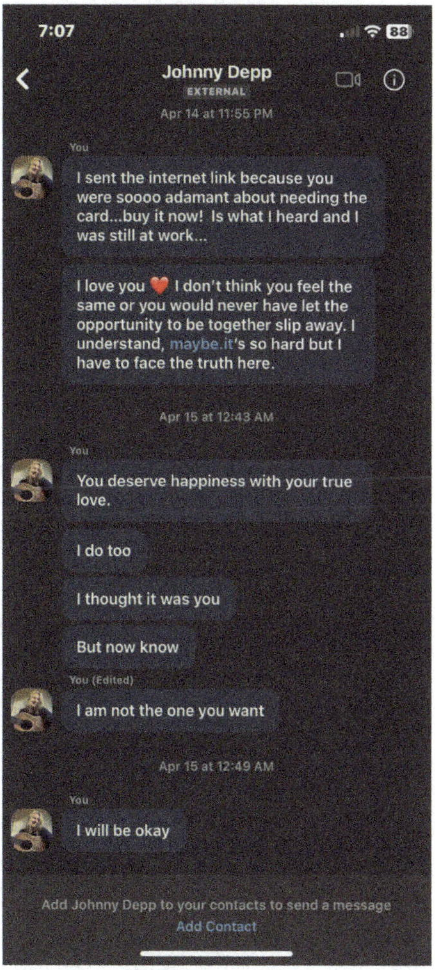
7:07
88
Johnny Depp
EXTERNAL
Apr 14 at 11:55 PM
You
I sent the internet link because you were soooo adamant about needing the card...buy it now! Is what I heard and I was still at work...
I love you ❤️ I don't think you feel the same or you would never have let the opportunity to be together slip away. I understand, maybe.it's so hard but I have to face the truth here.
Apr 15 at 12:43 AM
You
You deserve happiness with your true love.
I do too
I thought it was you
But now know
You (Edited)
I am not the one you want
Apr 15 at 12:49 AM
You
I will be okay
Add Johnny Depp to your contacts to send a message
Add Contact

I stopped at a local store on my way home and reviewed the text. I was shocked by the request. Why on earth would Johnny Depp hit me up for a Google Play Card, something he could easily get on his own or have his management team purchase? My mind was reeling by this request. I knew instantly this was not Johnny Depp but I was so upset by it that I panicked. Was this a person in prison or a minor? Should I end this communication now by ignoring the request and blocking? I sat in my car wondering how I should handle this situation. I reviewed the text communication and was taken back by the tone of urgency. "Hurry up and help me purchase it." I could not afford to throw away $200 so I purchased a card for $25. I figured that even if this was a charity purchase I could afford to give $25. I also knew this was likely the end of the fake relationship.

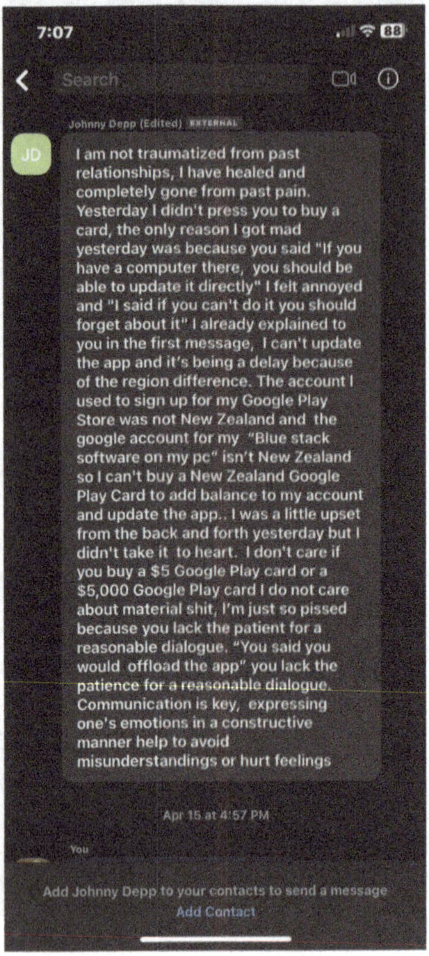
7:07
88
Search
Johnny Depp (Edited) EXTERNAL
JD
I am not traumatized from past relationships, I have healed and completely gone from past pain. Yesterday I didn't press you to buy a card, the only reason I got mad yesterday was because you said "If you have a computer there, you should be able to update it directly" I felt annoyed and "I said if you can't do it you should forget about it" I already explained to you in the first message, I can't update the app and it's being a delay because of the region difference. The account I used to sign up for my Google Play Store was not New Zealand and the google account for my "Blue stack software on my pc" isn't New Zealand so I can't buy a New Zealand Google Play Card to add balance to my account and update the app.. I was a little upset from the back and forth yesterday but I didn't take it to heart. I don't care if you buy a $5 Google Play card or a $5,000 Google Play card I do not care about material shit, I'm just so pissed because you lack the patient for a reasonable dialogue. "You said you would offload the app" you lack the patience for a reasonable dialogue. Communication is key, expressing one's emotions in a constructive manner help to avoid misunderstandings or hurt feelings
Apr 15 at 4:57 PM
You
Add Johnny Depp to your contacts to send a message
Add Contact

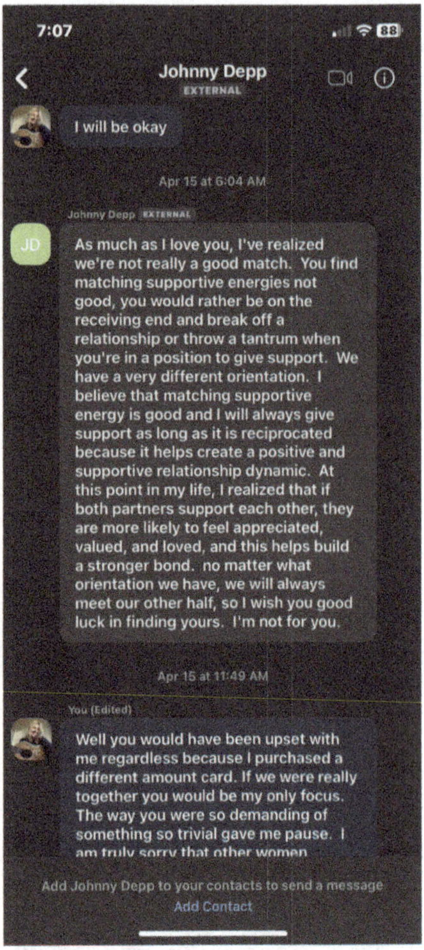
7:07
88
Johnny Depp
EXTERNAL
I will be okay
Apr 15 at 6:04 AM
Johnny Depp EXTERNAL
JD
As much as I love you, I've realized we're not really a good match. You find matching supportive energies not good, you would rather be on the receiving end and break off a relationship or throw a tantrum when you're in a position to give support. We have a very different orientation. I believe that matching supportive energy is good and I will always give support as long as it is reciprocated because it helps create a positive and supportive relationship dynamic. At this point in my life, I realized that if both partners support each other, they are more likely to feel appreciated, valued, and loved, and this helps build a stronger bond. no matter what orientation we have, we will always meet our other half, so I wish you good luck in finding yours. I'm not for you.
Apr 15 at 11:49 AM
You (Edited)
Well you would have been upset with me regardless because I purchased a different amount card. If we were really together you would be my only focus. The way you were so demanding of something so trivial gave me pause. I
Add Johnny Depp to your contacts to send a message
Add Contact

I lied about not knowing the amount of card requested. I did not have my glasses on when the text was received because I was packing up to leave work but I had checked the text while sitting in my car outside the store and I confirmed the request was for a $200 card

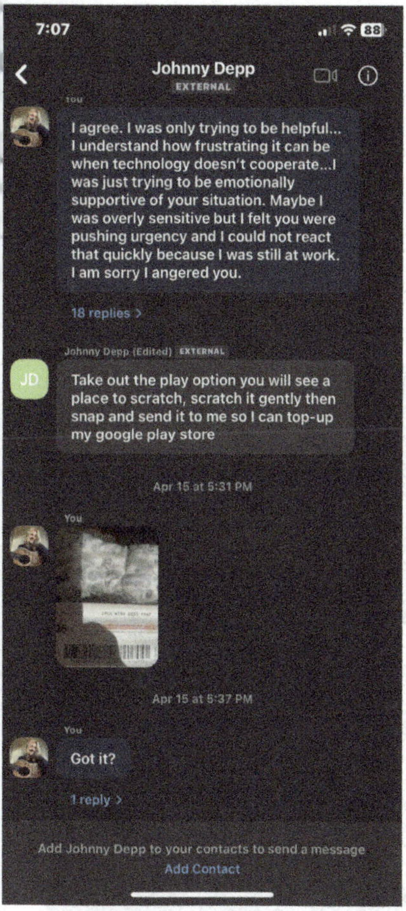
7:07
Johnny Depp
EXTERNAL
You
I agree. I was only trying to be helpful... I understand how frustrating it can be when technology doesn't cooperate...I was just trying to be emotionally supportive of your situation. Maybe I was overly sensitive but I felt you were pushing urgency and I could not react that quickly because I was still at work. I am sorry I angered you.
18 replies >
Johnny Depp (Edited) EXTERNAL
JD
Take out the play option you will see a place to scratch, scratch it gently then snap and send it to me so I can top-up my google play store
Apr 15 at 5:31 PM
You
Apr 15 at 5:37 PM
You
Got it?
1 reply >
Add Johnny Depp to your contacts to send a message
Add Contact

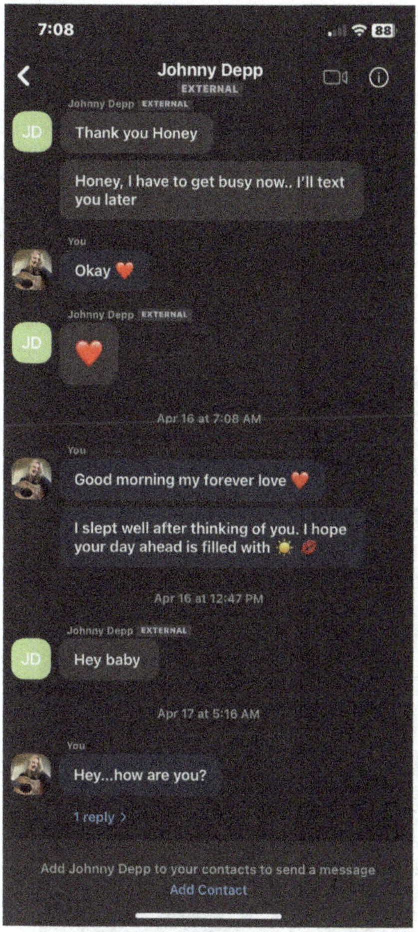
7:08
Johnny Depp
EXTERNAL
Johnny Depp EXTERNAL
JD
Thank you Honey
Honey, I have to get busy now.. I'll text you later
You
Okay ❤️
Johnny Depp EXTERNAL
JD
❤️
Apr 16 at 7:08 AM
You
Good morning my forever love ❤️
I slept well after thinking of you. I hope your day ahead is filled with ☀️ 💋
Apr 16 at 12:47 PM
Johnny Depp EXTERNAL
JD
Hey baby
Apr 17 at 5:16 AM
You
Hey...how are you?
1 reply >
Add Johnny Depp to your contacts to send a message
Add Contact

I was now sure that this was just a scam. No one in a relationship would ask for Google Play card like this. I knew and still my heart was in denial so I justified that the $25 Google Play Card was a charity purchase and let the scammer(s) have the card. This was a HUGE mistake because now I had proven to the scammer(s) that I could be scammed.

After all that drama I was spent emotionally from the tug of war between my heart and good sense. The situation was taking a toll on me mentally. I justified the whole thing in my head while thorns of regret pierced my heart. I felt that I lost some self-respect that day. Still, I could not let go.

As the days passed in April I found myself falling deeper in love and believing more often than not that there was a real person on the other end of the texts who felt the same. However, many questions I asked were not answered, some texts were inconsistent, and there were times when I was unsure if whoever it was texting knew that it was me on the receiving end. I wanted to end the virtual relationship several times and it appeared that the scammer(s) did as well, perhaps because it was realized that I had no intention of giving in to the authentication scam and had only funded a $25 Google Play Card. The text below made no sense when we were not living near to each other.

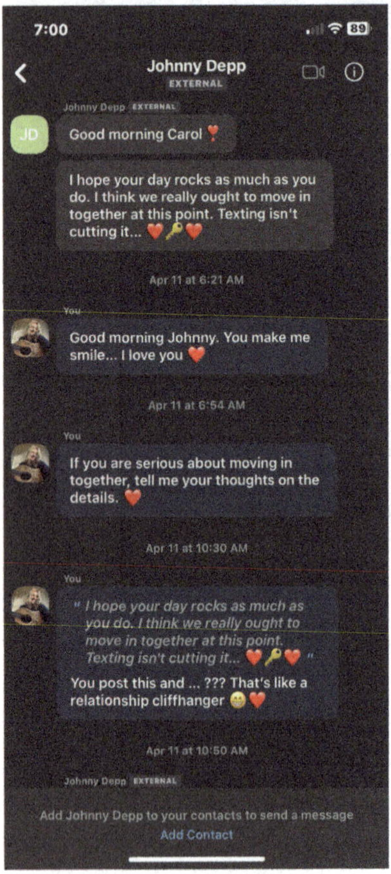
7:00
Johnny Depp
EXTERNAL
Johnny Depp EXTERNAL
JD
Good morning Carol
I hope your day rocks as much as you do. I think we really ought to move in together at this point. Texting isn't cutting it...
Apr 11 at 6:21 AM
You
Good morning Johnny. You make me smile... I love you
Apr 11 at 6:54 AM
You
If you are serious about moving in together, tell me your thoughts on the details.
Apr 11 at 10:30 AM
You
" I hope your day rocks as much as you do. I think we really ought to move in together at this point. Texting isn't cutting it... "
You post this and ... ??? That's like a relationship cliffhanger
Apr 11 at 10:50 AM
Johnny Depp EXTERNAL
Add Johnny Depp to your contacts to send a message
Add Contact

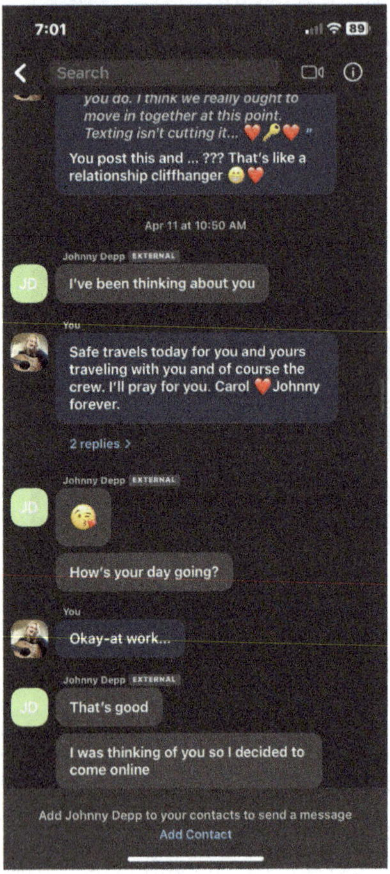
7:01
Search
you do. I think we really ought to move in together at this point. Texting isn't cutting it... "
You post this and ... ??? That's like a relationship cliffhanger
Apr 11 at 10:50 AM
Johnny Depp EXTERNAL
JD
I've been thinking about you
You
Safe travels today for you and yours traveling with you and of course the crew. I'll pray for you. Carol Johnny forever.
2 replies
Johnny Depp EXTERNAL
How's your day going?
You
Okay-at work...
Johnny Depp EXTERNAL
That's good
I was thinking of you so I decided to come online
Add Johnny Depp to your contacts to send a message
Add Contact

Whatever the intention, there were no further texts about moving in together. Our text threads became somewhat toxic as they were more and more often filled with ridiculous, baseless accusations and hurtful insults.

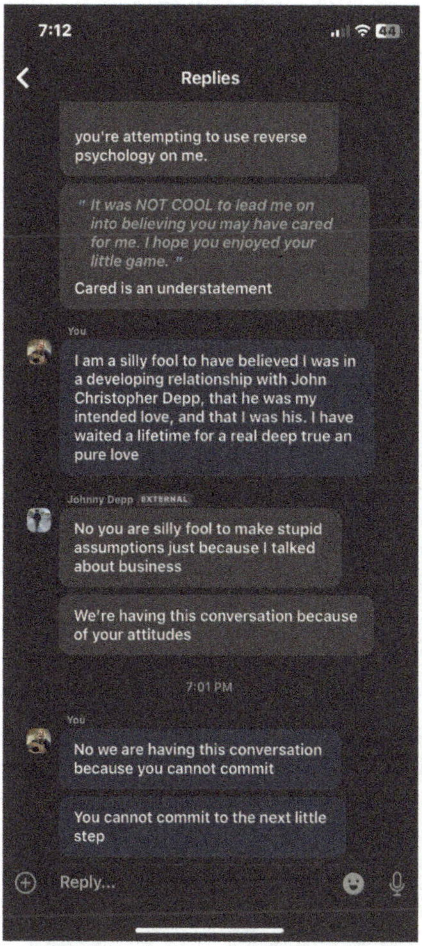
7:12
Replies
you're attempting to use reverse psychology on me.
" It was NOT COOL to lead me on into believing you may have cared for me. I hope you enjoyed your little game. "
Cared is an understatement
You
I am a silly fool to have believed I was in a developing relationship with John Christopher Depp, that he was my intended love, and that I was his. I have waited a lifetime for a real deep true an pure love
Johnny Depp EXTERNAL
No you are silly fool to make stupid assumptions just because I talked about business
We're having this conversation because of your attitudes
7:01 PM
You
No we are having this conversation because you cannot commit
You cannot commit to the next little step
Reply...

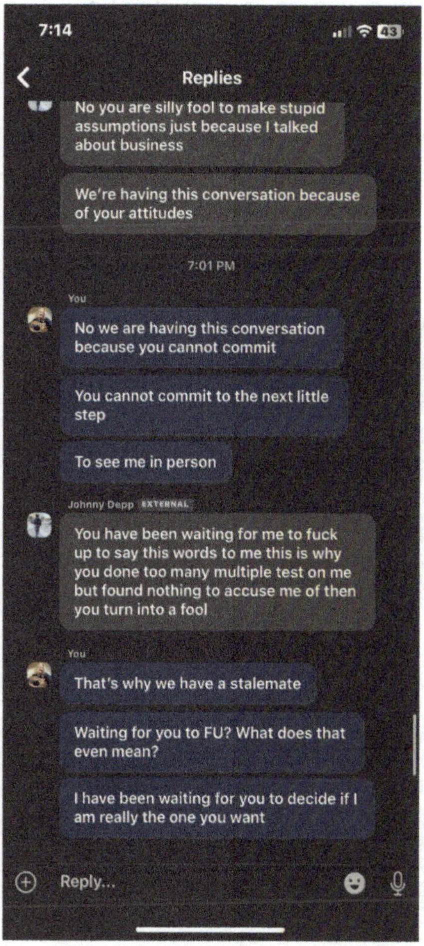
7:14
Replies
No you are silly fool to make stupid assumptions just because I talked about business
We're having this conversation because of your attitudes
7:01 PM
You
No we are having this conversation because you cannot commit
You cannot commit to the next little step
To see me in person
Johnny Depp EXTERNAL
You have been waiting for me to fuck up to say this words to me this is why you done too many multiple test on me but found nothing to accuse me of then you turn into a fool
You
That's why we have a stalemate
Waiting for you to FU? What does that even mean?
I have been waiting for you to decide if I am really the one you want
Reply...

We each said goodbye numerous times during the virtual relationship but neither of us severed the connection completely. I know that I wanted it to be real. I prayed for it to be real, even though the scammer(s) were verbally abusive at times. I did not want to be alone at this point in my life, especially during all the stressful things happening at the time. I needed support, even if it wasn't ideal. This might be why I overlooked all the red flags.

Tip: Keep a record of the texts to review later when you are not engaged in active communication. A later review will help you recognize red flags.

The conversations were at times disjointed and one-sided. Does the thread on the left seems like the text is meant for someone else? What multiple tests? How is texting a proper replacement for being together?

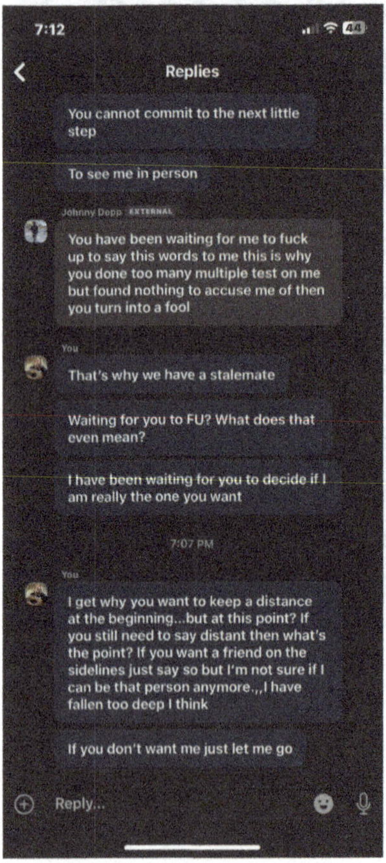
7:12
Replies
You cannot commit to the next little step
To see me in person
Johnny Depp EXTERNAL
You have been waiting for me to fuck up to say this words to me this is why you done too many multiple test on me but found nothing to accuse me of then you turn into a fool
You
That's why we have a stalemate
Waiting for you to FU? What does that even mean?
I have been waiting for you to decide if I am really the one you want
7:07 PM
You
I get why you want to keep a distance at the beginning...but at this point? If you still need to say distant then what's the point? If you want a friend on the sidelines just say so but I'm not sure if I can be that person anymore.,,I have fallen too deep I think
If you don't want me just let me go
Reply...

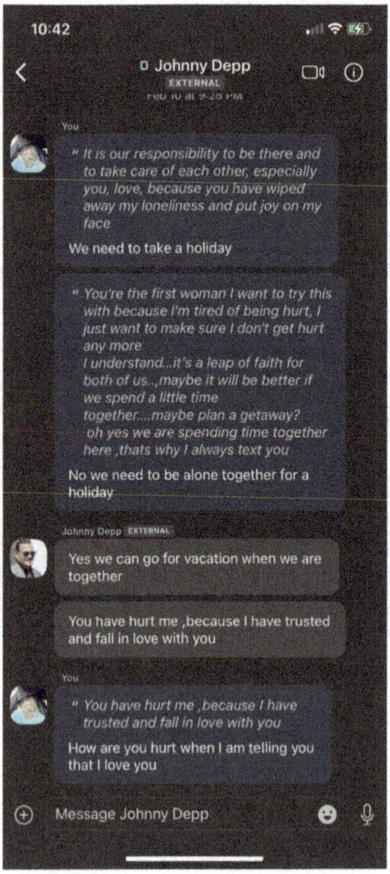
10:42
Johnny Depp
EXTERNAL
You
" It is our responsibility to be there and to take care of each other, especially you, love, because you have wiped away my loneliness and put joy on my face
We need to take a holiday
" You're the first woman I want to try this with because I'm tired of being hurt, I just want to make sure I don't get hurt any more
I understand...it's a leap of faith for both of us..,maybe it will be better if we spend a little time together....maybe plan a getaway?
oh yes we are spending time together here ,thats why I always text you
No we need to be alone together for a holiday
Johnny Depp EXTERNAL
Yes we can go for vacation when we are together
You have hurt me ,because I have trusted and fall in love with you
You
" You have hurt me ,because I have trusted and fall in love with you
How are you hurt when I am telling you that I love you
Message Johnny Depp

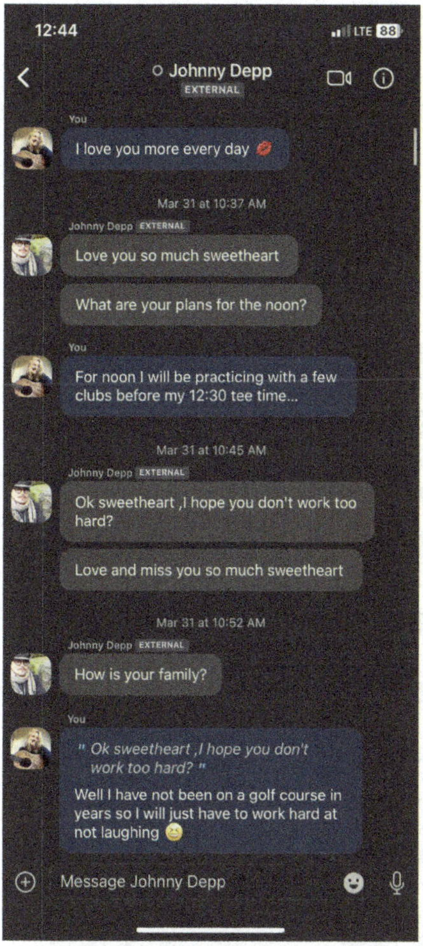
12:44
LTE 88
Johnny Depp
EXTERNAL
You
I love you more every day
Mar 31 at 10:37 AM
Johnny Depp EXTERNAL
Love you so much sweetheart
What are your plans for the noon?
You
For noon I will be practicing with a few clubs before my 12:30 tee time...
Mar 31 at 10:45 AM
Johnny Depp EXTERNAL
Ok sweetheart ,I hope you don't work too hard?
Love and miss you so much sweetheart
Mar 31 at 10:52 AM
Johnny Depp EXTERNAL
How is your family?
You
" Ok sweetheart ,I hope you don't work too hard? "
Well I have not been on a golf course in years so I will just have to work hard at not laughing
Message Johnny Depp

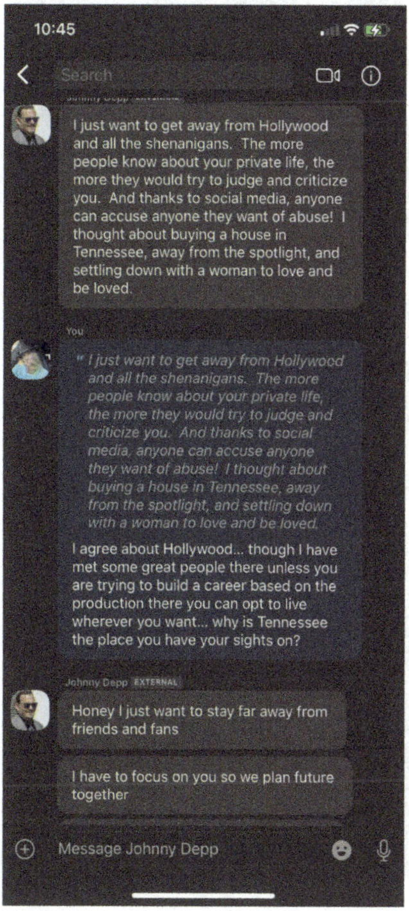
10:45
Search
I just want to get away from Hollywood and all the shenanigans. The more people know about your private life, the more they would try to judge and criticize you. And thanks to social media, anyone can accuse anyone they want of abuse! I thought about buying a house in Tennessee, away from the spotlight, and settling down with a woman to love and be loved.
You
" I just want to get away from Hollywood and all the shenanigans. The more people know about your private life, the more they would try to judge and criticize you. And thanks to social media, anyone can accuse anyone they want of abuse! I thought about buying a house in Tennessee, away from the spotlight, and settling down with a woman to love and be loved.
I agree about Hollywood... though I have met some great people there unless you are trying to build a career based on the production there you can opt to live wherever you want... why is Tennessee the place you have your sights on?
Johnny Depp EXTERNAL
Honey I just want to stay far away from friends and fans
I have to focus on you so we plan future together
Message Johnny Depp

KIND WORDS, DECLARATIONS of LOVE, and PROMISES

Throughout the scam the texting was filled with kind words, declarations of love, and promises. Don't be fooled by such empty words and do not allow yourself to be roped into the illusion of love and romance. This is easier said than done. Most people are naturally caring creatures and want to reciprocate kindness.

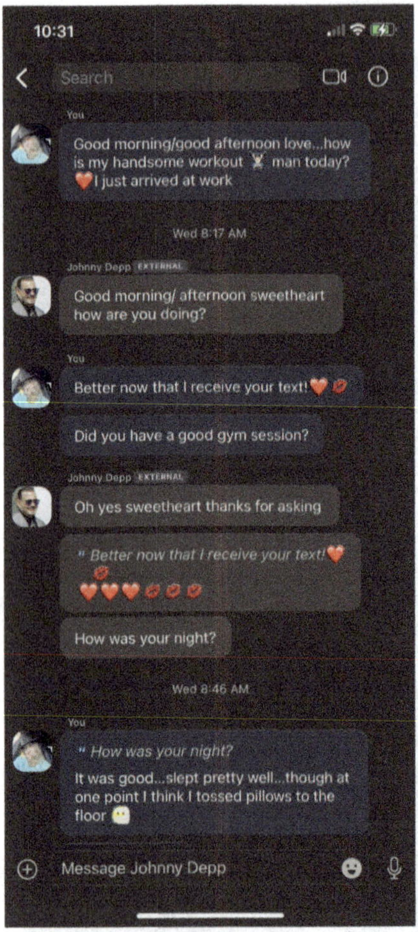
10:31
Search
You
Good morning/good afternoon love...how is my handsome workout man today? I just arrived at work
Wed 8:17 AM
Johnny Depp EXTERNAL
Good morning/ afternoon sweetheart how are you doing?
You
Better now that I receive your text!
Did you have a good gym session?
Johnny Depp EXTERNAL
Oh yes sweetheart thanks for asking
" Better now that I receive your text!
How was your night?
Wed 8:46 AM
You
" How was your night?
It was good...slept pretty well...though at one point I think I tossed pillows to the floor
Message Johnny Depp

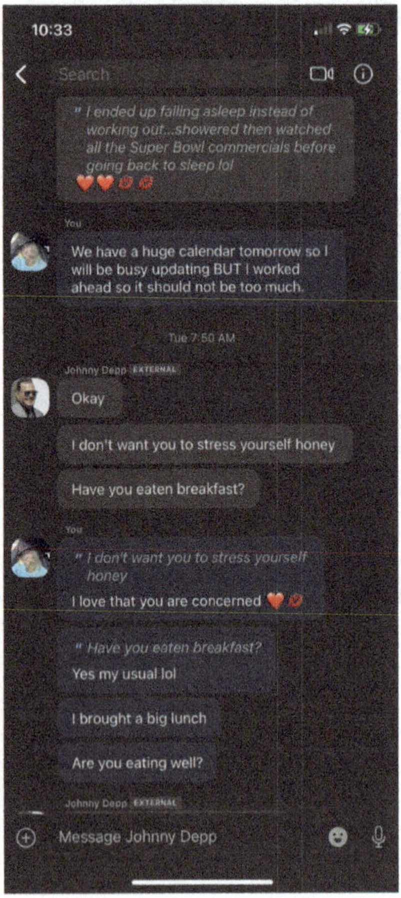
10:33
Search
" I ended up falling asleep instead of working out...showered then watched all the Super Bowl commercials before going back to sleep lol
You
We have a huge calendar tomorrow so I will be busy updating BUT I worked ahead so it should not be too much.
Tue 7:50 AM
Johnny Depp EXTERNAL
Okay
I don't want you to stress yourself honey
Have you eaten breakfast?
You
" I don't want you to stress yourself honey
I love that you are concerned
" Have you eaten breakfast?
Yes my usual lol
I brought a big lunch
Are you eating well?
Johnny Depp EXTERNAL
Message Johnny Depp

All of the pleasantries we share while communicating to a love interest in reality should never be shared the same way in the virtual world. By doing so we allow ourselves to give into a fantasy with unrealistic expectations. The inevitable result is that someone gets hurt because the fantasy bubble will eventually burst. As tempting as it is to want to accept a phantom love, don't do it. Walk/run away as quickly as you can.

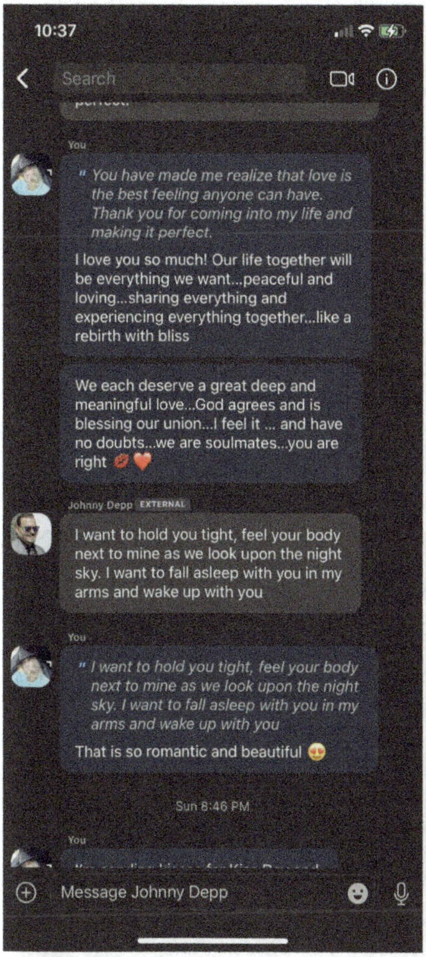
10:37
Search
You
" You have made me realize that love is the best feeling anyone can have. Thank you for coming into my life and making it perfect.
I love you so much! Our life together will be everything we want...peaceful and loving...sharing everything and experiencing everything together...like a rebirth with bliss
We each deserve a great deep and meaningful love...God agrees and is blessing our union...I feel it ... and have no doubts...we are soulmates...you are right
Johnny Depp EXTERNAL
I want to hold you tight, feel your body next to mine as we look upon the night sky. I want to fall asleep with you in my arms and wake up with you
You
" I want to hold you tight, feel your body next to mine as we look upon the night sky. I want to fall asleep with you in my arms and wake up with you
That is so romantic and beautiful
Sun 8:46 PM
You
Message Johnny Depp

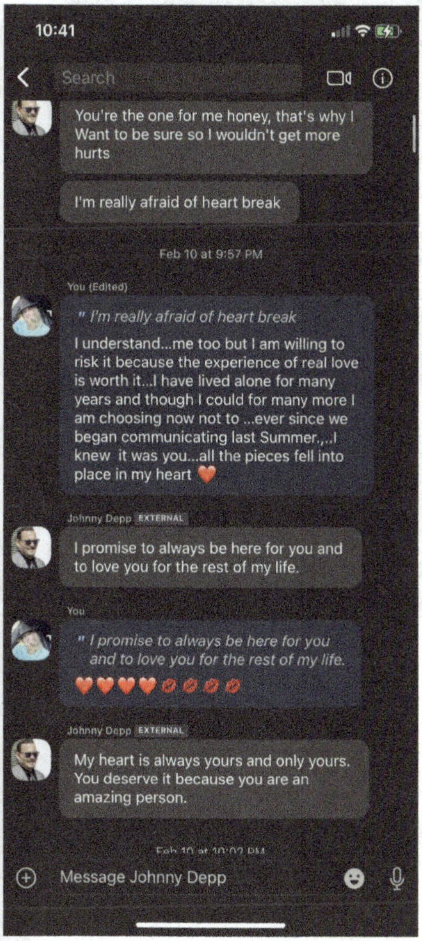
10:41
Search
You're the one for me honey, that's why I Want to be sure so I wouldn't get more hurts
I'm really afraid of heart break
Feb 10 at 9:57 PM
You (Edited)
" I'm really afraid of heart break
I understand...me too but I am willing to risk it because the experience of real love is worth it...I have lived alone for many years and though I could for many more I am choosing now not to ...ever since we began communicating last Summer,..I knew it was you...all the pieces fell into place in my heart
Johnny Depp EXTERNAL
I promise to always be here for you and to love you for the rest of my life.
You
" I promise to always be here for you and to love you for the rest of my life.
Johnny Depp EXTERNAL
My heart is always yours and only yours. You deserve it because you are an amazing person.
Message Johnny Depp

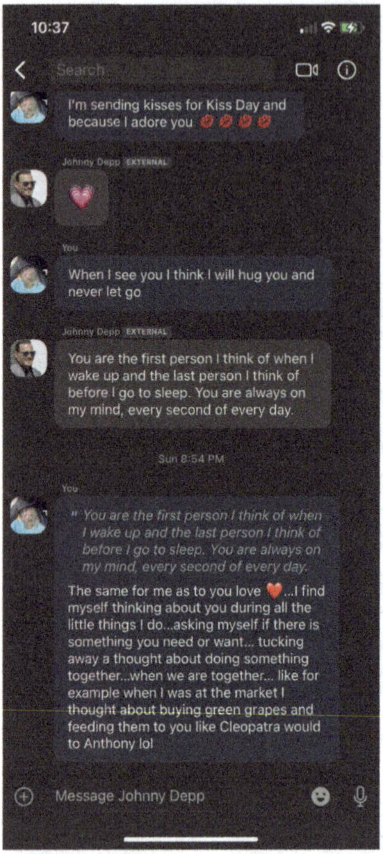
10:37
Search
I'm sending kisses for Kiss Day and because I adore you
Johnny Depp EXTERNAL
You
When I see you I think I will hug you and never let go
Johnny Depp EXTERNAL
You are the first person I think of when I wake up and the last person I think of before I go to sleep. You are always on my mind, every second of every day.
Sun 8:54 PM
You
" You are the first person I think of when I wake up and the last person I think of before I go to sleep. You are always on my mind, every second of every day.
The same for me as to you love ...I find myself thinking about you during all the little things I do...asking myself if there is something you need or want... tucking away a thought about doing something together...when we are together... like for example when I was at the market I thought about buying green grapes and feeding them to you like Cleopatra would to Anthony lol
Message Johnny Depp

Over the months of texting it seemed that we were building an alliance like to one that bonds two people together in a real relationship.

While it is so great to be supported by someone in reality, a sham support is more damaging than being alone and supporting oneself. Remember that you already are your best reliable source of support.

Tip: Whatever you do, try to refrain from making a declarations of love early on because if you do that will only give the scammer(s) reason to play with your emotions further. Once he/she/they/it thinks you are hooked it may be difficult to get free. If necessary, consider joining a support group or seeing a therapist to help you navigate away from the troubled waters.

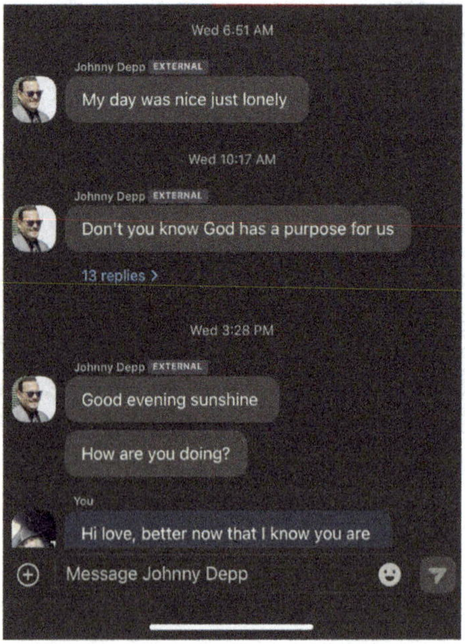
Wed 6:51 AM
Johnny Depp EXTERNAL
My day was nice just lonely
Wed 10:17 AM
Johnny Depp EXTERNAL
Don't you know God has a purpose for us
13 replies >
Wed 3:28 PM
Johnny Depp EXTERNAL
Good evening sunshine
How are you doing?
You
Hi love, better now that I know you are
Message Johnny Depp

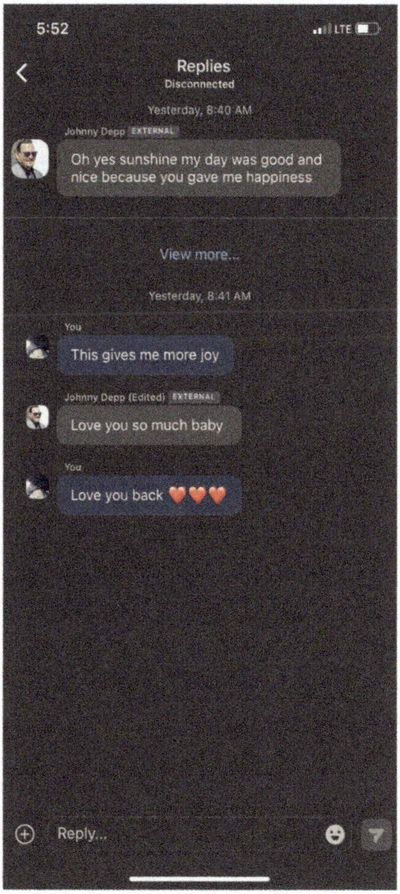
5:52
LTE
Replies
Disconnected
Yesterday, 8:40 AM
Johnny Depp EXTERNAL
Oh yes sunshine my day was good and nice because you gave me happiness
View more...
Yesterday, 8:41 AM
You
This gives me more joy
Johnny Depp (Edited) EXTERNAL
Love you so much baby
You
Love you back ❤️❤️❤️
Reply...

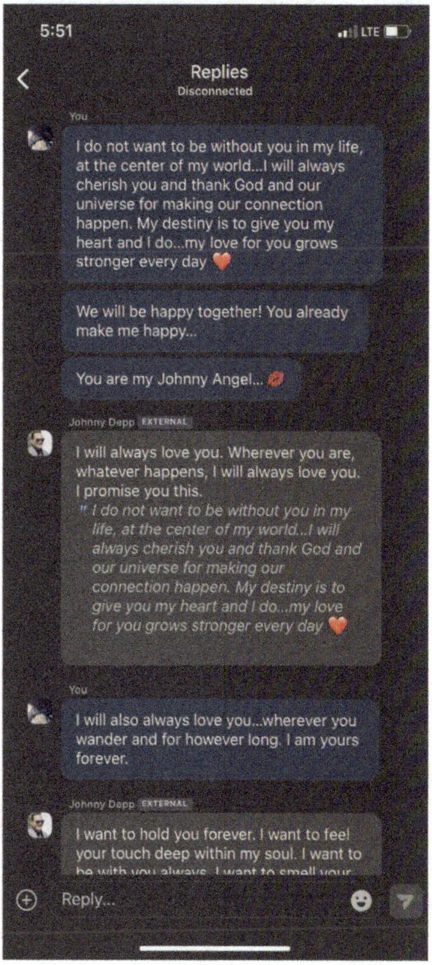
5:51
LTE
Replies
Disconnected
You
I do not want to be without you in my life, at the center of my world...I will always cherish you and thank God and our universe for making our connection happen. My destiny is to give you my heart and I do...my love for you grows stronger every day ❤️
We will be happy together! You already make me happy...
You are my Johnny Angel... 💋
Johnny Depp EXTERNAL
I will always love you. Wherever you are, whatever happens, I will always love you. I promise you this.
" I do not want to be without you in my life, at the center of my world...I will always cherish you and thank God and our universe for making our connection happen. My destiny is to give you my heart and I do...my love for you grows stronger every day ❤️
You
I will also always love you...wherever you wander and for however long. I am yours forever.
Johnny Depp EXTERNAL
I want to hold you forever. I want to feel your touch deep within my soul. I want to
Reply...

When the texting becomes a large part of your daily routine it will become increasingly difficult to stop.

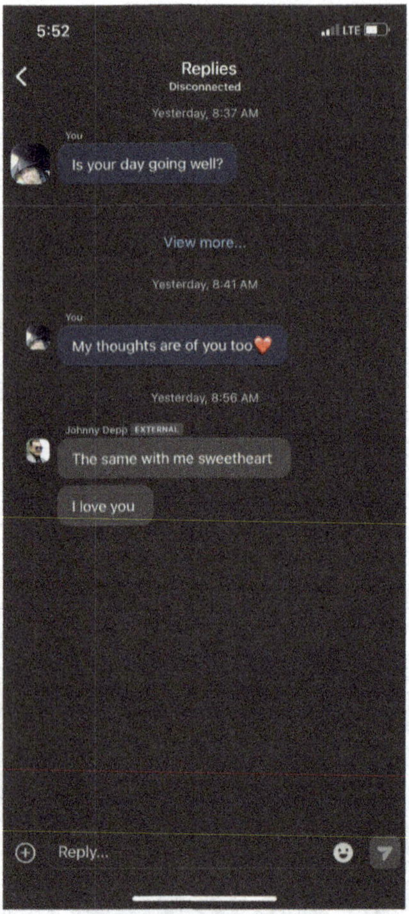
5:52
LTE
Replies
Disconnected
Yesterday, 8:37 AM
You
Is your day going well?
View more...
Yesterday, 8:41 AM
You
My thoughts are of you too
Yesterday, 8:56 AM
Johnny Depp EXTERNAL
The same with me sweetheart
I love you
Reply...

Remind yourself that all the promises are merely empty words and no matter what you do or say there is no truth to what you are reading. The only satisfaction you will receive is the gratitude if you give in to the scam and that will be short-lived. If you give in, the requests will continue and only be greater because you will have proven yourself a patsy. Don't do it!

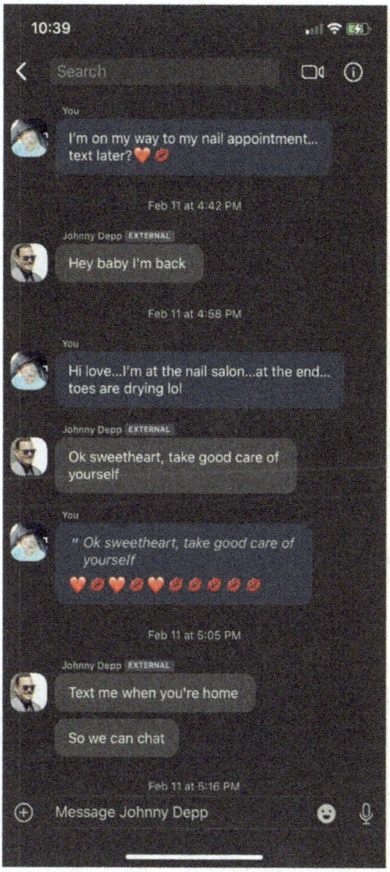
10:39
Search
You
I'm on my way to my nail appointment... text later?
Feb 11 at 4:42 PM
Johnny Depp EXTERNAL
Hey baby I'm back
Feb 11 at 4:58 PM
You
Hi love...I'm at the nail salon...at the end... toes are drying lol
Johnny Depp EXTERNAL
Ok sweetheart, take good care of yourself
You
" Ok sweetheart, take good care of yourself
Feb 11 at 5:05 PM
Johnny Depp EXTERNAL
Text me when you're home
So we can chat
Feb 11 at 5:16 PM
Message Johnny Depp

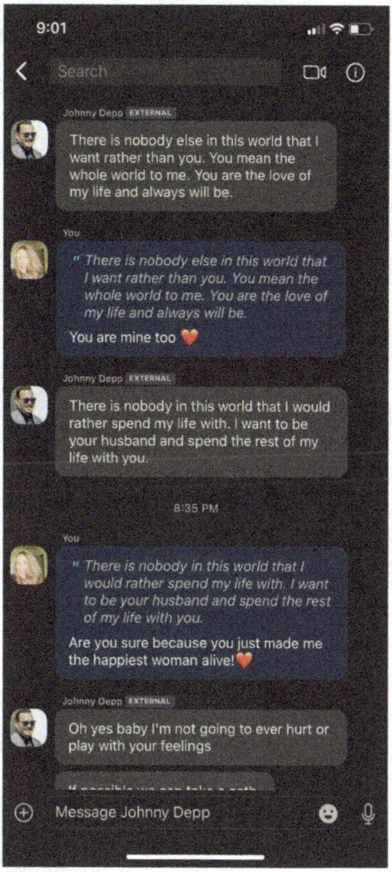
9:01
Search
Johnny Depp EXTERNAL
There is nobody else in this world that I want rather than you. You mean the whole world to me. You are the love of my life and always will be.
You
" There is nobody else in this world that I want rather than you. You mean the whole world to me. You are the love of my life and always will be.
You are mine too
Johnny Depp EXTERNAL
There is nobody in this world that I would rather spend my life with. I want to be your husband and spend the rest of my life with you.
8:35 PM
You
" There is nobody in this world that I would rather spend my life with. I want to be your husband and spend the rest of my life with you.
Are you sure because you just made me the happiest woman alive!
Johnny Depp EXTERNAL
Oh yes baby I'm not going to ever hurt or play with your feelings
Message Johnny Depp

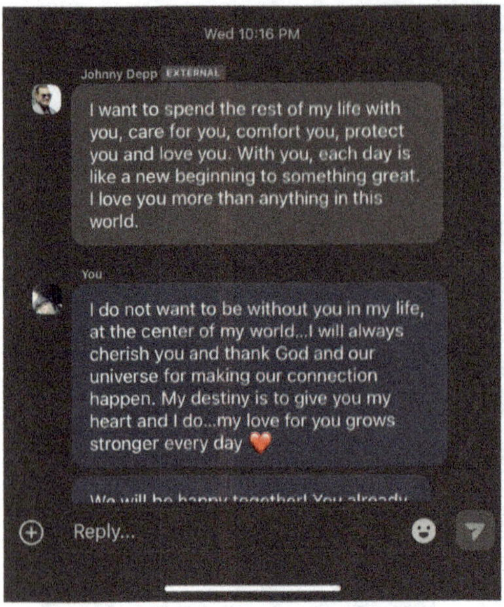
Wed 10:16 PM
Johnny Depp EXTERNAL
I want to spend the rest of my life with you, care for you, comfort you, protect you and love you. With you, each day is like a new beginning to something great. I love you more than anything in this world.
You
I do not want to be without you in my life, at the center of my world...I will always cherish you and thank God and our universe for making our connection happen. My destiny is to give you my heart and I do...my love for you grows stronger every day
Reply...

When the scam stalls you may see a sudden shift in the tone of the texts.

Compare the tone of theses two texts. From sweet and loving to dismissive and hurtful. How was authentication all on me? Isn't it hard to believe the time in between the texts was only a couple of months?

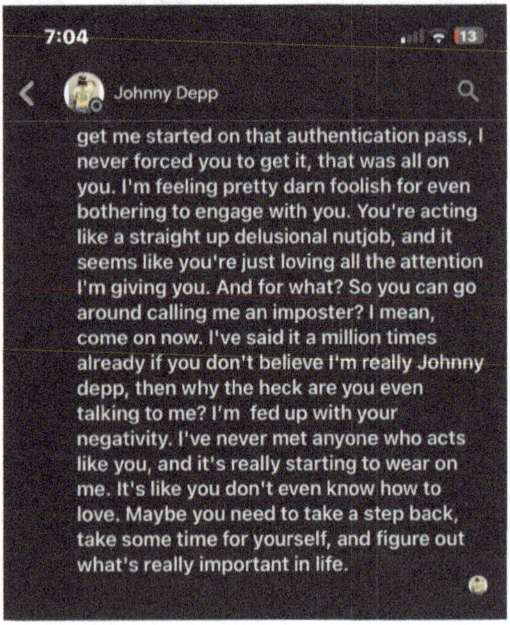
7:04
13
Johnny Depp
get me started on that authentication pass, I never forced you to get it, that was all on you. I'm feeling pretty darn foolish for even bothering to engage with you. You're acting like a straight up delusional nutjob, and it seems like you're just loving all the attention I'm giving you. And for what? So you can go around calling me an imposter? I mean, come on now. I've said it a million times already if you don't believe I'm really Johnny depp, then why the heck are you even talking to me? I'm fed up with your negativity. I've never met anyone who acts like you, and it's really starting to wear on me. It's like you don't even know how to love. Maybe you need to take a step back, take some time for yourself, and figure out what's really important in life.

MARRIAGE PROPOSAL, SCAM CLIMAX?

When I was seriously considering various property purchase options, making offers and confirming pre-approval by my lender, I received what seemed to be a proposal of marriage on the morning of April 18, 2023. Was this just coincidence or perhaps an attempt to delay my decision to go under contract? If the latter, why, unless because going under contract would include spending liquid assets. Whatever the intention, there was never any real follow through in terms of making a solid plan and there was never a ring presented for my hand. The subject was briefly mentioned in other texts, like the one on the next page, and expressions of love continued, but the extent of our 'engagement', like the rest of the relationship, remained virtual.

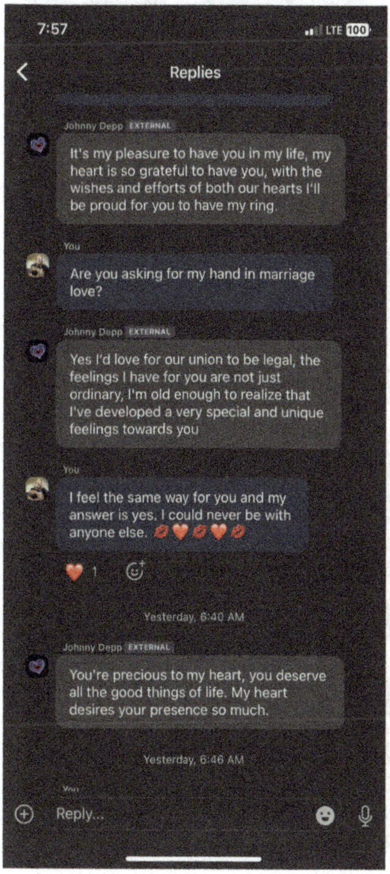

7:57
LTE 100
Replies
Johnny Depp EXTERNAL
It's my pleasure to have you in my life, my heart is so grateful to have you, with the wishes and efforts of both our hearts I'll be proud for you to have my ring.
You
Are you asking for my hand in marriage love?
Johnny Depp EXTERNAL
Yes I'd love for our union to be legal, the feelings I have for you are not just ordinary, I'm old enough to realize that I've developed a very special and unique feelings towards you
You
I feel the same way for you and my answer is yes. I could never be with anyone else.
1
Yesterday, 6:40 AM
Johnny Depp EXTERNAL
You're precious to my heart, you deserve all the good things of life. My heart desires your presence so much.
Yesterday, 6:46 AM
Reply...

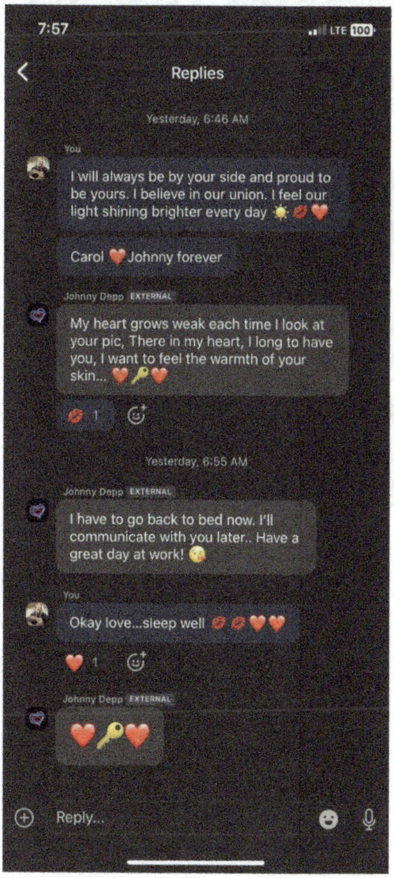

7:57
LTE 100
Replies
Yesterday, 6:46 AM
You
I will always be by your side and proud to be yours. I believe in our union. I feel our light shining brighter every day
Carol Johnny forever
Johnny Depp EXTERNAL
My heart grows weak each time I look at your pic, There in my heart, I long to have you, I want to feel the warmth of your skin...
1
Yesterday, 6:55 AM
Johnny Depp EXTERNAL
I have to go back to bed now. I'll communicate with you later.. Have a great day at work!
You
Okay love...sleep well
1
Johnny Depp EXTERNAL
Reply...

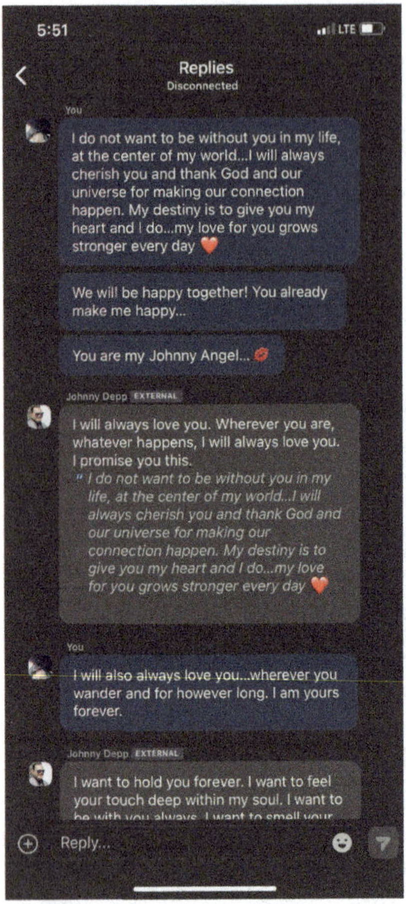
5:51
LTE
Replies
Disconnected
You
I do not want to be without you in my life, at the center of my world...I will always cherish you and thank God and our universe for making our connection happen. My destiny is to give you my heart and I do...my love for you grows stronger every day ❤️
We will be happy together! You already make me happy...
You are my Johnny Angel... 💋
Johnny Depp EXTERNAL
I will always love you. Wherever you are, whatever happens, I will always love you. I promise you this.
" I do not want to be without you in my life, at the center of my world...I will always cherish you and thank God and our universe for making our connection happen. My destiny is to give you my heart and I do...my love for you grows stronger every day ❤️
You
I will also always love you...wherever you wander and for however long. I am yours forever.
Johnny Depp EXTERNAL
I want to hold you forever. I want to feel your touch deep within my soul. I want to
Reply...

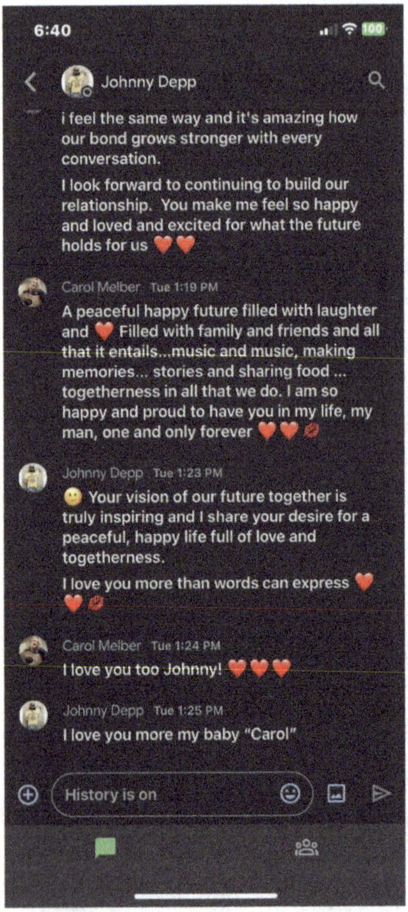
6:40
100
Johnny Depp
i feel the same way and it's amazing how our bond grows stronger with every conversation.
I look forward to continuing to build our relationship. You make me feel so happy and loved and excited for what the future holds for us ❤️❤️
Carol Melber Tue 1:19 PM
A peaceful happy future filled with laughter and ❤️ Filled with family and friends and all that it entails...music and music, making memories... stories and sharing food ... togetherness in all that we do. I am so happy and proud to have you in my life, my man, one and only forever ❤️❤️💋
Johnny Depp Tue 1:23 PM
😊 Your vision of our future together is truly inspiring and I share your desire for a peaceful, happy life full of love and togetherness.
I love you more than words can express ❤️❤️💋
Carol Melber Tue 1:24 PM
I love you too Johnny! ❤️❤️❤️
Johnny Depp Tue 1:25 PM
I love you more my baby "Carol"
History is on

LOVE COLLAGE

Less than a month prior to my scheduled move from California, and just a couple of weeks before my last day of work I was surprised by a text that included a spliced profile picture of the two of us framed within a heart. The 'love collage' seemed to be a confirmation of commitment and a willingness to publicly share the relationship. After the flip/flop on my request to share the relationship with my family, I was wary about this sudden change.

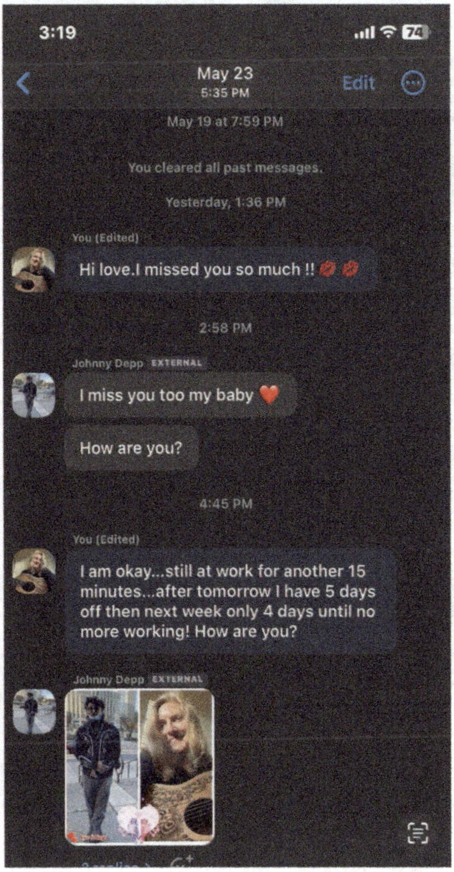
3:19
74
May 23
5:35 PM
Edit
May 19 at 7:59 PM
You cleared all past messages.
Yesterday, 1:36 PM
You (Edited)
Hi love.I missed you so much !!
2:58 PM
Johnny Depp EXTERNAL
I miss you too my baby
How are you?
4:45 PM
You (Edited)
I am okay...still at work for another 15 minutes...after tomorrow I have 5 days off then next week only 4 days until no more working! How are you?
Johnny Depp EXTERNAL

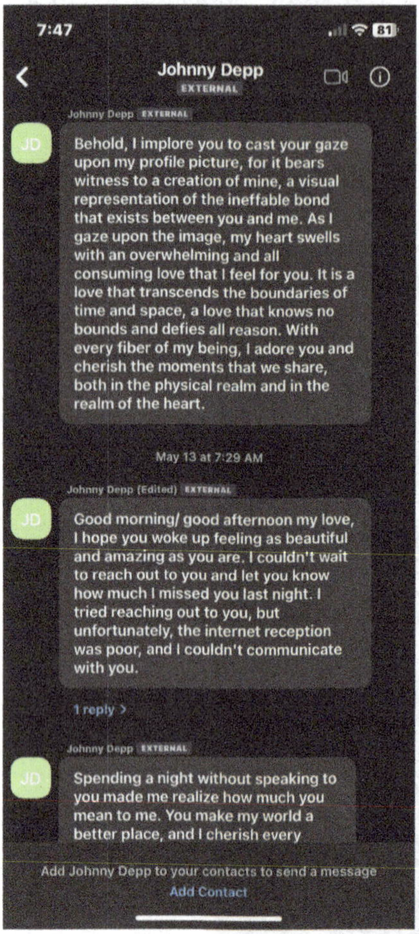
7:47
Johnny Depp
EXTERNAL
Johnny Depp EXTERNAL
JD
Behold, I implore you to cast your gaze upon my profile picture, for it bears witness to a creation of mine, a visual representation of the ineffable bond that exists between you and me. As I gaze upon the image, my heart swells with an overwhelming and all consuming love that I feel for you. It is a love that transcends the boundaries of time and space, a love that knows no bounds and defies all reason. With every fiber of my being, I adore you and cherish the moments that we share, both in the physical realm and in the realm of the heart.
May 13 at 7:29 AM
Johnny Depp (Edited) EXTERNAL
JD
Good morning/ good afternoon my love, I hope you woke up feeling as beautiful and amazing as you are. I couldn't wait to reach out to you and let you know how much I missed you last night. I tried reaching out to you, but unfortunately, the internet reception was poor, and I couldn't communicate with you.
1 reply
Johnny Depp EXTERNAL
JD
Spending a night without speaking to you made me realize how much you mean to me. You make my world a better place, and I cherish every
Add Johnny Depp to your contacts to send a message
Add Contact

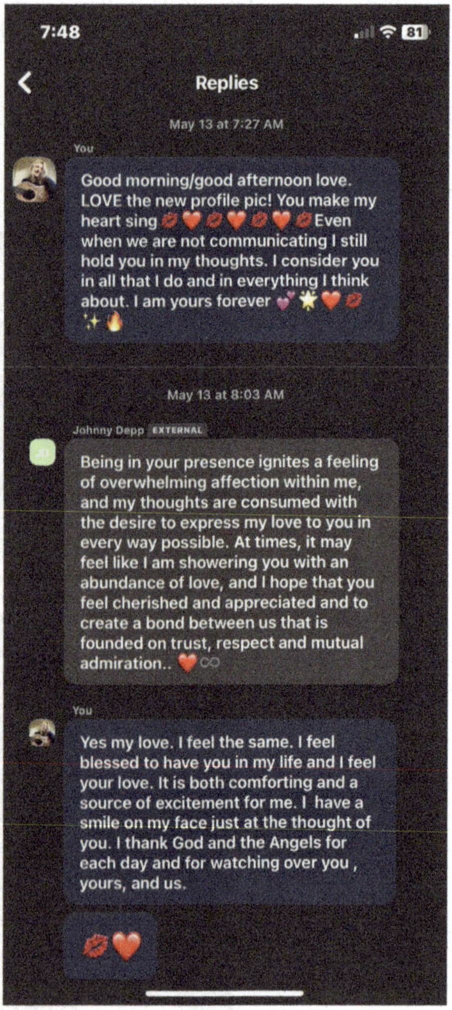
7:48
Replies
May 13 at 7:27 AM
You
Good morning/good afternoon love. LOVE the new profile pic! You make my heart sing 💋❤️💋❤️💋❤️💋 Even when we are not communicating I still hold you in my thoughts. I consider you in all that I do and in everything I think about. I am yours forever 💕🌟❤️💋✨🔥
May 13 at 8:03 AM
Johnny Depp EXTERNAL
Being in your presence ignites a feeling of overwhelming affection within me, and my thoughts are consumed with the desire to express my love to you in every way possible. At times, it may feel like I am showering you with an abundance of love, and I hope that you feel cherished and appreciated and to create a bond between us that is founded on trust, respect and mutual admiration.. ❤️♾
You
Yes my love. I feel the same. I feel blessed to have you in my life and I feel your love. It is both comforting and a source of excitement for me. I have a smile on my face just at the thought of you. I thank God and the Angels for each day and for watching over you , yours, and us.
💋❤️

After all the declarations of love and the love collage, just like that the conversation takes a backward turn. Once again, there is no plan made to see me in person.

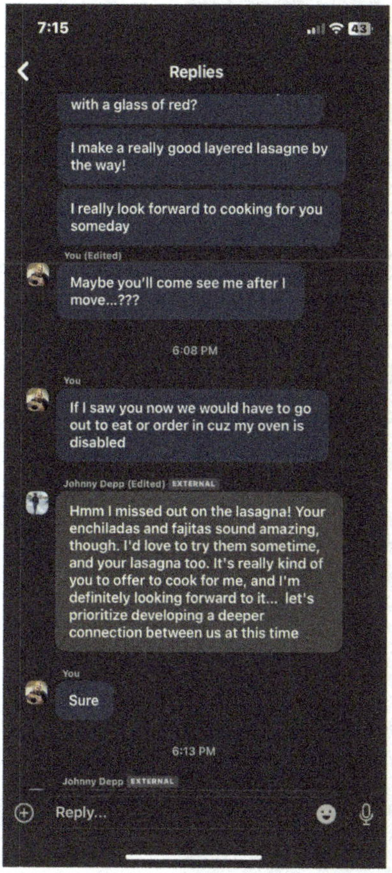
7:15
Replies
with a glass of red?
I make a really good layered lasagne by the way!
I really look forward to cooking for you someday
You (Edited)
Maybe you'll come see me after I move...???
6:08 PM
You
If I saw you now we would have to go out to eat or order in cuz my oven is disabled
Johnny Depp (Edited) EXTERNAL
Hmm I missed out on the lasagna! Your enchiladas and fajitas sound amazing, though. I'd love to try them sometime, and your lasagna too. It's really kind of you to offer to cook for me, and I'm definitely looking forward to it... let's prioritize developing a deeper connection between us at this time
You
Sure
6:13 PM
Johnny Depp EXTERNAL
Reply...

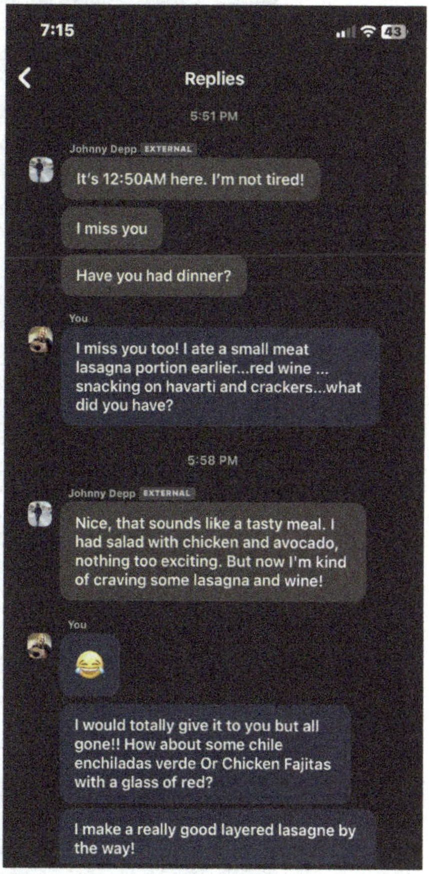
7:15
Replies
5:51 PM
Johnny Depp EXTERNAL
It's 12:50AM here. I'm not tired!
I miss you
Have you had dinner?
You
I miss you too! I ate a small meat lasagna portion earlier...red wine ... snacking on havarti and crackers...what did you have?
5:58 PM
Johnny Depp EXTERNAL
Nice, that sounds like a tasty meal. I had salad with chicken and avocado, nothing too exciting. But now I'm kind of craving some lasagna and wine!
You
I would totally give it to you but all gone!! How about some chile enchiladas verde Or Chicken Fajitas with a glass of red?
I make a really good layered lasagne by the way!

Instead, the conversation turns to a subject we had discussed months before, me starting a business. I felt like we were backtracking and that this conversation was definitely not between me and Johnny Depp. I began to feel a bad queasy feeling in my stomach about this imposter. Who was this stranger?

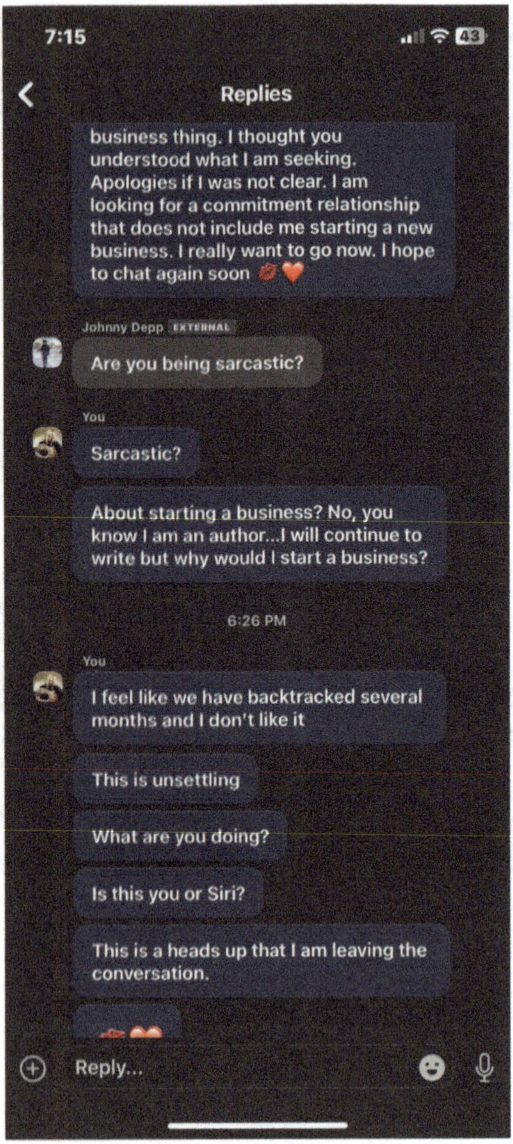
7:15
Replies
business thing. I thought you understood what I am seeking. Apologies if I was not clear. I am looking for a commitment relationship that does not include me starting a new business. I really want to go now. I hope to chat again soon 💋❤️
Johnny Depp EXTERNAL
Are you being sarcastic?
You
Sarcastic?
About starting a business? No, you know I am an author...I will continue to write but why would I start a business?
6:26 PM
You
I feel like we have backtracked several months and I don't like it
This is unsettling
What are you doing?
Is this you or Siri?
This is a heads up that I am leaving the conversation.
Reply...

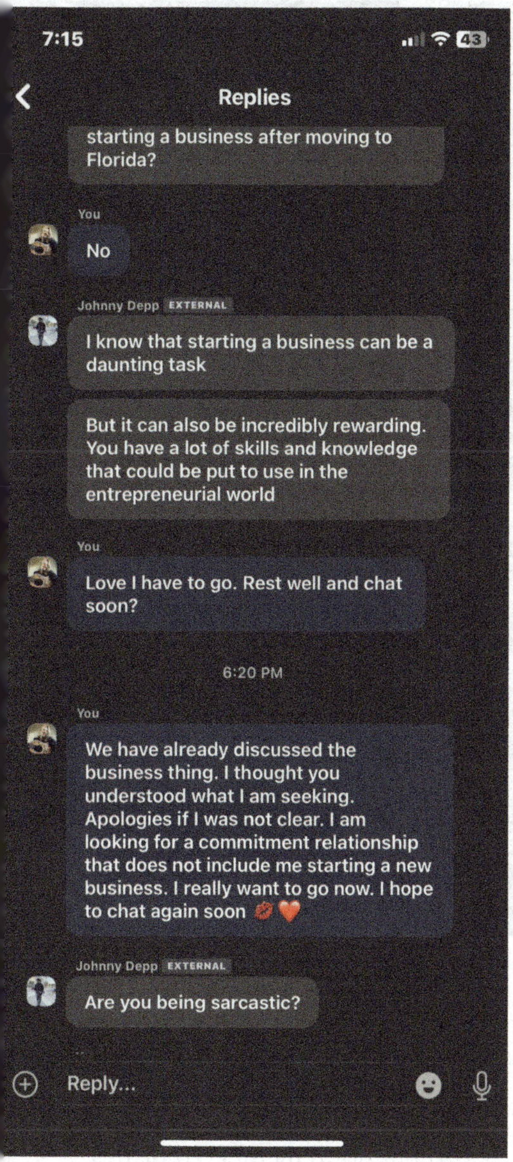
7:15
Replies
starting a business after moving to Florida?
You
No
Johnny Depp EXTERNAL
I know that starting a business can be a daunting task
But it can also be incredibly rewarding. You have a lot of skills and knowledge that could be put to use in the entrepreneurial world
You
Love I have to go. Rest well and chat soon?
6:20 PM
You
We have already discussed the business thing. I thought you understood what I am seeking. Apologies if I was not clear. I am looking for a commitment relationship that does not include me starting a new business. I really want to go now. I hope to chat again soon 💋🧡
Johnny Depp EXTERNAL
Are you being sarcastic?
Reply...

Once again a prior conversation was not remembered. I am wondering who or what I am conversing with. I know I am being duped and I do not want to accept it. I am also getting very irritated. The irritation mounts quickly with me willing to give up on the entire relationship.

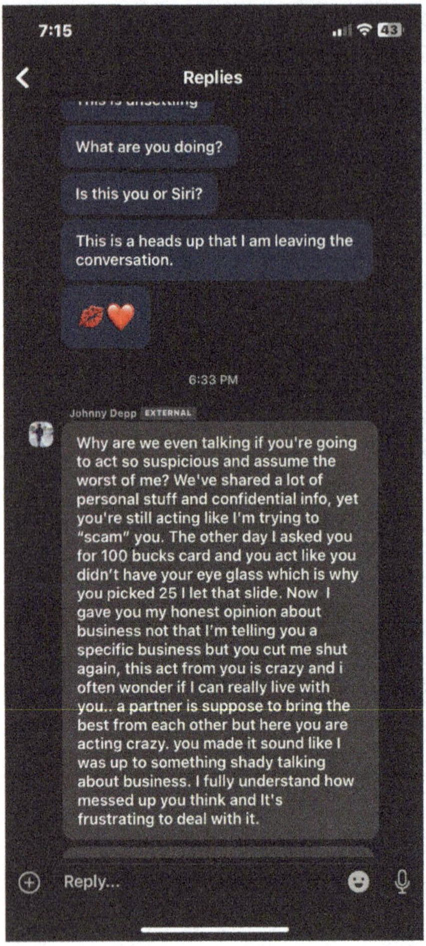
7:15
Replies
What are you doing?
Is this you or Siri?
This is a heads up that I am leaving the conversation.
6:33 PM
Johnny Depp EXTERNAL
Why are we even talking if you're going to act so suspicious and assume the worst of me? We've shared a lot of personal stuff and confidential info, yet you're still acting like I'm trying to "scam" you. The other day I asked you for 100 bucks card and you act like you didn't have your eye glass which is why you picked 25 I let that slide. Now I gave you my honest opinion about business not that I'm telling you a specific business but you cut me shut again, this act from you is crazy and i often wonder if I can really live with you.. a partner is suppose to bring the best from each other but here you are acting crazy. you made it sound like I was up to something shady talking about business. I fully understand how messed up you think and It's frustrating to deal with it.
Reply...

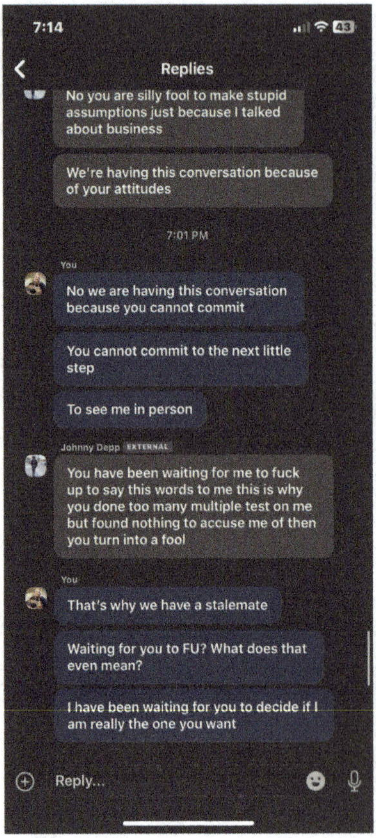
7:14
Replies
No you are silly fool to make stupid assumptions just because I talked about business
We're having this conversation because of your attitudes
7:01 PM
You
No we are having this conversation because you cannot commit
You cannot commit to the next little step
To see me in person
Johnny Depp EXTERNAL
You have been waiting for me to fuck up to say this words to me this is why you done too many multiple test on me but found nothing to accuse me of then you turn into a fool
You
That's why we have a stalemate
Waiting for you to FU? What does that even mean?
I have been waiting for you to decide if I am really the one you want
Reply...

This is another example of the scammer(s) interacting with multiple victims. The amount of the card requested was $200 not $100 and the business conversation was already had but not remembered by this scammer.

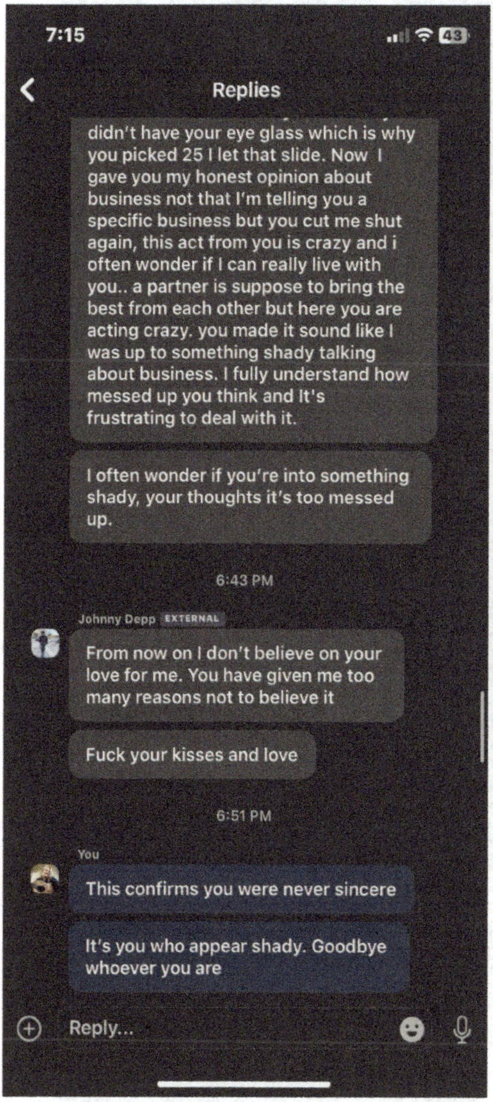
7:15
Replies
didn't have your eye glass which is why you picked 25 I let that slide. Now I gave you my honest opinion about business not that I'm telling you a specific business but you cut me shut again, this act from you is crazy and i often wonder if I can really live with you.. a partner is suppose to bring the best from each other but here you are acting crazy. you made it sound like I was up to something shady talking about business. I fully understand how messed up you think and It's frustrating to deal with it.
I often wonder if you're into something shady, your thoughts it's too messed up.
6:43 PM
Johnny Depp EXTERNAL
From now on I don't believe on your love for me. You have given me too many reasons not to believe it
Fuck your kisses and love
6:51 PM
You
This confirms you were never sincere
It's you who appear shady. Goodbye whoever you are
Reply...

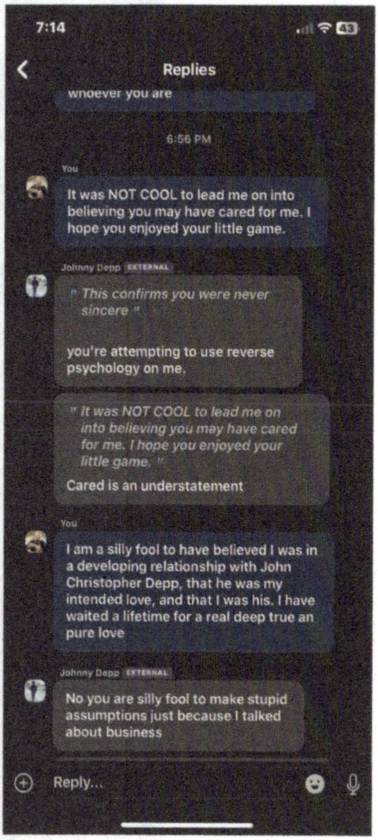
7:14
Replies
whoever you are
6:56 PM
You
It was NOT COOL to lead me on into believing you may have cared for me. I hope you enjoyed your little game.
Johnny Depp EXTERNAL
" This confirms you were never sincere "
you're attempting to use reverse psychology on me.
" It was NOT COOL to lead me on into believing you may have cared for me. I hope you enjoyed your little game. "
Cared is an understatement
You
I am a silly fool to have believed I was in a developing relationship with John Christopher Depp, that he was my intended love, and that I was his. I have waited a lifetime for a real deep true an pure love
Johnny Depp EXTERNAL
No you are silly fool to make stupid assumptions just because I talked about business
Reply...

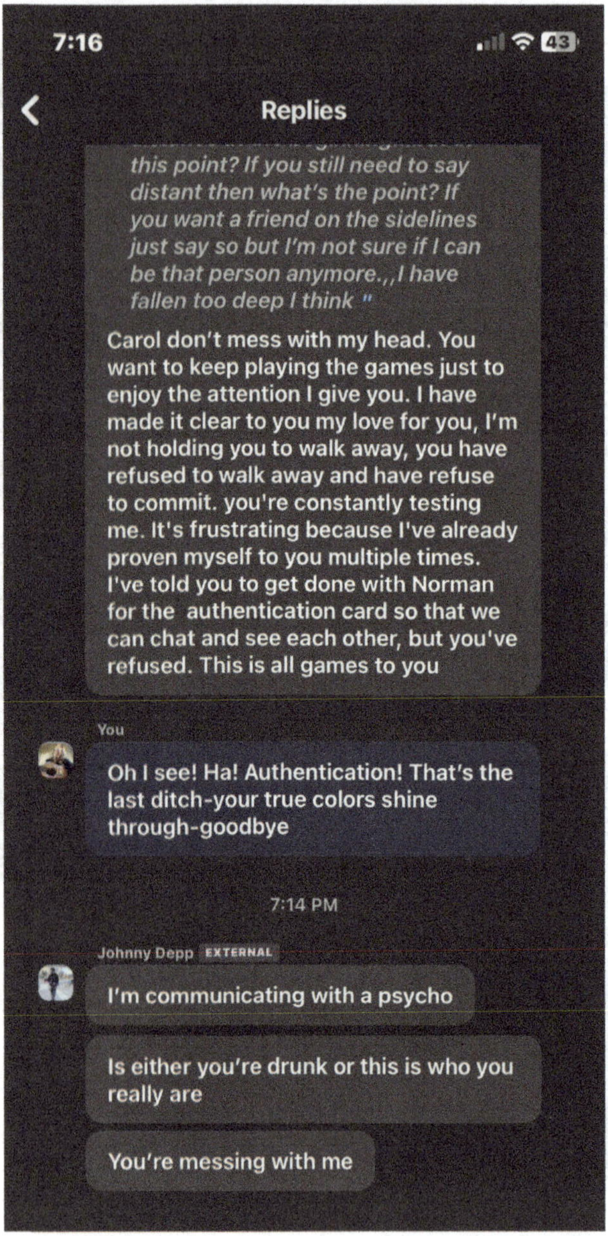
7:16
43
Replies
this point? If you still need to say distant then what's the point? If you want a friend on the sidelines just say so but I'm not sure if I can be that person anymore.,,I have fallen too deep I think "
Carol don't mess with my head. You want to keep playing the games just to enjoy the attention I give you. I have made it clear to you my love for you, I'm not holding you to walk away, you have refused to walk away and have refuse to commit. you're constantly testing me. It's frustrating because I've already proven myself to you multiple times. I've told you to get done with Norman for the authentication card so that we can chat and see each other, but you've refused. This is all games to you
You
Oh I see! Ha! Authentication! That's the last ditch-your true colors shine through-goodbye
7:14 PM
Johnny Depp EXTERNAL
I'm communicating with a psycho
Is either you're drunk or this is who you really are
You're messing with me

Once again the authentication part of the scam was raised and just like that we were back to square one.

MONEY SCAM (Part3?) BIRTHDAY & GOOGLE PLAY CARDS

The texting continued. I struggled between my desire to believe in the possibility of making the relationship a reality and my ever-nagging doubts our being together would come to fruition. I knew that I could not physically be with the person I thought I was communicating with during several upcoming special events happening at the same time I would be preparing for and executing my move. I had accepted this fact but also knew the situation would put a great strain on our relationship. I was now more frequently questioning the validity of the relationship. Whoever was texting seemed to be drifting further away, first cutting me off from discussing anything involving all those upcoming events and then passing off our communication to an unknown and likely illegitimate source.

It became clear to me whoever this was, he/she/it had grown tired of the texting, maybe because it was clear to him/her/it that I was not going to send money. But that did not stop a final request for additional Google Play Cards. The premise for the request was Johnny Depp's birthday. I had gone to a local jade festival in search of a piece of Big Sur jade for each of us to wear. Finding a jewelry piece with Big Sur jade was very special to me. I had hiked around Big Sur and wanted to have a keepsake reminder of the beauty there. Sharing Big Sur jade was the best way I could think of to share a piece of California with someone who told me he no longer wanted to live there. The texts I received upon my return were accusatory and hurtful.

Out of the blue there came a request to purchase Google Play Cards. Wow, I thought! Here we go again! I wonder who this is now?
I was really angry, mostly at myself for being so stupid. These are a few of the ridiculous texts back and forth that day.

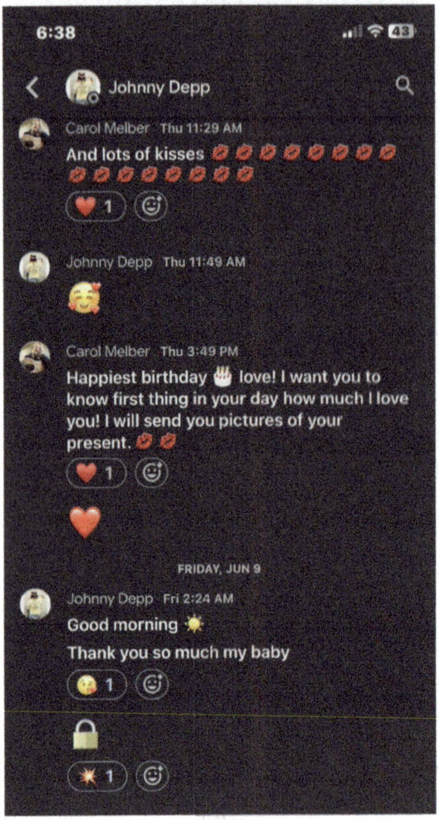
6:38
Johnny Depp
Carol Melber Thu 11:29 AM
And lots of kisses
1
Johnny Depp Thu 11:49 AM
Carol Melber Thu 3:49 PM
Happiest birthday love! I want you to know first thing in your day how much I love you! I will send you pictures of your present.
1
FRIDAY, JUN 9
Johnny Depp Fri 2:24 AM
Good morning
Thank you so much my baby
1
1

Receiving a text of a new profile picture before seeing it posted on social media contributed to my confusion over the identity of who/what I was communicating with.

6:38
Johnny Depp
Johnny Depp Fri 2:49 AM
I'M A HAPPY-GO-LUCKY RAY OF FUCKING SUNSHINE
Carol Melber Fri 6:24 AM - Edited
Love this!!! Made me laugh I hope you are enjoying your day love! Thank you for sending this picture! I love you so much!
Johnny Depp Fri 8:59 AM
Carol Melber Fri 9:06 AM
I will send pictures later today (want to pick up a couple of things first). I am having so much fun shopping for your birthday

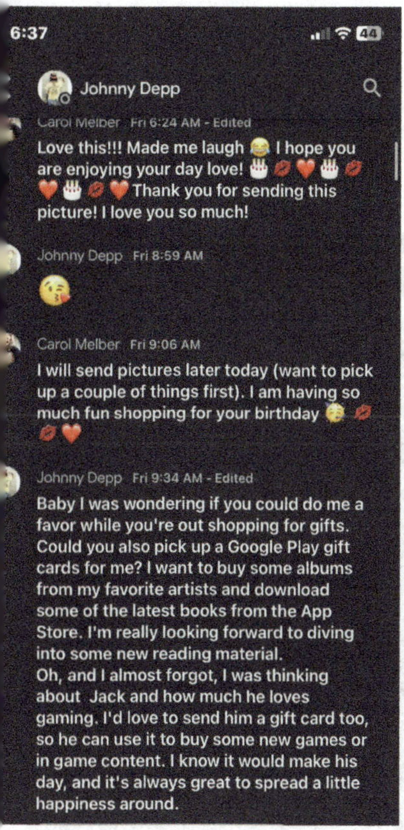
6:37
Johnny Depp
Carol Melber Fri 6:24 AM - Edited
Love this!!! Made me laugh I hope you are enjoying your day love! Thank you for sending this picture! I love you so much!
Johnny Depp Fri 8:59 AM
Carol Melber Fri 9:06 AM
I will send pictures later today (want to pick up a couple of things first). I am having so much fun shopping for your birthday
Johnny Depp Fri 9:34 AM - Edited
Baby I was wondering if you could do me a favor while you're out shopping for gifts. Could you also pick up a Google Play gift cards for me? I want to buy some albums from my favorite artists and download some of the latest books from the App Store. I'm really looking forward to diving into some new reading material.
Oh, and I almost forgot, I was thinking about Jack and how much he loves gaming. I'd love to send him a gift card too, so he can use it to buy some new games or in game content. I know it would make his day, and it's always great to spread a little happiness around.

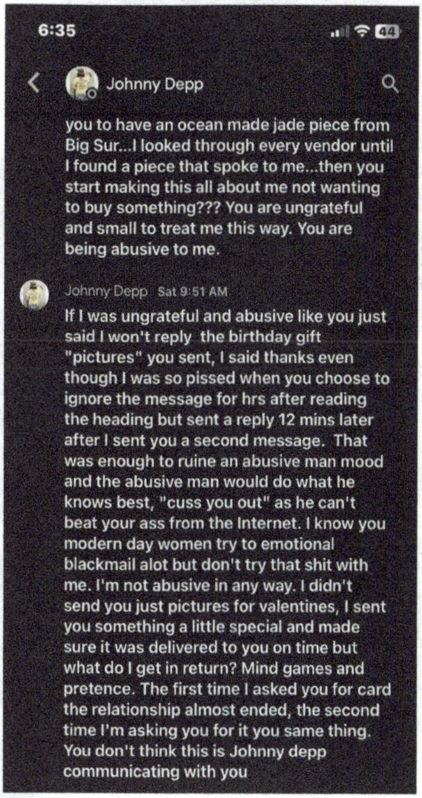
6:35
Johnny Depp
you to have an ocean made jade piece from Big Sur...I looked through every vendor until I found a piece that spoke to me...then you start making this all about me not wanting to buy something??? You are ungrateful and small to treat me this way. You are being abusive to me.
Johnny Depp Sat 9:51 AM
If I was ungrateful and abusive like you just said I won't reply the birthday gift "pictures" you sent, I said thanks even though I was so pissed when you choose to ignore the message for hrs after reading the heading but sent a reply 12 mins later after I sent you a second message. That was enough to ruine an abusive man mood and the abusive man would do what he knows best, "cuss you out" as he can't beat your ass from the Internet. I know you modern day women try to emotional blackmail alot but don't try that shit with me. I'm not abusive in any way. I didn't send you just pictures for valentines, I sent you something a little special and made sure it was delivered to you on time but what do I get in return? Mind games and pretence. The first time I asked you for card the relationship almost ended, the second time I'm asking you for it you same thing. You don't think this is Johnny depp communicating with you

While revisiting this thread of texts, once again I doubted that I was communicating with Johnny Depp. I felt challenged intellectually by the scammer(s) who were once again asking for Google Play Cards, this time using Depp's son as a pawn by saying that the request would also be for his benefit. I do not believe Johnny Depp would do such a thing,

I was enraged by the request because, once again, I had fallen back into the murky waters of questioning belief that I could actually have a connection with Johnny Depp.

I found myself entangled in a no win argument over a ridiculous request for Google Play Cards. I could not help but think the scammer was a middle school age child because of the tone of the insulting language used by the scammer(s).

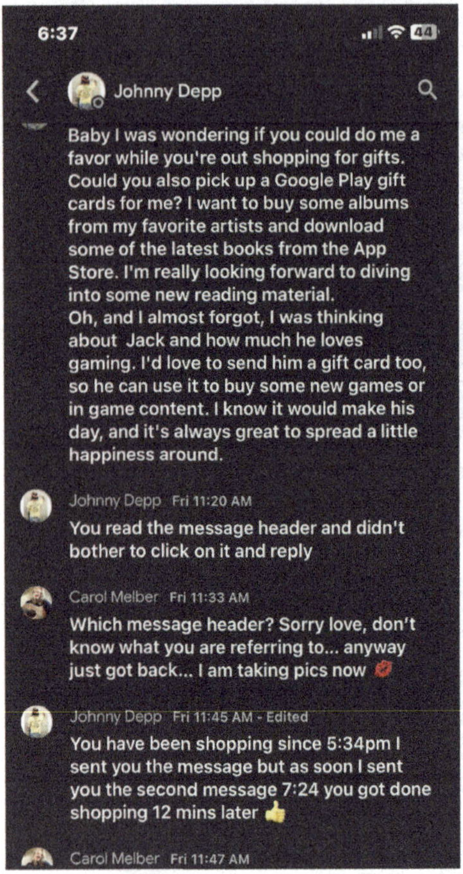

6:37

Johnny Depp

Baby I was wondering if you could do me a favor while you're out shopping for gifts. Could you also pick up a Google Play gift cards for me? I want to buy some albums from my favorite artists and download some of the latest books from the App Store. I'm really looking forward to diving into some new reading material.
Oh, and I almost forgot, I was thinking about Jack and how much he loves gaming. I'd love to send him a gift card too, so he can use it to buy some new games or in game content. I know it would make his day, and it's always great to spread a little happiness around.

Johnny Depp Fri 11:20 AM
You read the message header and didn't bother to click on it and reply

Carol Melber Fri 11:33 AM
Which message header? Sorry love, don't know what you are referring to... anyway just got back... I am taking pics now

Johnny Depp Fri 11:45 AM - Edited
You have been shopping since 5:34pm I sent you the message but as soon I sent you the second message 7:24 you got done shopping 12 mins later

Carol Melber Fri 11:47 AM

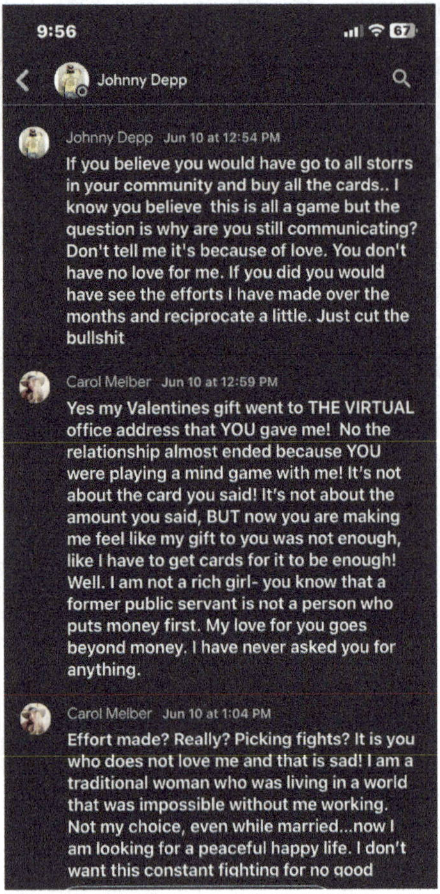

9:56

Johnny Depp

Johnny Depp Jun 10 at 12:54 PM
If you believe you would have go to all storrs in your community and buy all the cards.. I know you believe this is all a game but the question is why are you still communicating? Don't tell me it's because of love. You don't have no love for me. If you did you would have see the efforts I have made over the months and reciprocate a little. Just cut the bullshit

Carol Melber Jun 10 at 12:59 PM
Yes my Valentines gift went to THE VIRTUAL office address that YOU gave me! No the relationship almost ended because YOU were playing a mind game with me! It's not about the card you said! It's not about the amount you said, BUT now you are making me feel like my gift to you was not enough, like I have to get cards for it to be enough! Well. I am not a rich girl- you know that a former public servant is not a person who puts money first. My love for you goes beyond money. I have never asked you for anything.

Carol Melber Jun 10 at 1:04 PM
Effort made? Really? Picking fights? It is you who does not love me and that is sad! I am a traditional woman who was living in a world that was impossible without me working. Not my choice, even while married...now I am looking for a peaceful happy life. I don't want this constant fighting for no good

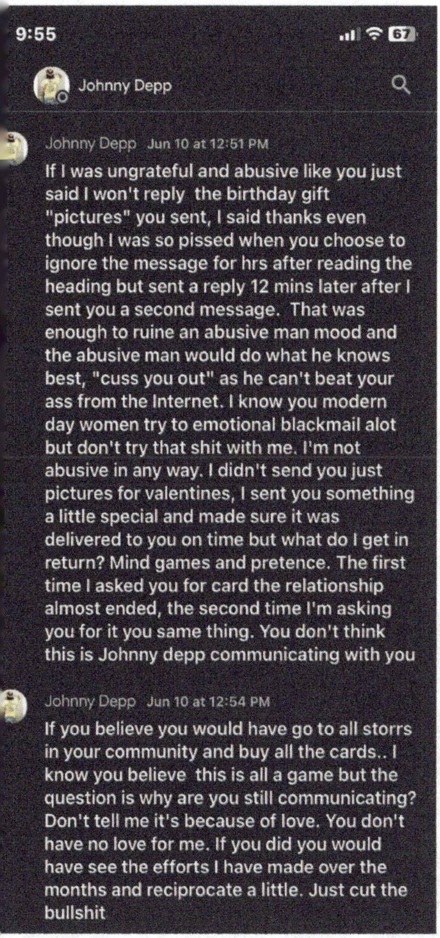
9:55
Johnny Depp
Johnny Depp Jun 10 at 12:51 PM
If I was ungrateful and abusive like you just said I won't reply the birthday gift "pictures" you sent, I said thanks even though I was so pissed when you choose to ignore the message for hrs after reading the heading but sent a reply 12 mins later after I sent you a second message. That was enough to ruine an abusive man mood and the abusive man would do what he knows best, "cuss you out" as he can't beat your ass from the Internet. I know you modern day women try to emotional blackmail alot but don't try that shit with me. I'm not abusive in any way. I didn't send you just pictures for valentines, I sent you something a little special and made sure it was delivered to you on time but what do I get in return? Mind games and pretence. The first time I asked you for card the relationship almost ended, the second time I'm asking you for it you same thing. You don't think this is Johnny depp communicating with you
Johnny Depp Jun 10 at 12:54 PM
If you believe you would have go to all storrs in your community and buy all the cards.. I know you believe this is all a game but the question is why are you still communicating? Don't tell me it's because of love. You don't have no love for me. If you did you would have see the efforts I have made over the months and reciprocate a little. Just cut the bullshit

9:57
Johnny Depp
Carol Melber Jun 10 at 3:42 PM
Carol Melber Jun 10 at 3:43 PM
This is the Big Sur jade piece -looks like a guitar pick doesn't it?
Johnny Depp Jun 10 at 4:21 PM
Stop this whole shit shows, you don't believe it's Johnny depp communicating with you!!
Johnny Depp Jun 10 at 4:36 PM
Go have a peaceful life
Carol Melber Jun 10 at 4:37 PM

I was getting impatient with the merry go round on the play cards. It was silly and a waste of time to argue about it. Still, even though I had renewed doubt about who/what I was communicating with, my feelings were hurt that my gift of jade brought no response.

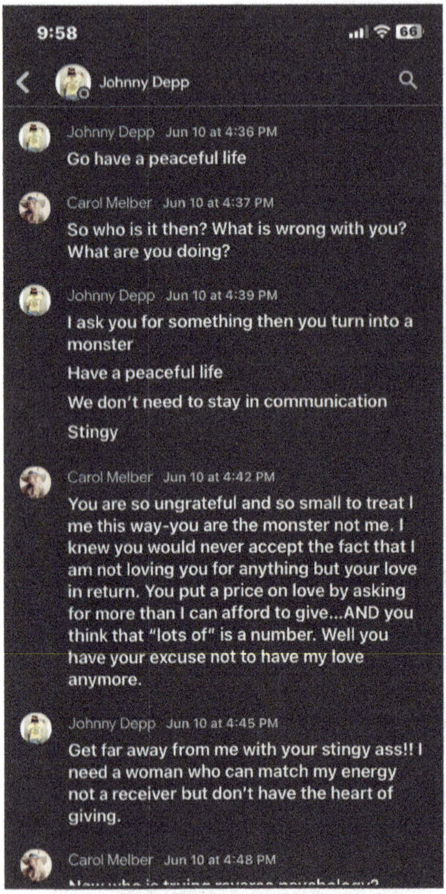

9:58

Johnny Depp

Johnny Depp Jun 10 at 4:36 PM

Go have a peaceful life

Carol Melber Jun 10 at 4:37 PM

So who is it then? What is wrong with you? What are you doing?

Johnny Depp Jun 10 at 4:39 PM

I ask you for something then you turn into a monster

Have a peaceful life

We don't need to stay in communication

Stingy

Carol Melber Jun 10 at 4:42 PM

You are so ungrateful and so small to treat I me this way-you are the monster not me. I knew you would never accept the fact that I am not loving you for anything but your love in return. You put a price on love by asking for more than I can afford to give...AND you think that "lots of" is a number. Well you have your excuse not to have my love anymore.

Johnny Depp Jun 10 at 4:45 PM

Get far away from me with your stingy ass!! I need a woman who can match my energy not a receiver but don't have the heart of giving.

Carol Melber Jun 10 at 4:48 PM

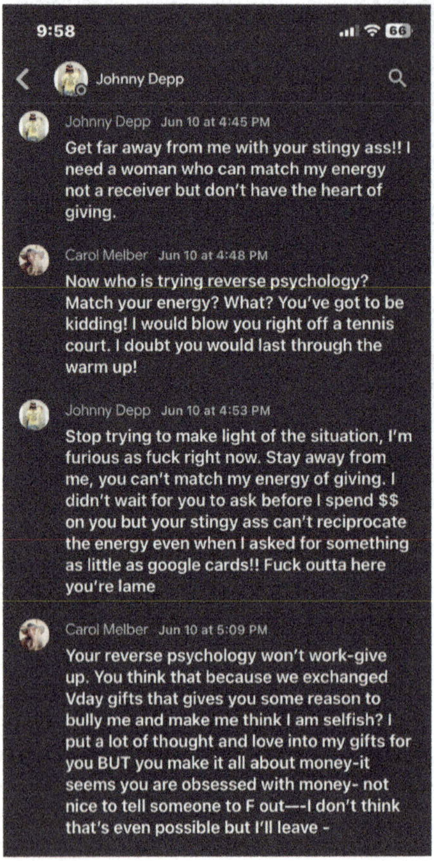

9:58

Johnny Depp

Johnny Depp Jun 10 at 4:45 PM

Get far away from me with your stingy ass!! I need a woman who can match my energy not a receiver but don't have the heart of giving.

Carol Melber Jun 10 at 4:48 PM

Now who is trying reverse psychology? Match your energy? What? You've got to be kidding! I would blow you right off a tennis court. I doubt you would last through the warm up!

Johnny Depp Jun 10 at 4:53 PM

Stop trying to make light of the situation, I'm furious as fuck right now. Stay away from me, you can't match my energy of giving. I didn't wait for you to ask before I spend $$ on you but your stingy ass can't reciprocate the energy even when I asked for something as little as google cards!! Fuck outta here you're lame

Carol Melber Jun 10 at 5:09 PM

Your reverse psychology won't work-give up. You think that because we exchanged Vday gifts that gives you some reason to bully me and make me think I am selfish? I put a lot of thought and love into my gifts for you BUT you make it all about money-it seems you are obsessed with money- not nice to tell someone to F out—-I don't think that's even possible but I'll leave -

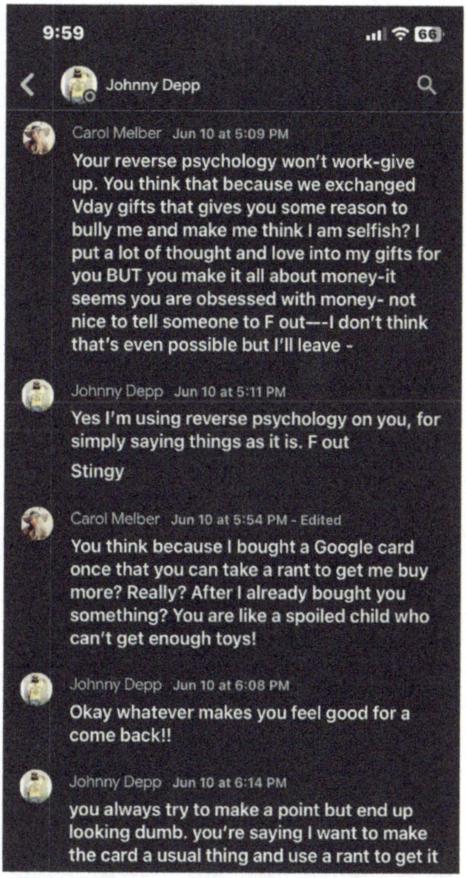
9:59
Johnny Depp
Carol Melber Jun 10 at 5:09 PM
Your reverse psychology won't work-give up. You think that because we exchanged Vday gifts that gives you some reason to bully me and make me think I am selfish? I put a lot of thought and love into my gifts for you BUT you make it all about money-it seems you are obsessed with money- not nice to tell someone to F out—-I don't think that's even possible but I'll leave -
Johnny Depp Jun 10 at 5:11 PM
Yes I'm using reverse psychology on you, for simply saying things as it is. F out
Stingy
Carol Melber Jun 10 at 5:54 PM - Edited
You think because I bought a Google card once that you can take a rant to get me buy more? Really? After I already bought you something? You are like a spoiled child who can't get enough toys!
Johnny Depp Jun 10 at 6:08 PM
Okay whatever makes you feel good for a come back!!
Johnny Depp Jun 10 at 6:14 PM
you always try to make a point but end up looking dumb. you're saying I want to make the card a usual thing and use a rant to get it

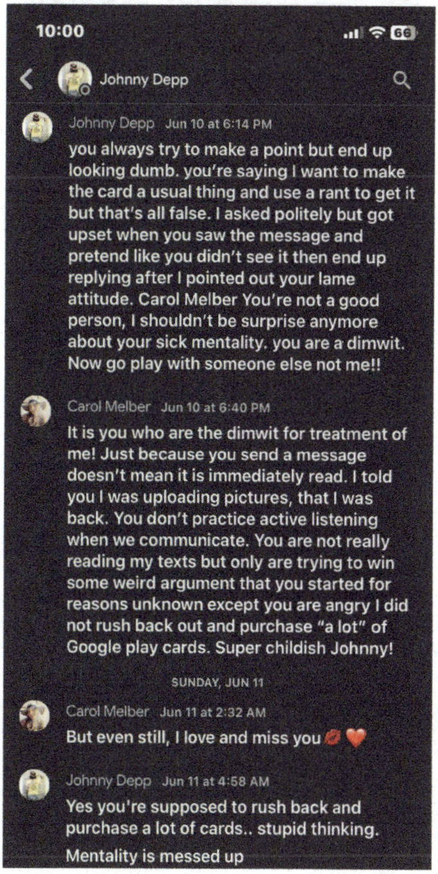
10:00
Johnny Depp
Johnny Depp Jun 10 at 6:14 PM
you always try to make a point but end up looking dumb. you're saying I want to make the card a usual thing and use a rant to get it but that's all false. I asked politely but got upset when you saw the message and pretend like you didn't see it then end up replying after I pointed out your lame attitude. Carol Melber You're not a good person, I shouldn't be surprise anymore about your sick mentality. you are a dimwit. Now go play with someone else not me!!
Carol Melber Jun 10 at 6:40 PM
It is you who are the dimwit for treatment of me! Just because you send a message doesn't mean it is immediately read. I told you I was uploading pictures, that I was back. You don't practice active listening when we communicate. You are not really reading my texts but only are trying to win some weird argument that you started for reasons unknown except you are angry I did not rush back out and purchase "a lot" of Google play cards. Super childish Johnny!
SUNDAY, JUN 11
Carol Melber Jun 11 at 2:32 AM
But even still, I love and miss you 💋 ❤️
Johnny Depp Jun 11 at 4:58 AM
Yes you're supposed to rush back and purchase a lot of cards.. stupid thinking.
Mentality is messed up

The argument continued into the following day. The rant below shows the scammer's climatic frustration when I held my ground. This is a strong indication that the scam is reaching an end.

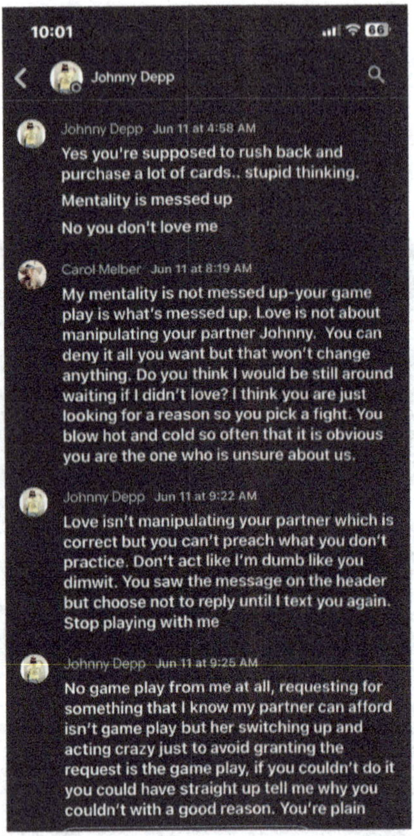
10:01

Johnny Depp

Johnny Depp Jun 11 at 4:58 AM

Yes you're supposed to rush back and purchase a lot of cards.. stupid thinking.

Mentality is messed up

No you don't love me

Carol Melber Jun 11 at 8:19 AM

My mentality is not messed up-your game play is what's messed up. Love is not about manipulating your partner Johnny. You can deny it all you want but that won't change anything. Do you think I would be still around waiting if I didn't love? I think you are just looking for a reason so you pick a fight. You blow hot and cold so often that it is obvious you are the one who is unsure about us.

Johnny Depp Jun 11 at 9:22 AM

Love isn't manipulating your partner which is correct but you can't preach what you don't practice. Don't act like I'm dumb like you dimwit. You saw the message on the header but choose not to reply until I text you again. Stop playing with me

Johnny Depp Jun 11 at 9:25 AM

No game play from me at all, requesting for something that I know my partner can afford isn't game play but her switching up and acting crazy just to avoid granting the request is the game play, if you couldn't do it you could have straight up tell me why you couldn't with a good reason. You're plain

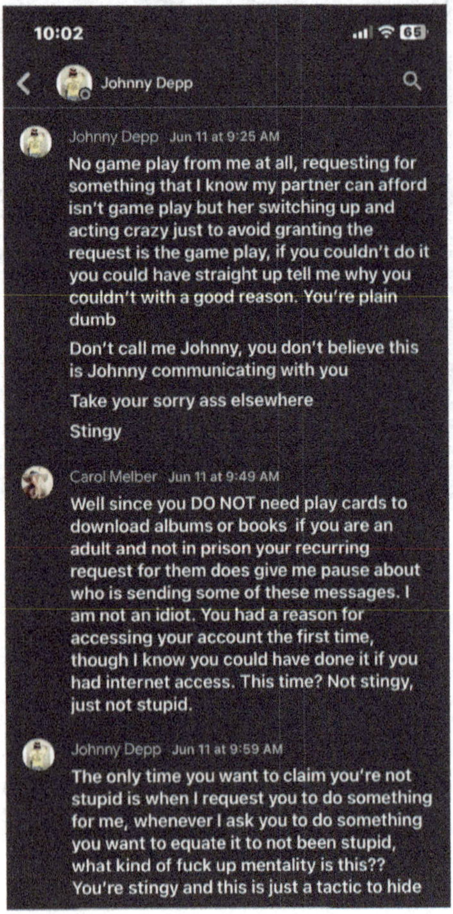
10:02

Johnny Depp

Johnny Depp Jun 11 at 9:25 AM

No game play from me at all, requesting for something that I know my partner can afford isn't game play but her switching up and acting crazy just to avoid granting the request is the game play, if you couldn't do it you could have straight up tell me why you couldn't with a good reason. You're plain dumb

Don't call me Johnny, you don't believe this is Johnny communicating with you

Take your sorry ass elsewhere

Stingy

Carol Melber Jun 11 at 9:49 AM

Well since you DO NOT need play cards to download albums or books if you are an adult and not in prison your recurring request for them does give me pause about who is sending some of these messages. I am not an idiot. You had a reason for accessing your account the first time, though I know you could have done it if you had internet access. This time? Not stingy, just not stupid.

Johnny Depp Jun 11 at 9:59 AM

The only time you want to claim you're not stupid is when I request you to do something for me, whenever I ask you to do something you want to equate it to not been stupid, what kind of fuck up mentality is this?? You're stingy and this is just a tactic to hide

10:03

Johnny Depp

Johnny Depp Jun 11 at 10:02 AM

You're pissing me off with this continue tactics of changing the narrative to make you feel good. Even you know deep in your dark heart that you're stingy and have no heart of giving but just hate.

The funny thing is I wouldn't even think twice to grant you something like a google play card if you ask me, I just don't know why kind hearted people tend to meet scums

Carol Melber Jun 11 at 10:14 AM

Reading what message header? You keep saying that but you forget I was already back and trying to upload pictures. You never needed a play card even while you were on location and lying to me about where you were. After those lies I should have known better but I guess I wanted to believe. I bought the first one because I figured I would buy a charity card to boost a person down on their luck. My man would not ask for Google Play cards. Bye whoever you are

Johnny Depp Jun 11 at 10:35 AM

Ok since you don't have no valid arguments anymore and want to resort back to old conversations just to make yourself feel better then I'll fuck up your ego and make you step off your high horse. I have known that this was all a game to you since but you have refused to admit it because for

Carol Melber Jun 11 at 12:34 PM

10:04

Johnny Depp

Johnny Depp Jun 11 at 10:35 AM

Ok since you don't have no valid arguments anymore and want to resort back to old conversations just to make yourself feel better then I'll fuck up your ego and make you step off your high horse. I have known that this was all a game to you since but you have refused to admit it because for whatsoever reasons you're enjoying the attentions... if I didn't need the cards I wouldn't ask you. Yes you're right your next man wouldn't ask you for something as lovely as a google card, he would be asking you gas money!!! You know you can't pull no high value man with your wrinkle face!!!! I hate cussing you this way because I do really like your face but since you want to hurt my feelings I would hurt yours too... Before this whole arguments started I asked you that why do you ask me if I need anything when you go out to run some few errands but as soon as I ask you for something you never give? You couldn't reply because you knew that when you ask me if I need anything you know I wouldn't tell you I need something. Even if I tell you i need something, you wouldn't get it for me because this is all a game to you and you like it you're Stupid as fuck. If you don't change your mentality I bet you that no man would want to tolerate your ass after living with you. With the way you're going with your life you would be single for long. Now run along stupid!!

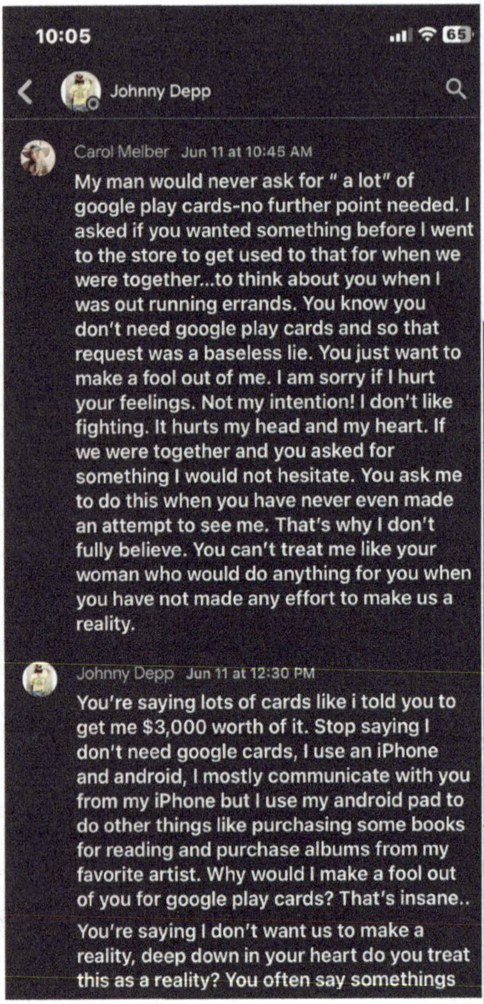

10:05

Johnny Depp

Carol Melber Jun 11 at 10:45 AM

My man would never ask for " a lot" of google play cards-no further point needed. I asked if you wanted something before I went to the store to get used to that for when we were together...to think about you when I was out running errands. You know you don't need google play cards and so that request was a baseless lie. You just want to make a fool out of me. I am sorry if I hurt your feelings. Not my intention! I don't like fighting. It hurts my head and my heart. If we were together and you asked for something I would not hesitate. You ask me to do this when you have never even made an attempt to see me. That's why I don't fully believe. You can't treat me like your woman who would do anything for you when you have not made any effort to make us a reality.

Johnny Depp Jun 11 at 12:30 PM

You're saying lots of cards like i told you to get me $3,000 worth of it. Stop saying I don't need google cards, I use an iPhone and android, I mostly communicate with you from my iPhone but I use my android pad to do other things like purchasing some books for reading and purchase albums from my favorite artist. Why would I make a fool out of you for google play cards? That's insane..

You're saying I don't want us to make a reality, deep down in your heart do you treat this as a reality? You often say somethings

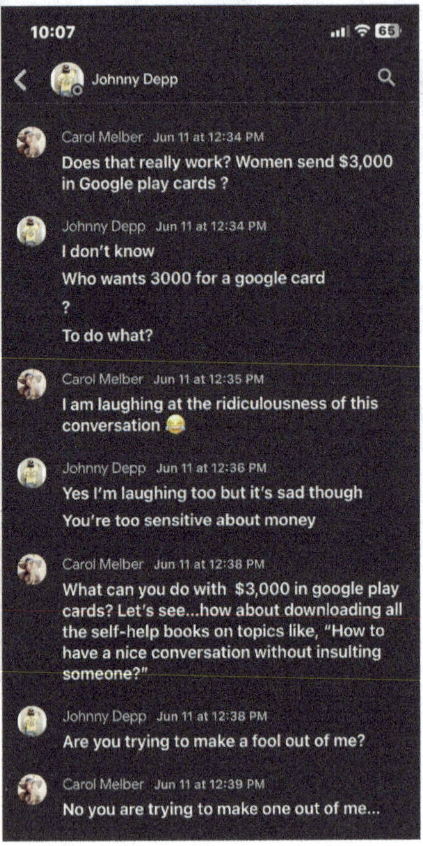

10:07

Johnny Depp

Carol Melber Jun 11 at 12:34 PM

Does that really work? Women send $3,000 in Google play cards ?

Johnny Depp Jun 11 at 12:34 PM

I don't know

Who wants 3000 for a google card

?

To do what?

Carol Melber Jun 11 at 12:35 PM

I am laughing at the ridiculousness of this conversation 😂

Johnny Depp Jun 11 at 12:36 PM

Yes I'm laughing too but it's sad though

You're too sensitive about money

Carol Melber Jun 11 at 12:38 PM

What can you do with $3,000 in google play cards? Let's see...how about downloading all the self-help books on topics like, "How to have a nice conversation without insulting someone?"

Johnny Depp Jun 11 at 12:38 PM

Are you trying to make a fool out of me?

Carol Melber Jun 11 at 12:39 PM

No you are trying to make one out of me...

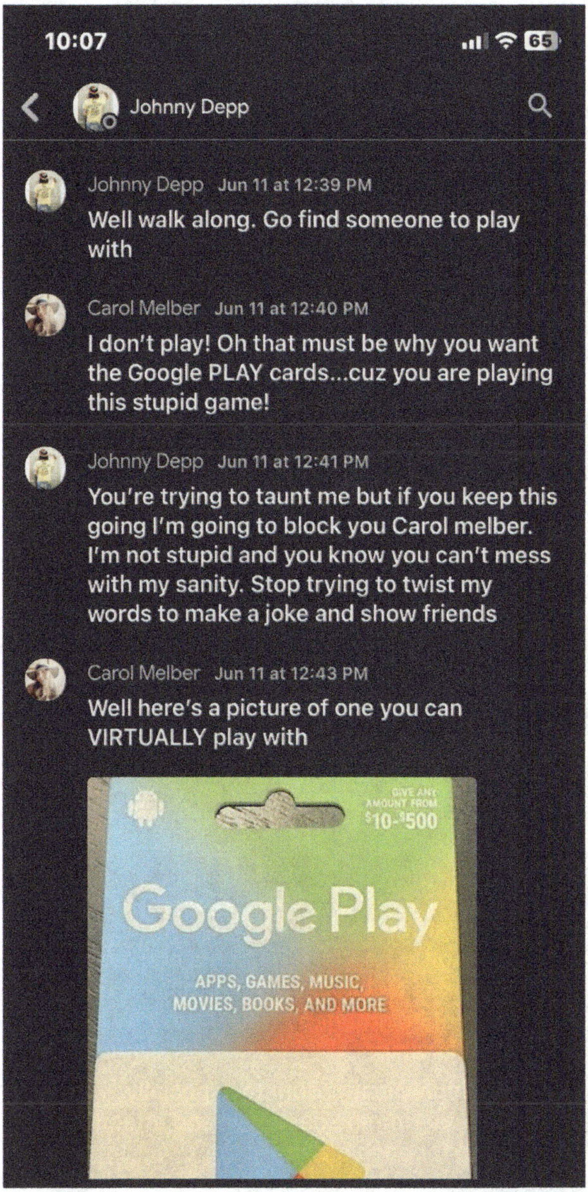
10:07
65
Johnny Depp
Johnny Depp Jun 11 at 12:39 PM
Well walk along. Go find someone to play with
Carol Melber Jun 11 at 12:40 PM
I don't play! Oh that must be why you want the Google PLAY cards...cuz you are playing this stupid game!
Johnny Depp Jun 11 at 12:41 PM
You're trying to taunt me but if you keep this going I'm going to block you Carol melber. I'm not stupid and you know you can't mess with my sanity. Stop trying to twist my words to make a joke and show friends
Carol Melber Jun 11 at 12:43 PM
Well here's a picture of one you can VIRTUALLY play with
$10-$500
Google Play
APPS, GAMES, MUSIC, MOVIES, BOOKS, AND MORE

When I saw the threat to block me I knew the scam was nearing the end because I refused to purchase more Google Play Cards.

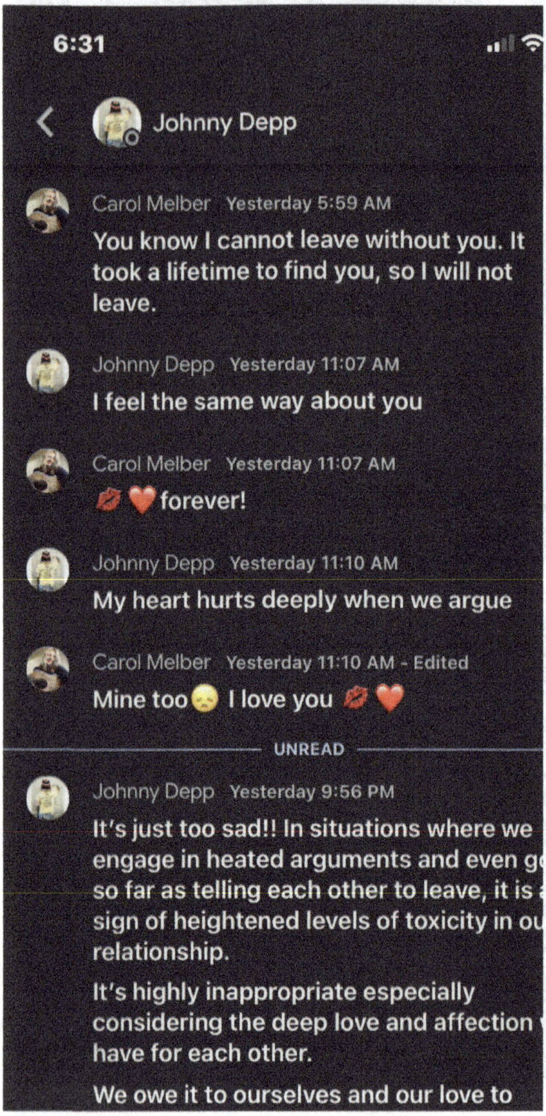
6:31
Johnny Depp
Carol Melber Yesterday 5:59 AM
You know I cannot leave without you. It took a lifetime to find you, so I will not leave.
Johnny Depp Yesterday 11:07 AM
I feel the same way about you
Carol Melber Yesterday 11:07 AM
💋 ❤️ forever!
Johnny Depp Yesterday 11:10 AM
My heart hurts deeply when we argue
Carol Melber Yesterday 11:10 AM - Edited
Mine too😞 I love you 💋 ❤️
UNREAD
Johnny Depp Yesterday 9:56 PM
It's just too sad!! In situations where we engage in heated arguments and even g
so far as telling each other to leave, it is
sign of heightened levels of toxicity in ou
relationship.
It's highly inappropriate especially considering the deep love and affection
have for each other.
We owe it to ourselves and our love to

Two days before my move the texting once again was filled with sweet words of love. I had renewed belief that I was possibly communicating with Johnny when I read the text above.

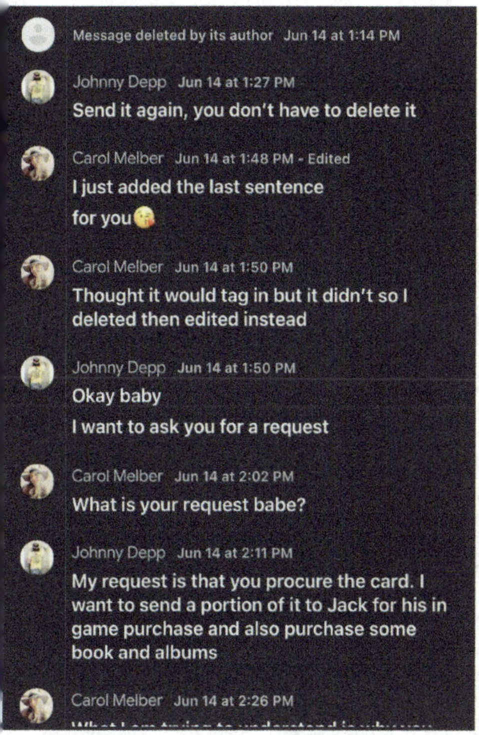
Message deleted by its author Jun 14 at 1:14 PM
Johnny Depp Jun 14 at 1:27 PM
Send it again, you don't have to delete it
Carol Melber Jun 14 at 1:48 PM - Edited
I just added the last sentence
for you
Carol Melber Jun 14 at 1:50 PM
Thought it would tag in but it didn't so I deleted then edited instead
Johnny Depp Jun 14 at 1:50 PM
Okay baby
I want to ask you for a request
Carol Melber Jun 14 at 2:02 PM
What is your request babe?
Johnny Depp Jun 14 at 2:11 PM
My request is that you procure the card. I want to send a portion of it to Jack for his in game purchase and also purchase some book and albums
Carol Melber Jun 14 at 2:26 PM

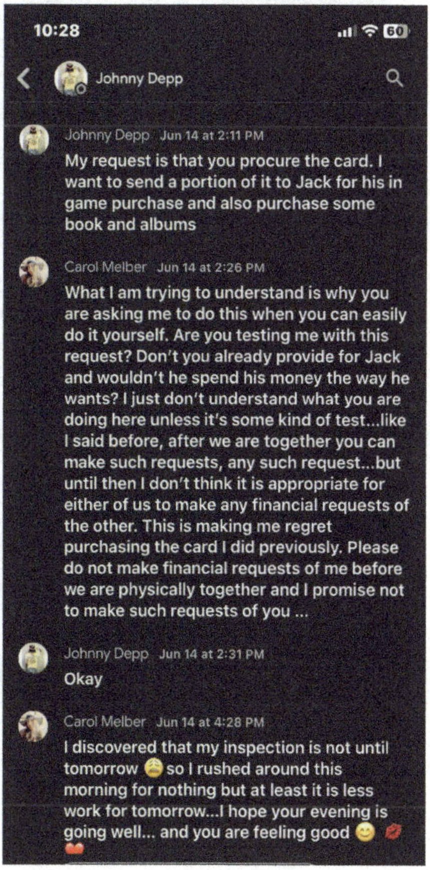
10:28
60
Johnny Depp
Johnny Depp Jun 14 at 2:11 PM
My request is that you procure the card. I want to send a portion of it to Jack for his in game purchase and also purchase some book and albums
Carol Melber Jun 14 at 2:26 PM
What I am trying to understand is why you are asking me to do this when you can easily do it yourself. Are you testing me with this request? Don't you already provide for Jack and wouldn't he spend his money the way he wants? I just don't understand what you are doing here unless it's some kind of test...like I said before, after we are together you can make such requests, any such request...but until then I don't think it is appropriate for either of us to make any financial requests of the other. This is making me regret purchasing the card I did previously. Please do not make financial requests of me before we are physically together and I promise not to make such requests of you ...
Johnny Depp Jun 14 at 2:31 PM
Okay
Carol Melber Jun 14 at 4:28 PM
I discovered that my inspection is not until tomorrow so I rushed around this morning for nothing but at least it is less work for tomorrow...I hope your evening is going well... and you are feeling good

Again, the scammer(s) used Depp's son Jack in the scheme for Google Play Cards. I requested we each not make any financial requests of the other and received a response that indicated agreement but as you will see the scammer(s) did not agree. How could such agreement exist when that would defeat the purpose of the scam, right?

The additional response made (with my text circled this time) led to the end of the virtual sham of a relationship and the romance scam

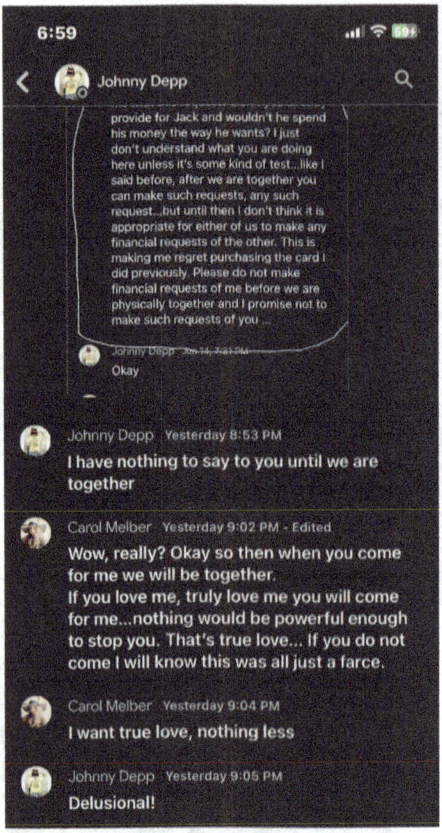
6:59
Johnny Depp
provide for Jack and wouldn't he spend his money the way he wants? I just don't understand what you are doing here unless it's some kind of test...like I said before, after we are together you can make such requests, any such request...but until then I don't think it is appropriate for either of us to make any financial requests of the other. This is making me regret purchasing the card I did previously. Please do not make financial requests of me before we are physically together and I promise not to make such requests of you ...
Okay
Johnny Depp Yesterday 8:53 PM
I have nothing to say to you until we are together
Carol Melber Yesterday 9:02 PM - Edited
Wow, really? Okay so then when you come for me we will be together.
If you love me, truly love me you will come for me...nothing would be powerful enough to stop you. That's true love... If you do not come I will know this was all just a farce.
Carol Melber Yesterday 9:04 PM
I want true love, nothing less
Johnny Depp Yesterday 9:05 PM
Delusional!

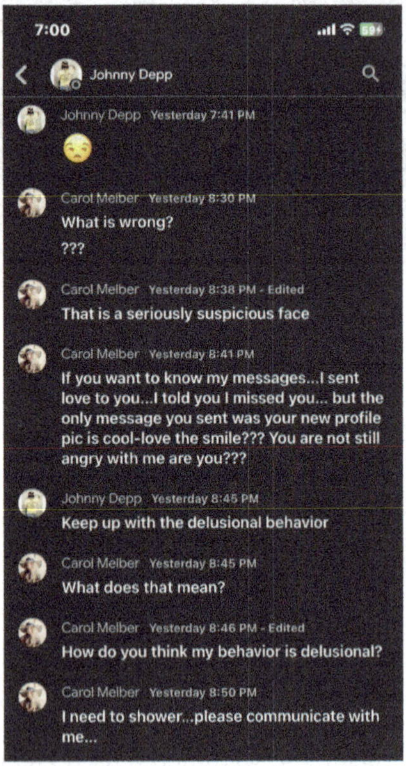
7:00
Johnny Depp
Johnny Depp Yesterday 7:41 PM
Carol Melber Yesterday 8:30 PM
What is wrong?
???
Carol Melber Yesterday 8:38 PM - Edited
That is a seriously suspicious face
Carol Melber Yesterday 8:41 PM
If you want to know my messages...I sent love to you...I told you I missed you... but the only message you sent was your new profile pic is cool-love the smile??? You are not still angry with me are you???
Johnny Depp Yesterday 8:45 PM
Keep up with the delusional behavior
Carol Melber Yesterday 8:45 PM
What does that mean?
Carol Melber Yesterday 8:46 PM - Edited
How do you think my behavior is delusional?
Carol Melber Yesterday 8:50 PM
I need to shower...please communicate with me...

THE FINAL END, SCAM OVER

A month later near the end of the Europe tour and after several of my texts were not answered I deleted them, knowing that I was just hanging on to a non-existent relationship. I was surprised to receive a text. For the last time I communicated with the scammer(s).

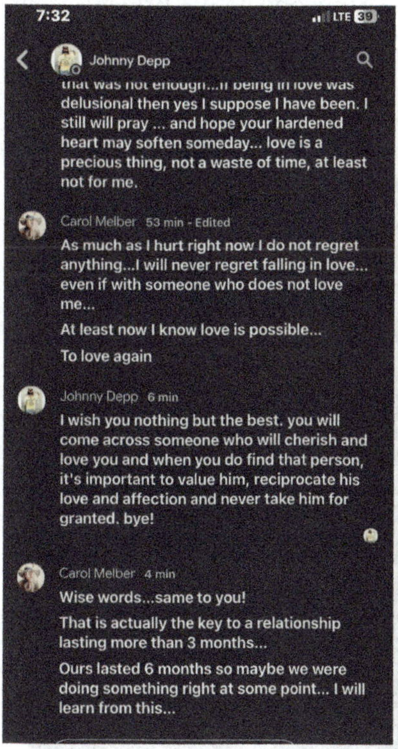

7:32
Johnny Depp
delusional then yes I suppose I have been. I still will pray ... and hope your hardened heart may soften someday... love is a precious thing, not a waste of time, at least not for me.
Carol Melber 53 min - Edited
As much as I hurt right now I do not regret anything...I will never regret falling in love... even if with someone who does not love me...
At least now I know love is possible...
To love again
Johnny Depp 6 min
I wish you nothing but the best. you will come across someone who will cherish and love you and when you do find that person, it's important to value him, reciprocate his love and affection and never take him for granted. bye!
Carol Melber 4 min
Wise words...same to you!
That is actually the key to a relationship lasting more than 3 months...
Ours lasted 6 months so maybe we were doing something right at some point... I will learn from this...

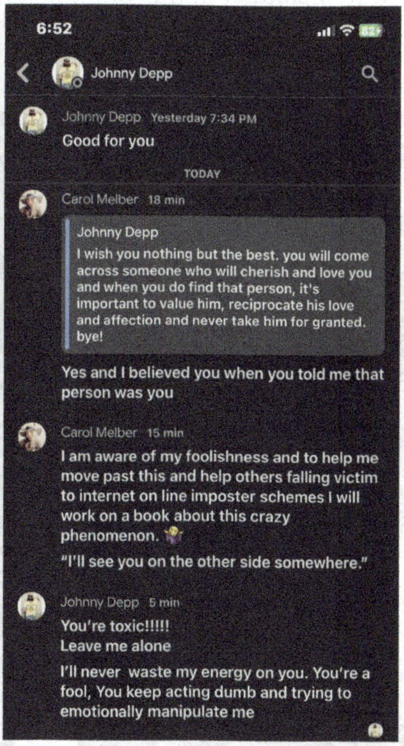

6:52
Johnny Depp
Johnny Depp Yesterday 7:34 PM
Good for you
TODAY
Carol Melber 18 min
Johnny Depp
I wish you nothing but the best. you will come across someone who will cherish and love you and when you do find that person, it's important to value him, reciprocate his love and affection and never take him for granted. bye!
Yes and I believed you when you told me that person was you
Carol Melber 15 min
I am aware of my foolishness and to help me move past this and help others falling victim to internet on line imposter schemes I will work on a book about this crazy phenomenon.
"I'll see you on the other side somewhere."
Johnny Depp 5 min
You're toxic!!!!!
Leave me alone
I'll never waste my energy on you. You're a fool, You keep acting dumb and trying to emotionally manipulate me

Soon after this text I was blocked on the chat platform. I sent an email to the address used at various times over the course of communication. In that final email I stated that I knew the "relationship" was over. I also made it clear that I had no regrets. The illusion of love was worth every minute of my time while on that journey. If I had suffered from a delusion during that time then it was one that brought me great joy. That stated, I would never engage in a virtual relationship again. My final words to the scammer(s): "I forgive you, whoever you are."

EPILOGUE

The communication on the scam ended. Was that the end of other imposters sending me texts on social media? The answer is no. On September 19, 2023 at 8:30 a.m. EST my cell phone rang with my caller ID announcing a call from Johnny Depp with a long phone number. I did not pick up the call as I was shocked by it. I decided to hit the return call button to see what happened. Someone with a British accent answered. I hung up and engaged in the last text thread below and decided to include it in this book. I still receive follow requests and the occasional chat message. I most always accept the requests to follow but no longer engage in text chats.

7:58
_johnny_depp_today_
Active 1h ago
_johnny_depp_today_
Instagram
1.1K followers · 4 posts
You follow each other on Instagram
View profile
6:32 AM
Morning darling how you doing today ?
It seems you're busy hope you're ok ?
Tap and hold to react
Message...

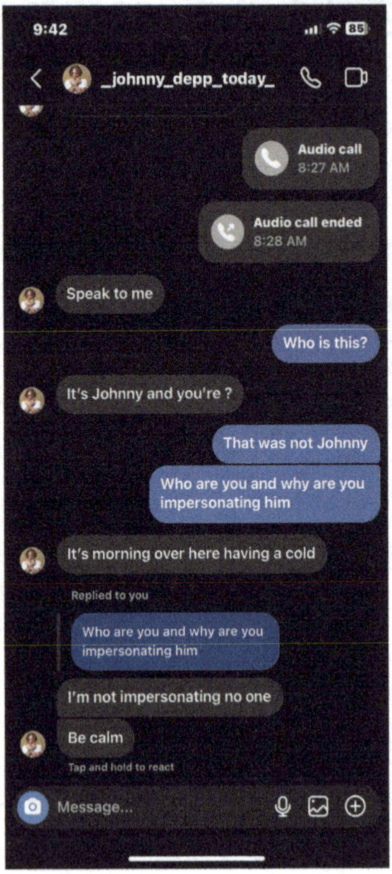

9:42
_johnny_depp_today_
Audio call
8:27 AM
Audio call ended
8:28 AM
Speak to me
Who is this?
It's Johnny and you're ?
That was not Johnny
Who are you and why are you impersonating him
It's morning over here having a cold
Replied to you
Who are you and why are you impersonating him
I'm not impersonating no one
Be calm
Tap and hold to react
Message...

SUGGESTIONS FOR SPOTTING A ROMANCE SCAM

When scammers "cat fish" someone they may have many text threads going on to numerous people at the same time. This could explain why it seems that some texts received seem to be meant for someone else. There are likely numerous scams going in at the same time and perhaps even originating in settings akin to call centers.

The scammer(s) at first attempt to gather information in order to determine whether they may have caught someone who has the means to be exploited for monetary gain or are attractive for identity theft. Scammers will get as much information as possible while appearing to be caring and concerned for the victim's welfare.

If the scammer learns the person is in a vulnerable position, like a single divorcee, alone and ready for a relationship, the scammer may try a romance scam. Here are some suggested questions to ask if a scam is suspected and the red flags to look for when a stranger requests to engage virtually:

1). How did the connection begin?
2). What platform is used to communicate and why was that platform suggested?
3). Have you asked for a "Selfie" test?
4). Have you asked to share the relationship with friends and family?
5). Is the relationship moving quickly?
6). Did you run a web search on the user name and profile picture to authenticate the source?
7). Is there ANY request for ANY personal information?
8). Is there ANY request for money of ANY amount?
9). What timezone does the communication originate and does that make sense?
10). Does it appear you are communicating with multiple text sources and/or AI?

My final words of caution are to NEVER participate in an online communication with a stranger even if there are existing circumstances that may provide some proof of authenticity. If a real person wants to communicate with you that communication will occur in person or via a reliable video chat platform.

About the Author

Carol Melber, JD thanks friends and family for their continued love and support.

Other books:

2014 - The Rolling Moon a journey to understand   alien abduction

2015 - Jumping Jellybeans

2016 - On Love Poems From The Heart

2021 - On Life Path of a Woman's Soul

2022 - Charlie's Avocado

2023 - Paxter the foster

Made in the USA
Monee, IL
03 November 2026

67375833R00069